The
Anthropology
of
Art

Elek Archaeology and Anthropology

General Editor: J. V. S. Megaw
Professor of Archaeology in the
University of Leicester

Already published

The Environment of Early Man in the British Isles
John G. Evans

The Roman Forts of the Saxon Shore
Stephen Johnson

Science and Society in Prehistoric Britain
Euan W. MacKie

Greek Architects at Work
J. J. Coulton

Parthian Art
Malcolm A. R. Colledge

Industrial Archaeology in the British Isles
John Butt and *Ian Donnachie*

The Anthropology of Art

Robert Layton

Columbia University Press   New York   1981

Published in 1981 in the United States of America by Columbia University Press

Library of Congress Cataloging in Publication Data

Layton, Robert.
   The anthropology of art.

   Includes bibliographical references and index.
   1. Art and anthropology.   I. Title.
N72.S6L39 1981   709'.01'1   80-39919
ISBN 0-231-05282-0

Printed in Great Britain

Contents

List of figures

List of plates

Acknowledgements

My warmest thanks to Peter Ucko and Peter Morton-Williams for teaching me about the Anthropology of Art. I am also very grateful to Howard Morphy for allowing me to quote unpublished material from his PhD thesis; to Anthony Forge, Daniel Biebuyck and Dover Publishing Inc., for permission to quote from published sources, and to the Museum of Mankind, Australian Institute of Aboriginal Studies and Howard Morphy for permission to reproduce photographs as plates. Tom Dewhurst and Anthea Whiting prepared the excellent line drawings. Ann Douglas, John Picton and Vincent Megaw made many useful comments on the draft text which helped me to improve the final version.

1
The art of other cultures

Primitive Art?

Anthropology's subject-matter is the study of Man, but it is not the only discipline with an interest in that field. Archaeology, linguistics and other specialized bodies of theory deal with particular aspects of human behaviour. Even the specific field of contemporary social life is by common consent divided between anthropology and sociology, sociology studying the large, urban, industrial society we belong to and anthropology those other societies still often vulgarly labelled 'primitive'. The subject of this book has in consequence sometimes been known as 'Primitive Art'. The term will not be used here, for reasons which help to explain the aim and scope of the present study.

The essential difficulty is that to use the term 'primitive' of recent, small-scale societies implies that the origins and early development of art can be seen in modern cultures. It is undeniably true that the first human societies were based on a hunting and gathering economy, and that such an economy persisted until recently among, for instance, the Australian Aborigines and African Bushmen studied by anthropologists. Clearly our own complex industrial economy has little in common with these systems, but to what extent are they alike among themselves? If the most parsimonious estimate for the origin of human societies placed their beginning at about 40,000 years ago, when *Homo sapiens sapiens* appeared, then (since agriculture probably began between 9,000 and 7,000 B.C.) hunting and gathering societies, far from representing a first step, would constitute 75 per cent of all human development. The hunter-gatherer artists of the Magdelenian, who painted at Altamira and Lascaux 15,000 years ago, were already far removed from both human origins and the earliest surviving forms of visual expression (fig. 1). The blurb writer who claimed that a certain history of art traces its evolution from 'primitive scribbles on cave walls to the work of Jackson Pollock' was either joking or the victim of a narrow theoretical outlook, but it is an outlook shared by many writers too interested in exploiting the art of other cultures for didactic purposes of their own. Greenhalgh, writing of *European interest in the non-European* (in Greenhalgh and Megaw, 1978), illustrates how Europeans have tended to assimilate the diverse and independent artistic traditions of other cultures to a

Figure 1   Prehistoric cave painting of a deer, from Altamira, northern Spain

monolithic evolutionary or diffusionist scheme at whose centre lie their own specific experiences. The prehistoric art of Western Europe alone spans a vast period, and the Magdelenian represents the work of a culture active ten thousand years after the first surviving pictorial representations of humans and animals in Europe (Ucko and Rosenfeld, 1967: 16, 26, 66). Modern hunter-gatherer cultures, let alone the many pastoralists and cultivators whom anthropology also studies, are correspondingly further removed in time from the origins of human society and they are also far in place from Western Europe.

The concept that hunter-gatherers or members of non-industrial pastoral or farming communities preserve, as living fossils, the original expressions of art, or those which subsequently occurred in our own distant past, could be valid only if there were a necessary correlation between art forms and broadly-defined economic or political practices. It is true that rather sweeping claims of this sort have been made. Hunter-gatherers, it has been asserted, are too busy struggling to obtain food to spare the time for art at all, or too enslaved to a life of constant movement in pursuit of game, to produce works of art that are durable and therefore cumbersome. We will consider Sahlins' comments on the first of these assertions in Chapter 2, but it is worth quoting here the outstanding example of the Hadza, a modern hunting and gathering culture of East Africa:

'Hadza women require, on a yearly average, only about two hours a day for necessary subsistence activities' (Ucko and Dimbleby, 1969, xvii, reporting the findings of Woodburn). Far from allowing more leisure, it is possible that more complex social systems require more labour to support them. The fallacy of the second assumption is demonstrated by the existence of durable and certainly immovable rock art among Bushmen, Aborigines and European palaeolithic cultures. The nomadism of modern hunter-gatherers in Australia was carefully circumscribed, and took place around repeated visits to base-camps, among which painted rock shelters number. The same may well have been true of prehistoric Europe.

It seems likely that, far from being 'living fossils' the contemporary art traditions of societies other than our own will show a wide diversity of forms all far removed from their origins. Nor is there anything unique about the recent past in this respect. As Ucko and Rosenfeld write of the Upper Palaeolithic in Europe: 'During this time [20,000 years] literally thousands of influences can be assumed to have affected cultural activity'. They conclude, 'It is clearly pointless to search for clear-cut improvements in artistic aptitude and expression over many thousands of years, except in the most general terms ... One can expect to find many "beginnings" and many "climaxes" of artistic expression at different points' during that period (op. cit.: 76-7).

The phrase 'Primitive Art' can surely be used of recent cultures only as one of those figures of speech which combine opposites for dramatic effect. Any community which possesses a tradition of artistic expression has more than a little sophistication in its culture. Dark (in Greenhalgh and Megaw, op. cit.: 32-4) reviews attempts to give the application of the term 'primitive' to recent, exotic art, a precise meaning. He concludes that the term has outlived its usefulness. If one extends the field of study to prehistoric cultures, further qualifications must be kept in mind. While prehistory can provide useful data on the creations of cultures similar in some respects to those studied by anthropology, even prehistoric art cannot, as Ucko and Rosenfeld pointed out (and as Dark reiterates), be seen as part of a single grand movement towards the art of Renaissance or industrial society. The impossibility of learning much about prehistoric artists' intentions or values, moreover, so severely limits the scope available for studying prehistoric art that it will rarely be referred to in the following chapters. The intention is rather to examine the recent art of small-scale societies around the world, looking on one hand for universal principles of artistic expression which they may reveal, and on the other for the diversity of fashions in which such principles have been put to effect.

The Anthropology of Art

The definition of art

If recent artistic traditions are so diverse, the definition of what is, or is not, art, is more of a problem. Art is a difficult phenomenon to define, both because there is an imprecise boundary between art and non-art whose location seems often to shift according to fashion and ideology, and because there appear to be at least two viable definitions of what is the core of art.

On the one hand, the same artistic impulse can be expressed and recognized in many media: poetry, dance, sculpture, painting: yet, within each of these media: language, body movement, the manufacture of three-dimensional forms or the use of pigments, there are many things that one would not consider art. The utilization of a particular medium, however, gives that form of art qualities which it will share with all other forms of expression in that medium. Poetry, like all language, must obey the rules of grammar; painting and sculpture must adopt a style to represent their subjects. The question is, what further qualities do expressions of art possess, which are distinctive within the medium, and comparable with parallel expressions in other media?

There are two approaches to the definition of art which are applicable across cultural boundaries, even if neither seems to have quite universal application. One deals in terms of aesthetics, the other treats art as communication distinguished by a particularly apt use of images.

Haselberger, one of those who has attempted to set out a framework for studying the anthropology of art (1961), adopts an aesthetic criterion: works of art can be identified in objects produced with the intention that they be aesthetically pleasing, not strictly, pragmatically functional. Boas (1955) carried out detailed and fascinating analyses on this basis which will be summarized later in the chapter. Certainly the approach has a long history in Western culture. It is based on the idea that the essential qualities of art lie in formal organization: the creation of balanced compositions which play with almost mathematical expressions of rhythm and harmony. 'Long before Plato', Finley writes of the Greeks, 'even before Pythagoras perhaps, the notion became entrenched in the arts that number was the key to harmony' (1966:153). Plato actually had a poor opinion of the arts, because they deal with images rather than the real objects craftsmen manufactured, and were thus two degrees from the ideals studied by philosophers like himself: 'He [the artist] will make his imitations, though he does not know whether a particular subject is good or bad, and he seems likely to imitate what appears beautiful to the ignorant majority' (*Republic*: x, 602;

translation by Grube, 1974). There is a recent discussion of the essence of Western art by Wollheim, to which the chapter will turn below, which has a certain affinity with Plato in considering the material efforts of the artist less important than the mental Types these express.

The second approach is exemplified by Aristotle, in his *Poetics*. Aristotle was not happy with a definition of poetry that focused on its 'beautiful form'. He pointed out that while poets make use of metre to order their words, a historian or a natural philosopher might choose to write his work according to a metre (as apparently some did in ancient Greece), but that although giving it a harmonious form this would not necessarily turn his work into poetry. Similarly, the use of unusual or ornate words may increase the impact of a poem without being peculiar to poetry. However, 'the greatest thing by far is to be a master of metaphor. It is the one thing that cannot be learned from others: and it is also a sign of genius, since a good metaphor implies an intuitive perception of the similarity in dissimilars' (*Poetics*, Chapter 22; translation by House, 1956). The structure distinctive of poetry is thus said to lie in its ordering of ideas rather than forms.

In most cases both definitions are equally applicable: we identify art works in a formal sense because we find them aesthetically pleasing and we find that they enhance our perception of the world around us through the apt use of images. But there are exceptions: sometimes the first criterion seems applicable but not the second; sometimes the second but not the first. The fact that both symbolism and aesthetics have so frequently been thought of as crucial elements of art — be it poetry, drama, sculpture or painting — seems to suggest rather that they may constitute alternative realizations of a more general goal, and that this more general quality is the core of art. What the core might be, and the diversity of ways in which it is realized, will certainly concern this study.

Art in small-scale societies

Although it is useful also to consider verbal arts such as proverbs or songs, our subject-matter in this study is primarily painting and sculpture. The following paragraphs will consider the applicability of the two definitions proposed above to plastic arts in small-scale societies.

To a significant degree the study must concern itself simply with 'the anthropology of visual representation', but while plastic arts devote themselves to visual representation, not all visual

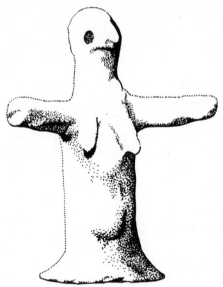

Figure 2 Initiation figure from East Africa: 'Kumburu settles down in the market place to gossip' — moral: pregnant women who stay too long at market risk the bewitching of their unborn child. *After Cory*

representation is art. There seems no reason to consider cartography an art form; nor road signs, at least by intention. Both, it is true, demand a skill in visual expression, and that means the choice of an appropriate style and the matching of visual motifs to ideas; but then a comparable skill with words is demanded in any form of effective verbal communication. And there are many forms of visual expression in the cultures of Africa (fig. 2), Aboriginal Australia etc., which do not need to be considered as objects produced for art: fetishes, initiation figures constructed to show the initiates how they should or should not appear (Cory, 1956). Someone with the wry sense of humour of a Marcel Duchamp might, it is true, place a road sign in an art gallery; even, perhaps, seeing in that object an artistic quality; but the important fact is that the sign was not designed, and nor does it function in use, as anything more than a pragmatic aid to road safety: a visual message about the hazards ahead. The errors of those who presume to read their own sentimental responses into works of art from Africa will be mentioned below.

AESTHETICS

Horton described how, among the Kalabari of southern Nigeria, sculptures are carved simply to be used as 'houses' for spirits (fig. 7). The sculptures are used in cults which seek to control the spirits of Kalabari religion, and the carvings provide an essential means by which such control is achieved, for they localize the spirit in the cult house where it is invoked (1965:8). The sculpture is compared to the *name* of the spirit, and Kalabari say 'the spirits come and stay in their names' (10).[1] The function of the sculpture, then, is the pragmatic one of manipulating spiritual forces. Horton writes: 'Perhaps the most striking thing one notices is the general apathy about sculpture as a visual object... Some evidence suggests that as visual objects, sculptures tend to evoke not merely apathy but actual repulsion. Thus one can refer to a man's ugliness by comparing his face with a spirit sculpture' (12).

But although beauty does not enter into them, there *are* criteria for judging whether a carving is a 'good' sculpture or a 'bad' one. The crucial thing is that a carved spirit figure should resemble the decayed object that it replaces: 'If an object is so crudely carved as to be virtually unrecognizable, it will certainly be rejected... Closely related to this criterion is the insistence that no cult-object should resemble that of any other spirit more than it resembles its own previous versions... Production of a cult-object appropriate to the wrong spirit is not only useless; it is positively dangerous to the carver' (22).

The reason is this: each spirit has a 'name', and each has a set of visual images which express that 'name' when they are incorporated into a sculpture. To make a carving where these elements are unrecognizable, or to depict the wrong elements, is to treat the spirit as a 'plaything' (22). If the correct elements are incorporated, then Kalabari judgement is satisfied: 'Various versions of a cult-object can differ quite widely in form and proportion; yet if they are all recognizable they will evoke little comment'. Horton observes: 'the situation is very much like that of handwriting in modern Western culture. So long as the minimum test of legibility (i.e. recognizability) is passed, one piece of handwriting is as good as another' (23). Here there seems to be a very good analogy with the place of poetry in the wider field of linguistic communication for (as Horton no doubt had in mind), in some instances other than modern Western culture, handwriting itself becomes elevated to an art tradition, in the form of calligraphy, and the caption, in effect, becomes part of the work of art.

The attitude of the Kalabari towards their sculptures does not imply that this culture has no art forms. According to Horton they put their aesthetic creativity and expressive skills into the dances which form another aspect of the spirit cults.

The Lega, another African people, provide an example of a cult where works of art are used alongside, and in many respects, to the

[1]Where successive references are taken from a single source, only the page number will be cited in text.

same ends as objects which in aesthetic terms seem to lie outside the field of art. The Lega live in dense equatorial or tropical rainforest in the eastern Congo, an environment of luxuriant vegetation and a rich fauna including monkeys, antelopes, rodents, elephants, buffalo and leopards. Their economy is based on a combination of hunting, fishing, gathering and an agriculture centred around banana cultivation. 'The durable parts of many wild species are used in large quantities as adornments, initiation objects and status and prestige symbols,' writes Biebuyck. 'Animal actors and hunting scenery abound in the oral literature of the Lega. Similitudes, metaphors and identifications drawn from the animal world fill the teachings that are given during circumcision rites and initiation ceremonies' (Biebuyck, 1973:27, condensed).

At the centre of Lega culture is the *Bwami* association. *Bwami* aims to satisfy the three major goals of life, namely: to have solid kinship links, to go through the intensive training associated with circumcision and to have many children. It controls sorcery. The initiation ceremonies in *Bwami* are a moral education, achieved through elaborate explanation in proverbs, dances and objects which include thousands of pieces of sculpture. (66).

During *Bwami* ceremonies, carved animal and human figures appear alongside utensils such as baskets and knives, as well as natural objects like leaves or animal claws. Biebuyck describes how he recorded at a single ceremony more than thirty-five varieties of leaf, selected, Biebuyck inferred from the accompanying explanation, for their ability to represent a tree's 'growth rate, tallness, and straightness, the breadth of its crown, the massiveness of its buttresses or aerial roots, its location in the forest or its relative prevalence in forest formations, and its usefulness to humans and animals (143). Substances extracted from trees are used as perfumes and dyes in *Bwami* ceremonies. A variety of animals provide skulls, beaks, feathers, tusks, bones, hoofs, claws, scales, hides and horns. Sometimes these appear in their natural state, sometimes decorated with beads, cloth or wickerwork. Some of the essentially utilitarian manufactured articles which figure in the cult are so decorated as to be 'outstanding examples of artistic excellence'. More importantly a single initiation basket will contain natural and manufactured articles (fig. 12). One basket, whose contents Biebuyck describes, had in it several animal skulls, vegetable objects, a pangolin scale, a carved animal and two human figurines. It was covered with bark cloth, to which a shield and spear were attached. The assemblage is an integrated whole, because the 'totality of ideas pertaining to a certain rite can be communicated only by the total configuration of assorted objects' (151). During the ceremony, the leaders of the dances pick up the objects, dance with them, show them to the seated candidates, sing proverbs associated with them, display and interpret them.

Like Horton, Biebuyck is struck by the way in which carvings are apparently used solely as vehicles for communication whose own qualities are superficially evaluated in a neutral fashion. He describes a class of sculptures which represent a human figure possessing a distended belly (fig. 3). These depict a woman who committed adultery while pregnant and, having thus ritually polluted herself, died as a result. In some communities, he records, a piece of naturally twisted wood may be substituted for the carving. In another instance, he was present at a ceremony which normally required the production of a large animal carving, but on this occasion the sculpture was replaced by four sticks of parasol wood laid on the ground, roughly in the form of an X (194). If a carving is broken or lost, or taken by an outsider, most initiates are not unduly worried, replacing it with 'something that is functional and' (adopting the same model as Horton) 'is *the semantic equivalent*' (164, my emphasis).

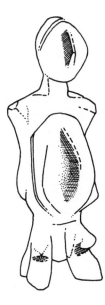

Figure 3   Lega carving (Central Africa): Wayinda, the pregnant woman who committed adultery. *After Biebuyck*

Yet, unlike the Kalabari, the Lega do express a positive evaluation of their carvings. The owners and users of the masks and figures claim all are *busoga*, good-and-beautiful; to do otherwise would be against the code of the *Bwami* (177). To an outsider such as himself, Biebuyck adds, carvings seemed to be of widely varying artistic merit, even though all were displayed together. He again parallels

Horton in his statement that, 'When the possessor of a particular carving traces its previous owners it is impossible to know whether he is talking about replacements or the original; what is important to him is the certitude that what he now has is the *true equivalent or substitute*, of what existed before' (178, my emphasis). However, the opposing point of view, that individual objects *are* valued for their own sake, appears to be expressed in the information that 'In recent decades, to protect their art objects against raids by the police, the military, catechists and Europeans, the Lega have hidden them in safer places [than their wives' huts], such as holes in trees.' (He adds: 'This practice led to irreparable damage of many pieces by rodents, termites and humidity' (166).) They may, of course, have been hiding them simply because it would be difficult to have produced enough 'semantic equivalents' for all of them, but this seems unlikely.

There is a series of terms which categorize the various kinds of object used in *Bwami*. Collectively, they are called *masengo*, whether natural or manufactured; but natural objects are called *mitume*, 'which seems to be related to the broad concept of "hunting for natural things in the environment" ' (159). Some are burnt after the ceremony; others are kept, and transmitted from initiate to initiate, like '*kisulukutu*, the great owl that passes and passes'. Manufactured objects are called *binkungankunga*, which means 'things pieced together, put together, or assembled', and these are in turn subdivided into insignia of rank and dance paraphernalia on one hand, and carved or constructed objects on the other. Insignia and paraphernalia are called *binumbi*, 'a crowd united for dance and joy', while the carved and constructed items — sculptures, assemblages of claws, seeds, etc. — are called *bitungwa*, 'something that is being tied together or something that is unifying' (160). These examples suggest that aesthetic values are not universally expressed in exotic carvings, or other forms of visual expression, but are rather specific to certain aspects of other cultures.

The artist's values

The investigation of the artist's intent (as far as he can express it), and the response of fellow members of his community, are of primary importance if we are not simply to take objects from them and see whether such objects can be appropriated by *our* culture as works of art in *our* terms. There is, however, a very valid philosophical objection which must be mentioned at this point. This is that it is impossible ever to investigate someone else's thoughts or intentions directly. They can be understood only *via* the means he uses to communicate them, and our understanding of such messages is based not on his experience, but our own. In the artist's case, his work of art *is* the primary means by which he expresses himself. If the artist could directly exhibit his thoughts, the production of art objects would presumably be superfluous. Nonetheless, it seems a reasonable enough comment that, if certain philosophers can satisfactorily express this objection of theirs to the rest of us, then they must allow others the possibility of sharing some media through which they too can at least hint at their intentions.

How then, might aesthetics be defined in a way that makes it applicable across cultures? The *Shorter Oxford Dictionary* is unhelpful here. Aesthetics, it says, may be defined either as 'The science of sensuous perception', or as 'The philosophy of taste, or of the perception of the beautiful'. If (as, unthinkingly, we probably do), we rely on aesthetic criteria in our identification of art objects from the culture of some other people, we are immediately presented with two problems. We cannot, as self-respecting anthropologists, assume right from the start that people the world over utilize the same aesthetic criteria as ourselves. Even in our own history, fashions have changed radically. Some peoples, moreover, deny any aesthetic criteria in evaluating what appear ostensibly to be art objects within their cultural repertoire. Haselberger rather sidesteps the issue when she poses the problem of identifying art objects at the beginning of her paper. Would one, she asks, include a pigmy wind-screen in the category of art works? Conceding that a strict division into art and non-art is probably impossible, she goes on to suggest that the screen is not a work of art because it is erected for purely practical purposes. Neither would she accept lines drawn as doodles on rock or sand: if the intent of the person responsible were nothing more than 'playful' then the product is not art. 'Art', she reasonably asserts, 'is involved only when the action produces results *designed to affect* someone and is not, like play, an end in itself' (342). As an example of something that *would* be art she then proposes 'a Melanesian paddle carved with *a beautiful form*', whether or not the form has been supplemented with ornament. Now, it seems to me that she has here begged the question, for she assumes that the beautiful form we perceive is the beauty which the artist intended to create. What right do we have to assume that our criteria of *harmony, rhythm and proportion* are those of other people?

Raymond Firth, another anthropologist who has written a general essay on the subject of the anthropology of art, explicitly confesses his willingness to assume that, although little study has been made of the aesthetic sense of traditionally non-literate peoples, 'there is strong indirect evidence that they share the same kind of aesthetic sensibilities and judgements as Western peoples'. 'A work of art makes a selection of elements of experience, imagination and emotion' in such a way that its *composition* will evoke reactions 'based on feeling tones which we call aesthetic' (1951:156); feelings evoked by the arrangement of lines, colours and movements.

There seems to be little difficulty in finding instances where people express, among other judgements, some form of aesthetic assessment of objects produced in their culture. One of the writers who comments on Haselberger's paper describes how, in one New Guinea society, the women 'frequently use any pieces of clay left over from making a batch of pots to fashion little figurines representing men and women'. The writer was told that these were made purely for pleasure, and kept in the house to look at (Blackwood, 1961:360).

Biebuyck, at whose study of the Lega we have just looked in some detail, shows how, for all the apparent interchangeability of sculptures and natural objects, the Lega have words which express the aesthetic appeal of the finest carvings. Some of these terms associate beauty with order; *kukonga*: to produce harmony and unison in singing together; *kwengia*: to be shiny like a well-polished chair or statue; *kwanga*: to be in good order like a country that thrives; *kuswaga*: to be at peace (129).

Among the natural objects the Lega use as symbols for beautiful and pleasing things are bongo antelopes, the white *bubulcus* birds that follow the herds and white *kinsamba* mushrooms. It is significant that all these are light-coloured and therefore somewhat shiny or glossy, and that the same qualities make ivory very attractive (178-9).

When an ivory carving is made, it lacks the patination which it will gain through repeated rubbing with ointments — castor oil sometimes mixed with red pigments, polished with leaves — a treatment which 'is called *kubongia*, meaning to bring in harmony, to produce unison... the reference is to beauty'. Initiates rub their own bodies with the same ointments, and apply the same terms to themselves, comparing themselves to *bubulcus* birds floating in the air. Ivory and well-polished wooden carvings which possess this quality are reserved for the highest grades of initiation (179). 'Among the other implicit characteristics of the Lega aesthetic code are smoothness of surface, lightness and smallness of the object, and overall simplicity of the forms, which are usually stripped of excessive ornamentation' (180); an aesthetic not apparently shared with baroque and rococo, even though both refer to the organization of forms.

Mountford, in his paper on Australian Aboriginal art in Marion Smith's book, *The Artist in Tribal Society*, provides a further example. He describes men among the Tiwi, a people who live on Melville and Bathurst Islands, near Darwin, manufacturing poles to erect beside a grave. He writes: 'there is no doubt that the artists gave much thought to the making of these, selecting the hardest and most durable eucalypts and carefully planning the designs to be painted on the poles'. Before the burial ceremony which Mountford witnessed, he was shown a design by one of the Aboriginal artists, days before the latter had even felled the tree which he was to decorate. He had scratched the design upon the back of a cigarette tin. Mountford notes that although the artists in any case enjoyed the task of decorating the poles 'they still desired the approbation of their fellows. Several of the Aborigines expressed the hope that when the men and women of the ceremony saw the poles for the first time in the final rituals, they would be pleased with their appearance' (1961:11).

Nonetheless, one must be careful in assessing what brought about the 'pleasure' and 'approbation'. An instance demonstrating this can be taken from another Aboriginal society of northern Australia, appearing in the work of a psychologist named McElroy. McElroy wanted to test a hypothesis put forward by Eysenck: that there was an inter-racial factor of good taste, which he called T. The Aboriginal community has its own art tradition, but McElroy asked forty of its members to rank classes of items with which they were relatively unfamiliar: coloured reproductions of butterflies, Scottish tartans; black-and-white photos of Aboriginal men etc. He gave the same tests to twenty white art students at Sydney University, and found that the two groups ranked the items in each class quite differently. Yet when we examine the bases for the Aborigines' judgements it is clear, as McElroy points out, that even though continuing to term the evaluations aesthetic ones (1952:91) not all are based on considerations of harmonious composition. In Aboriginal society, considerable prestige attaches to old men: the wisest and most experienced members of the group. The forty Aboriginal people tested ranked the photos of old men above those of younger individuals, whereas the Sydney art students — perhaps with more faith in youth and innovation — reversed the rank order (93).

Another exercise, in which an anthropologist asked members of a community to rank its own paintings in order of merit, also demonstrates the complexity of judgements that may be involved. Forge worked among a New Guinea society, the Abelam, who construct large ceremonial cult houses with elaborately painted façades (fig. 4) and within which painted panels are hung. Forge

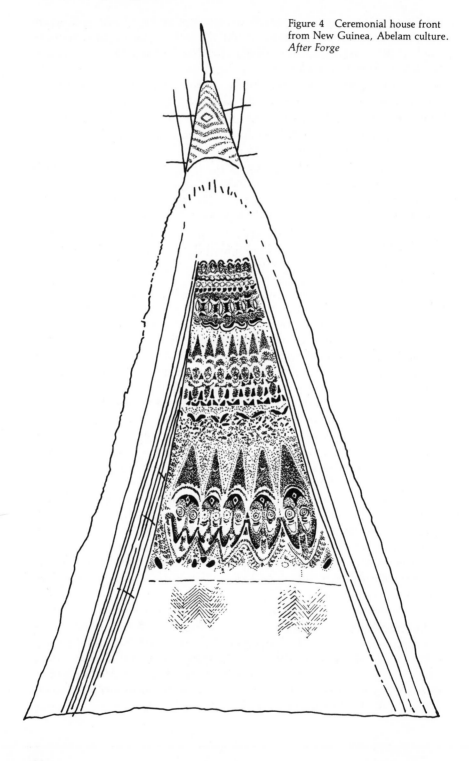

Figure 4   Ceremonial house front from New Guinea, Abelam culture. *After Forge*

invited members of the culture to arrange some of the cult house paintings in order of preference. As a result of this experiment, he reached the conclusion that Abelam artists had the same notions as himself as to what constituted the 'best' paintings, but he also found that to the general Abelam public 'best' meant 'most effective in ritual', effectiveness being measured by the quality of the yams the village subsequently grew (Forge, 1967).

> The artists, although they lack any specific terms, do talk about such things as form and proportion. Although not capable of, or not interested in, discussing art in the same terms, most non-artists asked to rate a group of figures or paintings in order of effectiveness, both in ritual power and secular prestige, rank them in the same order as do the artists and the ethnographer. Since, with Raymond Firth, I believe in a universal human aesthetic, this is not surprising; what is important, I think, is that the skilful artist who satisfies his aesthetic sense and produces beauty is rewarded not for the beauty itself but because the beauty, although not recognized as such, is regarded by the rest as power (82-3).

It is, in other words, the communities whose artists produce the most beautiful paintings, who appear also to be most successful at yam cultivation (cf. the Lega expression of aesthetic balance: 'to be in good order like a country which thrives'). Forge describes the fate of some innovative artists, and also how neighbouring communities desire to adopt the painting styles of villages who are successful at yam cultivation (Forge, 1965 and *op. cit.*).

Variations in aesthetic tradition

To demonstrate the expression of *an* aesthetic judgement is not to demonstrate that this aesthetic takes the same form in all cultures. Firth, whom we quoted arguing that everyone shares the same kind of aesthetic sensibilities and judgements also comments that 'similar psychological impulses can emerge in very different art forms because of different social conditions' (*op. cit.*, 162). Despite the somewhat summary conclusions about social causality implied here Firth is undoubtedly correct to point out that there can be many diverse traditions setting out how to devise harmony, rhythm and symmetry in one's work. Linton, in his classic book, *The Study of Man* (1936), wrote, 'The bulk of all cultures consist of what are, from the practical point of view, embroideries upon the fabric of existence' (301). Many elements of culture do not contribute in any direct way to the simple (biological) survival of the individuals who decorate or scar their bodies or load them with metal decorations; probably the reverse. Linton may be here a little harsh, perhaps overlooking some of the roles personal adornment can play in sustaining the organization of the community, but he has a specific point to make; the practical disadvantages of subjecting oneself 'are outweighed by the satisfaction which any individual takes in knowing that he is being admired, or at least approved, by the other members of his society' (302). One must admit that Wealth and Status, as well as Beauty, may evoke admiration, but Linton's argument is that, however universal the need for approval by one's community, 'the effectiveness of any element of culture for meeting such psychological needs depends *much less on its own inherent qualities* than *upon the associations which have been established within the culture* with regard to it. Thus no young lady in our own society feels an overwhelming desire for a gold nose-stud. In fact, if she were given one her first move would probably be to have it changed into an ear ornament...' (303).

What is needed is a method of abstracting from the multitude of forms found in art traditions across the world, some basic patterns of regularity on which a systematic comparison can be based.

There is a well-known criterion, which has long been used in Western art, for specifying aesthetically-pleasing dimensions in art and design. This is known as the *Golden Section*. In its simplest form, the relative dimensions of the parts in 'the Golden Section' can be shown by drawing a line, and dividing it so that the ratio of lengths of the shorter to the longer part is equal to the ratio of the longer part to the whole (approx. 5:9). Boas, in one of the best books ever written on the anthropology of art (Boas, 1955; originally published in 1927), conducts a detailed survey of regularities of form by means of a series of simple expressions in which recurring motifs are denoted by letter or number.

There are some limitations to his method. Boas disclaims any intent to discuss the ultimate sources of aesthetic judgement, arguing that it is sufficient in an inductive study to be able to demonstrate 'that regularity of form and evenness of surface are essential elements of decorative effect' (25). More than this, prehistoric examples are to Boas as valid as modern ones, whatever the probability of discovering the artist's intentions. To some extent, Boas is therefore vulnerable to the criticism, noted above, directed at commentators who rely on their subjective imputation of a motive to the artist. Nonetheless, Boas is conscious of the possibility that rhythm or balance may result from technical processes such as turning a pot upon a wheel, or the necessity of constructing a mechanically sound form. He deliberately attempts to isolate instances where such alternative causes have been turned to further effect, or where evidently aesthetic qualities cannot be attributed to purely technological considerations. For all this, there is an element of tautology in his basic proposition. The qualities for which he is searching are: symmetry, rhythm, and the emphasis of form by means of such devices as the application of decoration to the margin or prominent features of an artifact. When he concludes that such features 'may be observed in the art of all times and all peoples' (32), one is bound to ask by what independent means has he established what is or is not art.

Despite these qualifications, Boas' method is an interesting one, and his results valuable. He first discusses some instances where the craftsman has apparently taken pleasure in constructing symmetrical patterns in the design of his work without any attempt to communicate this to observers (a practice which Haselberger would presumably classify as 'play' rather than 'art'). He illustrates the type of design which the Fox Indians of North America made on sheets of rawhide that were to be sewn up into leather boxes: when laid out flat the designs are quite symmetrical; when the hide is cut into the shape of the box, the symmetry is completely lost, and in fact large parts of the design are hidden. Boas also cites a technique of mat weaving on the North-west Coast of North America in which the direction of the strands is regularly altered so as to create squares which, however, after a short period of use become almost completely invisible.

Particularly interesting is the technique Boas uses for describing and comparing patterns in decoration, demonstrating at once the widespread occurrence of rhythmic and symmetrical patterns, and the diversity of modes in which such aesthetic qualities are realized. This is achieved simply by identifying the repeated segments in particular designs and designating each by a letter, so that a sequence of letters reproduces the regularity of the design. A couple of his instances illustrate the method (fig. 5). One is that of the rhythmic repetition of beaded thongs on the fringe of a legging from among the Thomson Indians (op. cit., fig. 16). The rhythm is denoted by the sequence (where each letter is arbitrarily assigned to one form of strand on the fringe): abcba/abcba/ab... (etc.). This is one of his examples of a pattern concealed in use, since the strands do not hang individually. The second instance is that of a symmetrical design on a Peruvian textile (Boas, fig. 33). In the illustration there are two designs, designated 1 and 2, each of which is repeated four times, appearing oriented at a different angle in the top and bottom left, top and bottom right sectors of the textile. In some of the more complex cases Boas discussed there is further a rhythmic distribution of

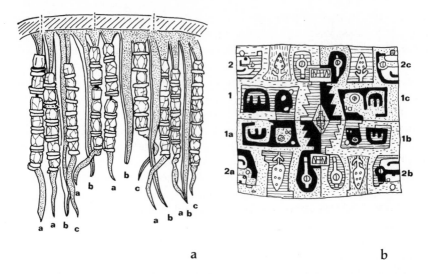

Figure 5   Rhythm in decorative art: (a) Thomson Indian fringe from legging, (b) Peruvian textile. *After Boas*

colours in the designs, often following a different sequence to the distribution of designs themselves. In the Peruvian textile illustrated here, the colouring of panel 1 matches that diagonally opposite (1b), and 1a plus 1c are similarly matched. The same pattern holds good for the other design, 2.

The most elaborate forms illustrated by Boas come from blankets, boxes and trays manufactured by the North-west Coast Indians. Boas himself documented how the individual motifs out of which the patterns on the blankets are constructed, each have meaning as pictures of creatures in the cosmology of these Indian cultures, filled with implications for the social status of the owner; yet he shows how a rather baroque elaboration of decorative form on some objects mitigates against a consistent 'reading' of such a cultural message. 'We find here, as well as in many other places, that elements which are in part derived from representations of parts of animals, have assumed a purely decorative function' (271).

Boas' conclusion is that: 'we cannot reduce this world-wide tendency to any other ultimate cause than to a feeling for form, in other words, to an esthetic impulse' (58). Finally, Boas argues that similar observations may be made of arts such as dance, music and poetry. Although poetry is necessarily concerned with the conveying of ideas through words, here (as in dance or music) 'rhythm and thematic forms follow stylistic principles that are not necessarily expressive [of ideas] but that have objectively an esthetic value' (63). Towards the end of his study, Boas discusses oral literature, music and dance in detail. Here he comments again, 'the investigation of primitive narrative as well as of poetry proves that repetition, particularly rhythmic repetition, is one of its fundamental esthetic traits' (310).

Such an applicability across media is also demonstrated by an elaborate analysis carried out by Lévi-Strauss and Jakobson upon a sonnet of Baudelaire (see Lane, 1970:202-22). The two authors of this essay, which has been described as a classic of structuralist method, are not content with pointing out such mundane elements of rhythmic construction as the rhyming scheme. They distinguish between masculine rhymes (those which end on a stressed syllable, such as såisón and måisón) and feminine rhymes (such as mágiqůes and mýstiqůes), denoting these with capital and lower case letters in designating the rhyming scheme aBBa CddC eeFgFg. They proceed with a detailed analysis of how the correspondences between grammatical structure and rhyme, the allusion to animate objects in the octet but inanimate ones in the sextet etc., all contribute to an elaborate structure in which meaning and form reinforce each other. Here, for the first time, is some suggestion of how the two definitions of art (that referring to aesthetics and that to fresh imagery) with which the chapter began, may be present as complementary elements contributing to the quality of a work as a whole.

ART AND ART IMAGERY

Sometimes works of art appear to derive their effect as much from their imagery as from their form. Aristotle considered the question of form misleading. Like form, imagery is a quality one can evaluate in more than one medium; certainly it is as applicable to verbal as to plastic arts.

The Dinka, a cattle-herding people of East Africa, have a song:

Spring rain in a dry spell, strikes the ants on the head with a club
And the ants say: (it is the work of Divinity)
And they do not know whether he helps people
And they do not know whether he injures people.

Lienhardt, who quotes the song, explains that Dinka commonly compare themselves with ants, before God. The second phrase in the second line is actually: 'My father has seen!' which Lienhardt describes as an idiomatic expression equivalent to the one given in parenthesis above. In another song, the Dinka depict the moon disappearing behind cloud with the image:

The black bull of the rain has been released from the moon's byre.
(Lienhardt, 1961:38, 54)

Clearly, no attempt to understand such imagery can progress without knowledge about the way of life of those who compose and sing the songs. The Lega, another African people, whose use of natural and carved objects in ritual we have mentioned above, make extensive use of proverbs and aphorisms with the qualities of poetic imagery, in *Bwami* ceremonies.

Indeed, Biebuyck writes that there is no synthesis of *Bwami* philosophy; it can only be construed behind the 'thousands' of such sayings which depict the significance of *Bwami* in Lega society, the attributes of the initiate and the responsibilities of office-holders within the cult.

The imagery of Lega proverbs comes first from the animals and plants of the Lega environment and, after that, from geographical features of their surroundings, from their technology and social system. The proverbs are always explained to initiates in an attempt to make their meaning clear, but this may not be sufficient elucidation. The parallel content of verbal, and other art forms is demonstrated by the further illustration, or realization of the proverbs' meaning in accompanying dances and in the production of natural and manufactured articles.

Biebuyck recognizes four structures according to which the imagery of a Lega proverb may be built up. In the first type, the first phrase establishes an identity between two entities, and the second indicates something they have in common. Note that the property of the image is applied to the subject. Biebuyck's example is:

The senior (initiated man, is) a turtle.
He was born (for) long distances.

That is, no matter how far he travels, he will always find relatives, a powerful matter in a culture based on extended kinship. A second example, provided elsewhere in his book, is:

A child: a dug-out canoe; you carve it, it takes you across (138).

The second type first mentions two characters perhaps well-known in story and evidently both therefore already having associations of imagery, and being linked with one another, the second part summarizes an event which happened to them or a pattern of behaviour which characterizes them:

The blue pheasant and the turtle.
Animals that challenge each other over territory.

In a third type the first part acknowledges a pattern of behaviour or a situation which the second verse criticizes or extends:

You may refuse the senior the meat
(But) you shall give him the liver.

In still another type the first part makes a statement, or a concession, which is contrastively completed in the second part:

The ibulungu tree may be somewhat on the side
But every distance between two rivers has its ibulungu tree (55).

It is interesting to note, remembering Lévi-Strauss and Jakobson, the way in which the statements in the proverbs interact with the form to create a simple, but balanced whole.

Perhaps the most dramatic use of visual metaphors in the recent art of the West is in the work of Magritte, or some of Max Ernst's Surrealism. But maybe it is more apparent in the West's poetry than its painting. Among non-literate cultures, however, the visual expression of the imagery of myth is common. One excellent example is provided by the art of the Asmat of New Guinea: the Asmat were traditionally head-hunters, and much of their imagery is concerned with head-hunting. They conceive of Man being created by an ancestral hero who carved a ceremonial house-full of wooden figures and brought them to life: for them, man and tree are related concepts. So, too, are the concepts man and praying mantis. This identification, writes the anthropologist (Gerbrands, 1967), is based partly on the human-like behaviour of the mantis: the way it moves its limbs; the fact that the female bites the head off the male after mating. But the mantis also resembles a piece of wood: when it moves, it is like a cluster of twigs come to life; and so the mantis epitomizes the man-tree link, having elements of both. Not unnaturally, the mantis features prominently in Asmat sculpture (see fig. 46a). Sometimes it is carved relatively naturalistically; sometimes the figure is deliberately rendered so that it suggests equally men and mantis: a visual expression of their symbolic identity.

Another good example of such a tradition is the art of protodynastic Egypt (*circa* 3,000 B.C.); the period when Egypt was in the process of becoming unified; passing from a series of petty chiefdoms to two kingdoms — Upper and Lower Egypt — and then, with the conquest of Lower by Upper Egypt, to unity and the establishment of the First Dynasty. A low-relief carving from a slate palette of the period depicts what has been interpreted as a record of a victory by the ruler of Upper Egypt over a town in Lower Egypt (fig. 28). The king (identifiable by his crown), grasps a victim and is about to execute him with a mace. Over the victim stands a falcon, symbolic of the kingship, grasping the beard of a similar victim. The six papyrus shoots growing from the second victim's back state (if they already had the meaning attributed them later in Egypt) that 6,000 captives were taken. But when we look closely at the falcon, we see that, although it stands on its victim with a falcon's foot, it clutches his beard with a human hand: a visual expression, one assumes, of his identity with the king. In a fragment of a similar carving, beasts probably emblematic of the various chiefdoms whose confederation united Upper Egypt, are represented each attacking a walled town with picks (fig. 6): an action no doubt in reality conducted by their human representatives, the soldiers of the confederation.

The sculpture of the Kalabari, which seemed to fail to satisfy aesthetic criteria, appears more eligible for consideration as art on the grounds of its visual imagery. The motifs by which each spirit is represented are often the visual expression of similes and metaphors in Kalabari thought. To take one instance, *Opu Adamu* is a 'water spirit' (fig. 7). In Kalabari cosmology, water spirits live in the creeks and swamps around settlements. They are associated with extra-social forces, both natural events and human deviancy: successful or unsuccessful innovation. The Kalabari express the position of the

Figure 6 Fragment of protodynastic Egyptian palette: fortified settlements attacked by emblematic animals

Figure 7 Spirit sculpture from West Africa: *Opu Adamu*, a Kalabari water spirit. *After Horton*

water people, outside the social world of the other spirits (lineage ancestors and village heroes), in the simile: 'the water people are like men and also like pythons' (Horton, 1960:213). The python is the major animal associated with the creeks. The Kalabari simile is given tangible expression in dance, where actors representing water spirits move with a 'horizontal, slithering motion' opposed to the 'rather rigid verticality' which represents humans. In the sculpture this same simile is expressed by giving the figure a human face, but the body of a snake — indicated in Kalabari convention, by the black, white and blue diamonds painted on a brown background that decorate the trunk of the carving.

Despite the evident fact that many of the *verbal* images quoted at the beginning of this section can only be understood if one knows, for instance, how the Lega look on the relative significance of the liver and meat referred to in the aphorism about the senior man, many commentators have been prepared to interpret *visual* imagery unaided. Such a willingness probably derives from the assumption, criticized below, that if carvings or pictures 'look like what they depict' then they can be 'read' by members of alien cultures. In fact, there are two separate problems here: identification of the subject-matter of the depiction, and knowledge of its cultural significance. In a general essay on African art Biebuyck (1969) has himself attacked art critics on these points. One instance he mentions is the common Lega representation of the woman with the distended belly (fig. 3). Far from appreciating her significance as a warning against committing adultery while pregnant, those who have seen examples of the figure in museums or art galleries have frequently interpreted her as the product of a fertility cult. Another common Lega sculpture is that depicting a human figure with one arm raised, a gesture sometimes interpreted as an appeal to the gods of the sky. But the Lega, writes Biebuyck, are not concerned with sky gods; for them the gesture is one of prohibition.

Firth, in the paper cited above, makes similar comments. Art works, he says, express themselves through their use of symbols (I would prefer to substitute 'visual images'). One cannot assume that the meanings certain art objects evoke in us, as foreigners, are those the artist intended. To illustrate his point he quotes the case of an art critic who, in reviewing an exhibition of African sculpture, claimed to be repelled by what he saw as 'terror, cruelty and a pathetic acceptance of the unknown' behind the form of the carvings. The masks he had seen had *'cunning* eyes', *'fiercely* protruding lips' and so on. Such an emotional content, Firth insists, is supplied by the observer, and however legitimate such a practice may be if one is describing one's private reaction to the work as an expression of one's model of an alien culture, it is quite illegitimate to infer that there is any parallel between such a reaction and the conditions in which the work was produced. To understand the artist's aims we must understand the symbolism he utilized. The art object one observes is merely the tangible expression of a cultural, and therefore a mental construct, expressed according to that culture's conventions of visual representation.

Ideas and objects

The significance of the fact that an art object is an expression of mental images is dramatically highlighted by Richard Wollheim, in his book *Art and its Objects* (1970). The object we can handle or the performance we can watch or hear is never, he maintains, the 'work of art'. Wollheim draws his data solely from Western culture, but instances from small-scale, non-literate cultures are as appropriate. In the end, I think, Wollheim overstates his case, but not without having presented some most valid arguments. These arguments follow two lines, for he believes that in certain arts there is *no* physical object with which a work could conceivably be identified, whereas in others there are such objects, *even though it would still be wrong to identify them as the works of art*. I will summarize his argument here because it at least underlines the importance of relating art objects to their cultural milieu.

In the case of music or literature, Wollheim believes, it would be impossible to point to a physical object that could be said to be 'the work of art'. It may be that one has a copy of *Ulysses* on one's table, and it may be that one can go to listen to a performance of a symphony; but one couldn't conclude from that that The Novel or Symphony were simply one's own copy or a single evening's performance. For if one lost one's copy of *Ulysses*, *Ulysses* itself would not be lost; and if one disliked the evening's performance of the symphony, it would not necessarily imply that one disliked the symphony itself. Suppose it were argued that in making such a claim one had in fact identified the work of art with the *wrong* object. It could be said that *Ulysses* was in fact the author's original manuscript. Yet, Wollheim points out: 'the critic who admires *Ulysses* does not necessarily admire the manuscript. Nor is the critic who has seen or handled the manuscript in a privileged position (as such) when it comes to judgement on the novel'. Further, the manuscript of the novel could be lost and, providing copies of it survived, nothing of the Novel itself could be said to have been lost. If the work of art that is a symphony were identified with the composer's sheets of music, the mistake would be even clearer. Not only do the same arguments as those just mentioned apply; further, whereas the symphony should be listened to, the score sheets cannot be 'heard'.

Having thus dismissed the claim that there exist physical objects that are the works of art one appreciates in music or literature, Wollheim then turns to other arts, where he believes a more plausible identification with physical objects *could* be made. These are painting and sculpture. One can point to Renaissance sculptures and paintings and assert apparently plausibly that these objects are works of art. (The plausibility derives, presumably, from the fact that these objects are unique. Wollheim would have had less difficulty had he been dealing with traditions of sculpture such as those of the Kalabari and Lega, where successive representations of a single spirit or heroic figure are considered of equal value.) The way in which Wollheim deals with his Renaissance objects may seem rather less convincing than his earlier arguments. He quotes critics who have attributed to such works properties that the physical objects in question could not possibly possess. A sculpture of St George was said by Vasari to 'move with life'. Yet, while some physical objects might be said to move with life, this is certainly not so of a block of marble. A painting is said to be 'exalted and dignified', but *no* physical object — let alone a canvas painted with oils — could of itself be exalted and dignified; it is the ideas expressed that have these properties. If these arguments do appear spurious, it is worth remembering the comments by Biebuyck and Firth on critics who, with only the object at their disposal, had been quite misled as to its significance.

How does Wollheim deal with the problem he has raised? His solution is to suggest that the physical objects that we find in art may be labelled *tokens*, of a *type* — a purely conceptual, platonic entity — which is the work of art. Each performance of the symphony is a token, each copy of the novel. This helps to underline the importance of the criticisms which Firth made of the English commentator visiting the exhibition of African sculpture. If the critic imagined the works had 'cunning eyes' and 'fiercely protruding lips', Firth objected, he was indulging in a creative act of his own that had little significant relation to that of the artist. For the artist the sculpture is a token of one type. The English commentator unconsciously seizes on it as a token for his own preconceptions of African culture.

In addition to its value in characterizing the relationship between a series of sculptures and the cultural construct which they represent, Wollheim's notion of the 'many tokens of one type' is most relevant to the study of myth and ritual; for rituals correspond to Wollheim's case of the symphony (only there is no traditional form of score or written notation, simply a series of repeated performances), and myths to Wollheim's case of the novel. Indeed, one of the problems most frequently encountered in recording a myth is that of variation each time one hears it told. What, one must decide, is the essential myth that generates all these tellings? A further point of interest in Wollheim's argument is the observation that there may be some difficulty in deciding what are the tokens of, for instance, a symphony: are they the various scores that have been printed, or the various performances? They are, rather, all tokens, in different media. A perhaps more valid instance presents itself in anthropology where each telling of a myth would be regarded as a token, each dramatization of that story in ritual as another kind of token of the same 'type' and each depiction of the mythological characters in art as yet a third form of token.

A final point of interest in Wollheim's argument is one which to some extent undermines his position. He notes that not all 'tokens' of a single 'type' may be identical (even though interchangeable); a point again illustrated by the Lega and Kalabari. The reason provided by Wollheim for this phenomenon is that the construction of a token very often involves a certain amount of *interpretation*, and interpretation, according to Wollheim, involves the addition of something to the type: a little further creation. He suggests that the degree of necessary interpretation may depend on the nature of the medium in which the token is created, and further argues that the kind of interpretation carried out by the performers of a symphony or play is not essentially different to the kind of interpretation which the audience make as they listen or watch. He quotes with approval the French poet, Valéry, who claimed that all artists demand that the spectator engage in such creative interpretations. No doubt one can, for anthropological purposes, exclude interpretations of the 'fierce-lips-and-cunning-eyes' syndrome, because one is interested in that cultural entity, the 'type' which inspires indigenous artists. Yet, if realization of the token is said to be a creative act, the possibility is admitted that the token may also embody some artistic quality. One of the objections to forgeries is very often that apart from expressing less exalted ideas, they embody workmanship inferior to the artist's own creation.

A more fundamental objection to Wollheim's treatment of the phenomena he has revealed is this: if an idea is to belong to culture, then it must be shared. And if it is to be shared then it must be communicated through tangible media. These sensible messages are none other than Wollheim's 'tokens'. Yet, in calling them tokens they are somehow made to appear very subordinate appendages to the ideas they express. It may be true that, if one copy of *Ulysses* were lost, the work of art would survive, but it could not survive the loss of all copies. The loss of a single Renaissance painting would be correspondingly more serious; no modern copy would be considered an adequate substitute. Saussure, who founded modern linguistics, argued that the idea and its tangible expression in the sounds of speech are so equal in value, and inseparable, that both together must be called the linguistic *sign*, and each sign therefore has two inseparable and necessary components — the idea and its expression. The particular way in which an artist expresses his idea in his painting, or the skilled performance of an accomplished musician has a lot to do with Art. Horton's distinction between ordinary handwriting and calligraphy is germane, so too are Wollheim's comments on the importance of interpretation. However clear the non-artist's mental image of good handwriting, or the sound of a tune within his head, if he cannot realize those types he will not be an artist.

The intimate relationship between the art object and the idea to which it gives tangible form is excellently illustrated by Edmund Carpenter, in a further comment on Haselberger's paper. Carpenter describes the Eskimo carver working at a piece of ivory in a way that sculptors in our own culture have portrayed their approach to a block of marble. The carver holds his unworked ivory and asks it: 'Who are you? Who hides there?' Then he sees the inner form: 'Ah, Seal!' It is rare, writes Carpenter, for the artist to set out with the deliberate intention of representing a specific animal; rather he carves aimlessly until he sees it, humming and chanting as he works. Again, 'it was always there: he didn't create it; he released it; he helped it step forth' (Carpenter, 1961:361). The author goes on to argue that Eskimo language and the physical environment itself match, or promote, such an emphasis on the artist's role in giving tangible form to a pre-existing idea. In the monotony of snow, ice and long nights no feature stands out and what the Eskimo construct is quickly obliterated again: 'Theirs is a world which has to be conquered with

Plate 1   Eskimo miniature carving: arrow straightener. *British Museum*

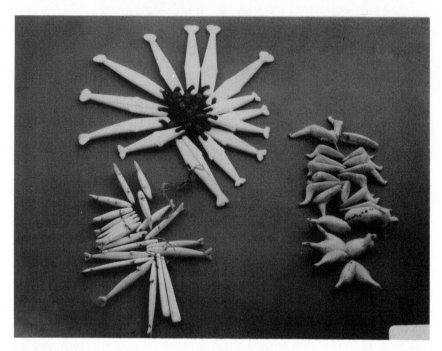

Plate 2 Eskimo amulets: (a) Fish carvings from western Eskimo, (b) Carved duck from Hudson Bay area. *British Museum*

each act and statement, each carving and song — but which, with each act accomplished, is as quickly lost ... Words for the Eskimo are like the knife of the carver: they free the idea, the thing, from the general formlessness of the outside'. Carpenter deduces that for the Eskimo it is the 'artistic act' of giving tangible form to their carvings that is important; once made, the objects are abandoned: 'When spring comes and the igloos melt, the old habitation sites are littered with waste, including beautifully-designed tools and tiny ivory carvings, not deliberately thrown away but, with even greater indifference, just lost' (plate 2). He concludes, in a phrase that Wollheim might approve, 'It's senseless to assume that when we collect these silent, static carvings, we have collected Eskimo art' (362).

The interplay of concept and tangible form is, I think, also illustrated by Biebuyck's comments on how the Lega artist realizes cultural 'types' in his carvings (although I admit that the artist probably forms a mental image of his specific carving before executing it). 'Constrained diversity — that is creative originality', writes Biebuyck, is one the basic goals of all Lega carving (1973:179). He illustrates how this process can take place by describing some of

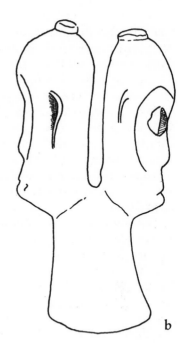

a   b

Figure 8   Lega carving (Central Africa): two realizations of the figure, 'Mr Many-Heads'.
After Biebuvck

the ways in which the 'fundamental prototype' 'Mr Many-Heads' can
be realized (fig. 8): some carvers represent two free-standing heads
on one body, others portray two free-standing bodies with separate
heads; others depict two bodies merged together with separate
heads, others construct carvings consisting solely of heads superimposed on,
and opposed to, one another ... 'These astonishingly varied forms,
all elaborated on one basic idea, fulfil identical social functions and
reveal a common meaning' (180). Initiates who use these carvings in
their ritual 'appreciate expressions of individuality and originality,
and readily accommodate themselves to what is available for use in
the *Bwami* rites' (230).

Orders of representation

What must be kept in mind is that an art object probably has
representational qualities at a number of cultural levels. It depicts a
form which may exist in nature or may, like Mr Many-Heads, be one
that draws on natural models while not, specifically, existing outside
the shared imagination of the Lega. This depicted form, however,

itself stands for cultural notions of wisdom and impartiality among high initiates (see Biebuyck's text accompanying 1973, plate 86), and they in turn are realizations of fundamental values in Lega culture. Panofsky has analysed these orders of representation in European art, in his essay *Iconography and Iconology* (1955). Here he attempts to distinguish between levels at which the critic can assess an object without resort to the artist's cultural background, and levels at which he needs a progressively more detailed knowledge of that context. Panofsky distinguishes between form and subject matter in the artist's product, and isolates three aspects of subject matter. In order to express the differences between his categories he suggests how they might be applied to the analysis of an event lying outside the field of art. His discussion is summarized here both to explain what he means by Iconography and Iconology, and to show the relevance of his analysis to the anthropology of art. Suppose, suggests Panofsky, we see an acquaintance approaching us in the street, raising his hat to greet us. From a purely *formal* point of view, all we see is a change in certain details within a general pattern of colours and lines: in other words, a formal analysis (if the event were treated as art) would have to employ the kinds of aesthetic analysis illustrated by Boas, and by Lévi-Strauss and Jakobson in their analysis of Baudelaire's sonnet. To interpret the particular configuration which we have seen undergo change in front of our eyes as a *gentleman* is, writes Panofsky, to enter the first stage of the analysis of subject matter. To see that he is in a good or bad temper is to develop this, but so far, Panofsky asserts, we are doing something that a person of any culture could do: we are concerned with 'natural meanings', and have not yet entered the realm of iconography. The 'fierce-lip-cruel-eye' syndrome casts some doubt on the extension of this conclusion to artistic representations, but for Panofsky it is not until we interpret the gentleman's raising his hat as a *greeting* that we enter the realm of culture-bound analysis. The gesture is a conventional one characteristic of the interpersonal ritual of Western culture, and it is here, writes Panofsky, that we are making an analysis of subject matter analogous to the study in art of *iconography*: specific motifs whose imagery is evoked and instantly understood by members of our culture as referents to particular, consciously-held ideas. Here, we are at the level of the Lega images of the adulterous woman or the gesture of prohibition.

Finally, Panofsky argues, if we were to co-ordinate our many memories of the acquaintance, and his behaviour on different occasions, we could learn something of his social standing, his national and educational background. This, the deepest level of analysis, is for Panofsky *iconology*, the realm of cultural premises. In art, *iconography* is concerned with the identification of the characteristic motifs employed in particular art traditions: the recognition that certain figures portray the Holy Family, or particular saints; whereas *iconology* is taken up with assessing the underlying cultural premises from out of which the artist's work was drawn, and which he may quite unconsciously express in what he produces.

Religion and art

Many of the anthropological examples discussed in this chapter demonstrate the integral part which religion plays in the beliefs and assumptions of other cultures. Both the iconography and the underlying iconology of art in small-scale societies are frequently embedded in religion. In view of this fact, a discussion of how best to approach exotic religions is probably essential to an appreciation of the anthropology of art. It is with this that the chapter will conclude.

In the late nineteenth century, the religions which proved to play so great a role in many of the cultures being discovered by explorers and missionaries were generally dismissed as mere superstition. According to the evolutionary concepts popular at the time, mankind was believed to exhibit a progress from an irrational devotion to spirits and deities, to the rational, scientific outlook of the writers then establishing anthropology. Nor were the 'irrational' precursors of science only to be found in distant historical records; they flourished in cultures contemporaneous with that of nineteenth-century Europe. It was Durkheim, at the turn of the century, who opened the way to a sympathetic understanding of the part religious beliefs and practices play in the life of a small-scale society. His book *The Elementary Forms of the Religious Life* was first published in 1912 and translated into English three years later. Durkheim here stated his position in no uncertain terms, declaring: 'It is an essential postulate of sociology that a human institution cannot rest upon an error ... If it were not found in the nature of things it would have encountered in the facts a resistance over which it could never have triumphed [for so long]' (1915:2).

To understand Durkheim's argument it is necessary to know a little about Durkheim's general approach to sociological analysis, but it is an approach which will be referred to several times during this study. Throughout his writing runs the idea that the distinctive features of social life derive from the *association* of individuals; that in the association features emerge that cannot be explained by recourse to individual psychology. Durkheim believed this 'social reality' is felt, at its simplest, whenever people assemble in a crowd: a crowd is prone to be gripped by a collective emotion that fills each participant with sentiments quite different from those which he or she would feel when alone. He argued that it is man's constant awareness that he is surrounded by a social force constraining and directing his individual actions which generates religious belief. Because Durkheim still tended to conduct his analysis within an evolutionary framework, he hoped to discover the 'origin' of religion in the simplest *extant* human societies, hunter-gatherers.

The recently-published reports of two excellent observers who were working in Central Australia (Spencer and Gillen), provided Durkheim with the information that each of the small groups, into which the Aborigines of that region were divided, possessed an animal or plant totem. He argued that, although the Aborigines were aware of the collective force of their social group, they could only express this awareness through 'symbols', and it was these that the totem supplied. Durkheim attached particular importance to the *material objects* used in ritual to represent the totems: 'if left to themselves, individual consciousnesses are closed to each other; they can communicate only by means of signs which express their internal states' (230). The sacred objects, some of which are works of art in their own right, were the concrete realization of the sense of social unity felt by the actors.

Despite its value, Durkheim's argument has some important defects. He never proved that it was, specifically, an awareness of 'social forces' which generated religious belief, simply asserting that these forces were *sufficiently* powerful to account for the persistence of religion over thousands of years. Horton, the anthropologist who worked with the Kalabari, is one recent writer to criticize Durkheim and those who accepted his view that the celebration of a religion 'signified acceptance of certain social relationships'. Citing one of our main authorities on the subject, Horton comments, 'Christ himself condemns the scribes and pharisees for using religious ritual as a status-symbol and points to their attitude as the essence of irreligion' (1960:204). The Kalabari, he continues, feel the same way: any Kalabari individual who uses his religious alignments — either pagan or Christian — as an expression of his political position is condemned by his neighbours as irreligious.

Horton, like Durkheim, emphasizes the importance of symbols in thought and communication. Instead, however, of seeing social life as the real source of the forces worshipped in religion, Horton sees social life as the source of the *models* small-scale societies frequently employ in order to conceptualize the nature of the less-readily grasped forces they experience. He argues that in such societies, the social structure provides 'the most markedly ordered and regular area of their experience, whereas their biological and inanimate environment is by and large less tidily predictable'. Complex, literate cultures are different; they experience social interaction as a field subject to significant and rapid change, and uncertainty. Social models cease to have so much of an appeal. Consequently members of such societies turn (as they did in classical Greece and in seventeenth-century Europe) to look elsewhere, in the natural world, for their models. We are prone to forget, Horton wrote, that scientific theories such as the molecular theory of physics, or Newton's laws of mechanics, rest on models. (Horton's paper was published two years before Kuhn popularized the idea of a scientific paradigm (Kuhn, 1962).) Rutherford, attempting to conceive of the structure of the atom, visualized it as a minuscule planetary system with the electrons, like planets, orbiting a larger central mass. The idea that light or sound is transmitted as waves has a clear model in one's everyday perception of waves on a pond or in the sea. On the basis of this argument Horton gives a specific form to the general definition of religion as a belief in spiritual forces: 'Religion can be looked upon as an extension of the field of people's social relationships beyond the confines of purely human society'. He adds that, in order to exclude pets from this definition, it should be qualified as an extension in which 'the human beings involved see themselves in a dependent position *vis-à-vis* their non-human *alters*' (211).

Although Horton follows Durkheim in demonstrating the intellectual content of religion in small-scale societies, it is interesting to note that he has reversed the direction of the process in which models are said to be selected and applied to puzzling areas of experience. Where Durkheim had the animal and plant world yielding totems emblematic of social groups, Horton has social relationships providing a model of forces in the natural world. Despite the fact that Central Australian totemism is more complex than Durkheim was led to believe, it is the case that Central Australian cultures have an ordered taxonomy of plant and animal species and indeed, a sophisticated knowledge of the variety of their natural environment. Aboriginal myths frequently present parables of social life in the form of adventures befalling part-human and part-animal ancestors (fig. 9). But as Stanner (1963) points out, the power of these ancestral heroes lies precisely in their ability to cross the otherwise unbridgeable boundary between the animal and human worlds (fig. 10). It seems likely that Horton and Durkheim have both documented aspects of religious thought, but that it is actually in the construction of analogies between the social and natural worlds that

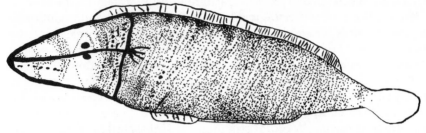

Figure 9   Australian totemic ancestor as animal: Tjimpritja the Rock Cod, Doubtful Bay, Kimberleys

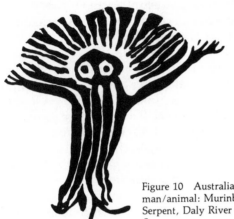

Figure 10   Australian ancestor figure as composite man/animal: Murinbata painting of the Rainbow Serpent, Daly River area, Northern Australia. *After Stanner*

underlying order is perceived in both (see e.g. Layton, 1970, and Blundell and Layton, 1978, for a more detailed discussion of the relationship between Australian Aboriginal religion and social life).

It is perhaps not surprising that Horton has been criticized for claiming that there is an essential affinity between religious and scientific thought. Beattie published a critique of Horton's proposition in which he argued that scientific thought is unique in testing and verifying or rejecting the applicability of its models to the phenomena it is investigating. 'Myth dramatizes the universe, science analyses it', he wrote (1966:60). 'Magical and religious rites are very much more like the arts than they are like science as we understand it in this century'. Since it has been argued here that one of the fundamental qualities of art is the construction of images and metaphors, the idea that there is an essential connection between art and religion is attractive. It is important nonetheless to avoid the evolutionary trap of seeing religion as a precursor of science; a less efficacious mode of explanation which becomes progressively displaced as science develops. All cultures — including those of farmers, herders and hunter-gatherers — necessarily possess a complex body of technological knowledge, acquired and maintained by practical experience. Religion provides rather an account of the most general features of experience: problems of morality and the invisible forces behind what we observe in the natural world.

If we want to judge other cultures by our own standards we have to be very careful. One measure of the rationality of another culture is the degree of internal coherence in its view of the world. In our culture we would look at the logical construction of scientific theories; in others, religious beliefs might be so examined. A second test consists of examining the consequences of applying a body of beliefs to action: is the action appropriate to the goal it aims for? There is a useful collection of essays on the rationality of other cultures' beliefs and practices (Wilson, 1970) which debates the issues involved in making such judgements. Some of the authors' arguments can be summarized here.

The possibility of internal order in another culture's world view is expressed by Beattie, the author whose view of the similarity between religion and art was cited above: 'even though these [religious] premises are founded in metaphor and drama rather than controlled hypothesis-testing of science, they have, or may have, their own order' (Wilson, op. cit.: 259). Is internal coherence necessarily to be valued? Gellner, in the same volume (42), repeats Marx's observation that a politically-dominant group might foster unnoticed contradictions in a society's beliefs to encourage acceptance of its own position.

To what extent can we evaluate the content of someone else's world view? The spiritual beings inhabiting a cosmology are not themselves accessible to our investigation. 'God's reality', as Winch expresses it, 'is certainly independent of what any man may care to think' (81). One thing we can investigate is whether people seem correctly to have described how spirits *affect the workings of the visible world*, but very often we close our eyes to the patterns on which someone else's religion focuses attention. One of the studies most frequently cited in Wilson's volume is Evans-Pritchard's analysis of witchcraft and magic among the Azande, an African society (Evans-Pritchard, 1937). One of Evans-Pritchard's examples of how a belief in witchcraft can explain events is that of a granary collapsing on a sleeping man. The Azande know termites eventually destroy the supports of granaries and they know the mid-day sun drives people to sleep in the shade; but *why* did that granary collapse at the time that man was asleep beneath it? What for us is a coincidence is for the Azande evidence of the intervention of the spiritual force controlled by witchcraft. The idea of magic, Winch

35

argues, may 'express an attitude to contingencies' which reflects a particular sense of the significance of human life (104-5).

A second way of partially circumventing the impossibility of studying spiritual beings is to look, like Horton, at the areas of experience from which religious *models* of these spirits derive, which can in turn help us to understand what motivates ritual action. An appreciation of why people behave the way they do is crucial to anthropology. Winch has an apposite example: 'A historian of art must have some aesthetic sense if he is to understand the problems confronting the artists of his period'. Without it he would experience only 'a rather puzzling external account of certain motions which certain people have been perceived to go through' (5).

The second test, that of the aptness of behaviour based on other world-views, is also a difficult one. As Gellner (24) and Winch (82) point out in Wilson's volume, we cannot evaluate the appropriateness of someone else's behaviour against *reality*, only against our own (scientific) *interpretation* of how the world works. 'If our concept of rationality is a different one from his, then it makes no sense to say that anything does or does not appear rational for *him* [to do] in *our* sense' (97). Winch and Beattie both take up Evans-Pritchard's careful demonstration that the Azande have developed successful techniques of pottery, agriculture, housebuilding etc., and that it is this area of Azande culture that should be compared with our applications of science. There is no parallel in our culture for the integral role of magic in guiding Azande behaviour, and therefore no simple way of 'translating' it into our own concepts. Winch argues that the particular quality of the rationality in the behaviour of members of another culture can only be understood with reference to the problems created by acting that way in *that society*. He cites (87) Evans-Pritchard's admission that following Azande magical procedures (for determining who is bewitching whom, etc.) while he lived with the Azande proved to be 'as satisfactory a way of running my home and affairs as any other I know of'. He does not, however, mention Evans-Pritchard's comment that he once saw a witch moving, as a white light, through his vegetable garden. On the whole, because of their primary interest in the workings of society, anthropologists have tended to examine how acting according to the tenets of a religion affect the social order rather than the spiritual forces they are evidently directed at. One line of thought on this stems directly from Durkheim, identifying the spiritual forces themselves as an expression of society, while another sees the social consequences of ritual as an unintended by-product of its actions. Since the two following chapters will largely be taken up with a discussion of art traditions used in a ritual context, it is worth outlining the theoretical approaches that have been used in treating such material.

Anthropologists and ritual

Ritual certainly seems to present a greater intellectual problem than religious belief. We can readily appreciate the dramatic power of visualizing creatures and forces in the world around us as conscious, moral beings, but when such a world-view is translated into action towards these entities it is less easy (given our concepts of how the world works) for us to accept such behaviour as appropriate. Anthropologists have long debated whether ritual *really* attempts to communicate with the weather, disease, animals of the chase etc., or whether it is essentially concerned with relations *in society* transposed onto the outside world in order to make *social* behaviour more manageable.

Durkheim's view was essentially of the latter type, but Malinowski, whose approach to religion owed as much to his nineteenth-century predecessors in Britain, the Animists, as to Durkheim, found it impossible to accept that all ritual was carried out at collective festivals in which participants celebrated their social solidarity. Rejecting part of Durkheim's analysis, he fell back on the evolutionary notion that small-scale cultures retained an irrational ingredient which science and technology had not yet completely displaced. His interpretation was based on his own study of the Trobriand Islanders, off the coast of mainland New Guinea. When the Trobrianders dig and weed their gardens, he wrote, they periodically resort to magical ritual in the midst of their technological activity. That this is so does not mean that they lack empirical knowledge of how best to cultivate crops: 'if you were to suggest to a native that he should make his garden mainly by magic and skimp his work, he would simply smile on your simplicity' (1948:28). Even people with the simplest of agricultures must, he admitted, have a detailed knowledge of soil types, periodicity of rainfall, plant growth etc. The Trobrianders' accumulated experience has, Malinowski argues, also made them aware of many natural forces which they cannot control: plagues of insects, droughts and storms which, if they strike, may ruin the crops. It is towards these technologically uncontrollable forces that the Trobrianders are said to direct their magical ritual gaining confidence from the illusion that natural disasters are thus controllable. Just as technological activity is punctuated by magical acts, so social interaction is periodically interrupted by religious rituals. These occur at moments of crisis such as sickness or death, when the uncontrollable forces of aging and disease threaten social cohesion, and are similarly intended to renew the participants' confidence. The difference, for Malinowski, was that while magical ritual claimed to act on uncontrollable natural forces, and was therefore irrational, religious ritual *obliquely* achieved its effect because, in worshipping together, the congregation does re-affirm its solidarity. The implication remains that, with the development of agricultural and medical knowledge magic and religion would progressively be displaced.

Satisfying though it may be to the anthropologist to show that even if ritual seems to him misdirected in its stated aim, it still has a useful component in communicating social values, it is important to realize that exotic ritual is not the only kind of behaviour with such a component. Suppose an alien anthropologist discovered that our impression we could travel from one place to another by car were to him illusory. He could still point to the symbolism of car-owning, so important in expressing our social standing. Since it appears many suburban cars are in motion for less than ten per cent of their lives, the alien anthropologist would have understandable reason for saying we really continued to buy cars because of their expressive functions.

Two opposed views of the nature of ritual have thus arisen among social anthropologists. Are the social consequences of ritual intended, or an unwitting by-product of behaviour directed to the environment? Goody has followed Firth and others, in adopting the second view: 'by ritual we refer to a category of standardized behaviour (custom) in which the relationship between the means and the end is either irrational or non-rational' (1961:159). Beattie, in the critique of Horton which we have already reviewed, criticized Goody for being so negative. 'When we speak of ritual', he wrote, 'we are speaking of something which is basically expressive' (1966:65), a view in line with his interpretation of religion as a phenomenon more closely related to art than to science. Other writers would agree with Beattie, although they would differ as to whether all expressive behaviour is ritual, or only that conducted with reference to religious beliefs. For many anthropologists, too, the simple expressive gestures studied by ethologists which are analogous to the ritualized aggression and mating of animals, are significantly different from the elaborate ceremonies evoked by the word ritual.

It would be difficult to deny that explanations which show the social consequences of ritual to be deliberate seem the more intellectually satisfying. Equally important, perhaps, it is possible to study the social consequences of ritual, whereas spiritual forces are rather more mysterious qualities. Tambiah (1968) has analysed

Malinowski's material on Trobriand gardening and fishing ritual and argued that the Trobrianders appear consciously to use their spells as mnemonic devices for impressing on their *own* minds the correct sequence and value of the accompanying technological acts, as if they were reminding themselves of how best to make the plants grow, not to eat more than available resources allow, and so forth. To the extent that this is true, such an interpretation would account for the proliferation of ritual in small-scale societies in terms of the specific fact of their lacking a written language in which to codify such procedures, rather than the general hypothesis of their relative intellectual development.

One of the most comprehensive, and satisfying analyses of ritual in terms of its deliberately-sought social effects, is Lienhardt's account of ritual among the East African cattle-herders, the Dinka. This can be illustrated with his discussion of a rite to remove the consequences of an incestuous relationship in which a man had slept with a junior wife of his father. The guilty couple and their kin were taken to a pool of water. Prayers were made over them, then the whole group entered the pool, accompanied by a ram which was later to be sacrificed. When all had washed the guilty couple, everyone came out. The ram was then taken a short distance away and slaughtered by being cut in half longitudinally. Special care was taken to cut in two its sexual organs. This was held retroactively to neutralize the consequences of the incestuous relationship: for instance, the development of skin diseases by the guilty couple, or the potential death of the girl in childbirth (Lienhardt, 1961:284-5). Lienhardt argues that communication among the participants of a certain view of social solidarity is not *incidental* to the rite's explicit purpose but a central function.

He points to evidence for conscious symbolism in the ritual actions. When the guilty couple were washed in the pool by their kinsmen, their impure condition was said to be transferred to the ram, also in the water. If this were not symbolic, Lienhardt argues, then surely the Dinka would have considered the impurity also to have transferred itself to the kinsmen in the water. When the ram is cut in half, special emphasis is placed on dividing the sexual organs; and this, Lienhardt suggests, can only refer to the severing of the illicit sexual union established by the offending couple.

Furthermore, Lienhardt then states, such action is not some kind of delusion, or conjuring trick, fooling the participants into believing something that is really untrue. Incestuous relationships are not physical entities; they exist only because a human culture defines certain sexual relationships as incestuous. This being the case, if one wishes to deny that an incestuous relationship continues to exist, one can do so only by affirming this in the minds of those who participate in and keep alive that culture. 'The symbolic actions described above thus recreate, and even dramatize, situations which they aim to control, and the experience of which they effectively modulate. If they do not change actual historical or physical events — as the Dinka in some cases believe they do — they do change and regulate the Dinka's experience of those events' (291).

Conclusion

There is, of course, some justification for our judging how other peoples' behaviour measures up to our criteria of rationality. Our interest in cross-cultural comparison sometimes rises above the level of ridiculing the exotic which seems to typify peoples' attitudes to their neighbours the world over. Also, we consider that our theories of how the world works are tested and revised more frequently than other peoples' (although no doubt only against areas of experience that interest us). Nonetheless, the fact that we stand in the reflected glory of our culture's scientific achievements should not make us forget that we, as individuals, almost invariably lack the technical expertise, and equipment, to carry out the tests which characterize scientific method. As Horton comments: 'the layman's ground for accepting the models propounded by the scientist is often no different from the young African villager's ground for accepting the models propounded by one of his elders' (1960:171): both are recognized authorities. We don't have to look far into the history of science to find, in specific instances, a credulity among our immediate forebears about diet, medicine and space flight quite like that we attribute to members of small-scale societies, and this alone should make us cautious in judging others.

When, in the following chapters, we consider the religious symbolism of art in other societies, and the use of art objects in ritual, we should beware of dismissing the basis of such phenomena as 'mere superstition'.

2
Art and social life

'Primitive art', wrote Raymond Firth, 'is highly socialized' (1951:71). The art objects of small-scale societies are very often also objects of everyday, technical use which have been decorated with artistic designs. Whereas in Western culture one tends to think of *real art* as being something too expensive for the average citizen to afford, in small-scale societies art objects are found in many domestic contexts. The artist in such a society is in consequence primarily a craftsman. He makes things which will, on the whole, serve material ends and, although they give pleasure, such things often also have a pragmatic role to play in the life of the household or community. Even songs have social functions. On the Pacific island of Tikopea, where Firth has worked over a considerable period, funeral dirges are sung by people who have a specific kin relationship with the deceased, the chosen song is one which expresses this social link, and singing is an activity which brings material reward. In contrast to the image of the artist we hold in our own Western society, the artist in a small-scale society is not divorced from his public. Generally he is a part-time specialist, at most, and shares to a very large extent the values of those around him.

Firth's set of contrasts between the Western artist and the artist of small-scale societies is a useful one, but rather too dichotomous, allowing neither for popular art in our society, nor for the differentiation of exclusive sub-cultures in other parts of the world. His essay also suffers from the common tendency to view a people's ideas and concepts of the world around them as a mere appendage to their social life, rather than as a genuinely creative order of experience. Accurate though the statement is that many 'primitive' art objects have a utilitarian purpose, it disregards the fact that many others do not and are primarily vehicles for the communication of ideas, rather than axes, or bowls, or canoes with a decorative frill. Without denigrating the value of Firth's paper, it does seem that this deficiency is apparent when he proceeds to outline the two fields which he considers a contextual analysis of ethnographic art should take into account: the art-work's relation to a system of ideas, and its part in a system of social relationships. It may be that art provides a medium for the expression of universal human emotions but, as Firth aptly observes, all art is composed in a social setting and has its context in a specific body of beliefs and values. He proposes two goals in the analysis of the social role of art. The first is to discover the consequences that producing and using art objects have upon the society within which they are manufactured; the second, to discover 'the nature of the values which are expressed by the formal characteristics of the [art] objects'. What, in other words, writes Firth, paraphrasing himself, does art *do* in a small-scale society? Unfortunately, the two genuine problems of analysis, which will form the theme of this chapter, are by Firth related to one another in such a way as to make the second dependent upon the first, for he gives the general answer that in addition to affecting social interaction in certain ways, the use of art objects expresses a system of images which 'correspond to' that system of social relationships. It is important also to avoid simply cataloguing the various social roles played by particular types of art object such as masks, or human figurines.

Much although not all of Haselberger's *Method of studying ethnographic art*, published ten years later (1961), is taken up with the construction of a series of boxes by means of which art objects can be put into their social context. She proposes to achieve this by looking at the status of the artist within his society, and by investigating the connection between the production of art works and other social activities. Like Firth, Haselberger emphasizes that art is always the concern of a community, and like him, she sees this epitomized in its social purpose: is it utilitarian, ritual, educational, commercial, concerned with prestige or social control or, finally and perhaps by implication residually, a work of art produced entirely for art's sake?

Not that these questions are unimportant. The present chapter will certainly ask them of the examples it considers. But while vital for the complete analysis of any particular instance of an art tradition, they are a weak basis for comparative study. Once used for comparison rather than a simple contextual analysis, they fall into the sort of superficial listing of similarities and differences which so outrage Lévi-Strauss when he discusses Radcliffe-Brown's form of structuralism. What other methods of comparison are available to anthropology? For Radcliffe-Brown, sociological analysis had to 'combine with the intensive study of structural systems observable in particular communities, the systematic comparison of many societies (or structural systems of *different types*)' (Radcliffe-Brown, 1952: my emphasis). Lévi-Strauss' structuralism has been directed at showing that social or, more properly, cultural systems are not all types unto themselves, but can be reduced to variations on a limited number of themes in which a few basic rules of social behaviour or cultural logic will generate the great variety of ways of life suggested by superficial comparison.

Rather than attempt to list and compare the functions of specific categories of art *object*, such as figurines or masks, this chapter will follow Lévi-Strauss in examining the role of art objects, regardless of their surface morphology, within two basic variants of West African culture: the chiefless society and the traditional kingdom. Further, we will attempt not to reduce the ideas and values given expression in art objects to a servile reflection of social interaction, but rather assess their impact as agents of an ideology upon the form of social relations.

If one were, as I think Firth and Haselberger would recommend, to adopt a Radcliffe-Brownian approach to the comparative study of art in social life, one would soon find that the attempt to discover *The Role of Masks* in society, or *The Functions of Figurines*, is likely to result in the kind of puzzle encountered in, for instance, the application of the term *Feudal* to traditional States outside Mediaeval Europe, or the attempt to discover a universal form of the family. Just as institutions, such as clientage and fief-holding, perform different functions in different social systems, and are differently articulated with other institutions in each case; and just as there are a number of ways of running a household or raising children; so it is unlikely that masks or figurines perform constant functions (fig. 11), or functions which cannot equally well be performed by other means. For Lévi-Strauss the specific content of gift, trade or matrimonial exchanges is less important than the basic types of reciprocity which they realize, and the specific imagery of myth less important than the fundamental principles of cognition to which they give tangible form. It is the frequent lack of a constant correlation between form and function which is likely to reduce one to a mere cataloguing of differences when such a purely formal study is applied cross-culturally.

When Haselberger's paper was published, Leach had already attacked Radcliffe-Brown's method in his essay *Rethinking Anthropology*. 'Comparison', he wrote, 'is [for these people] a matter of butterfly collecting — of classification, of the arrangement of things according to their types and sub-types. The followers of Radcliffe-Brown are anthropological butterfly collectors' (1961:2). Radcliffe-Brown's proposal for cross-cultural analysis 'is equivalent to saying that you can arrange your butterflies according to their colour, or their size or the shape of their wings, according to the whim of the moment' (3).

Although the kind of comparative anthropology Leach was engaged in at the time he wrote this essay owed a lot to Lévi-Strauss,

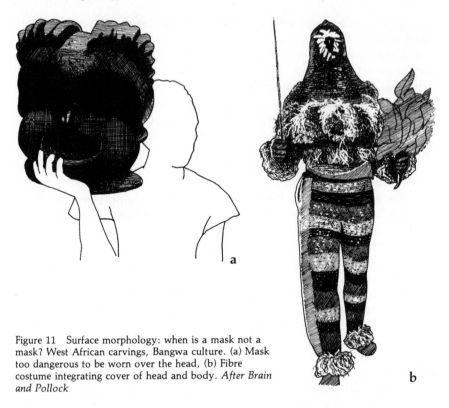

Figure 11   Surface morphology: when is a mask not a mask? West African carvings, Bangwa culture. (a) Mask too dangerous to be worn over the head, (b) Fibre costume integrating cover of head and body. *After Brain and Pollock*

he made some important criticisms of Lévi-Strauss' reductionism, demonstrating that the consequences of one of Lévi-Strauss' basic types of reciprocity could have quite different consequences if embedded in different social systems. Leach's own analysis relied more on examining several permutations on a single type of social system, and it is at this level that the comparisons which follow will be carried out. To compare a limited number of societies which, although quite different can be reasonably assumed to have a common origin and to exhibit different arrangements of a common set of institutions provides something more like a controlled experiment. The examples to be used here are all taken from West Africa, although coming from both centralized states and societies without centralized government.

On the subject of methods of comparison, however, there is a final point to note. If one is comparing societies which are historically related and yet have developed differently, the question soon presents itself: why have the differences developed? If the reasons are held to be extraneous to the social system (to be differences of the physical environment, for instance), then they are not necessarily very germane to one's analysis of the internal dynamics of social life. If, however, it can be shown that the differences arise partly through the actual processes of social interaction — whether or not they are precipitated by technological innovation or contact with other societies — then the way in which societies develop or preserve an equilibrium becomes critical to one's analysis of 'how they work'. Marx was a writer who expressed this very clearly, and as anthropologists have felt free to pass beyond the ahistorical approach of Radcliffe-Brown, Marx has become a popular source of models for analysis. Marxist anthropologists have also criticized Lévi-Strauss for his failure to use models which would generate social change simply through the operation of patterns of interaction. In his classic analysis of the rise of capitalism in Europe, Marx uses concepts closely akin to the more recent ideas of positive and negative feedback. A certain pattern of production and trade may set up an equilibrium, but once new methods of production and new concepts of exchange arise in the society, social relationships may undergo a progressive transformation until they become so unstable as to precipitate yet new social systems. While Marx tended, as was typical of his time, to view such processes as an instance of unilinear evolution, some anthropologists to whom we will refer below have borrowed his ideas to describe cyclical developments in society. One of these, indeed, has reanalysed Leach's own data (Friedman, 1975). We will examine how art objects participate in the social processes of continuity and change in a few, detailed examples.

Uncentralized societies in West Africa

Anthropologists have sometimes maintained that there are relatively few differences between centralized states in West Africa and neighbouring peoples who lack a centralized government. For the purposes of comparison this is a useful hint. Fortes (1940), comparing the Tallensi of northern Ghana (who lack a single, traditional leader) with the neighbouring chiefdom of Mamprusi, writes that the Mamprusi simply 'exhibit a somewhat different variant of the [same] culture'; they live in more scattered settlements, they have a 'more complex economic system and they have a paramount chiefship'.

Any understanding of the part which art objects play in realizing or maintaining an uncentralized political system seems therefore to depend on examining the kind of fluctuations which may exist within these societies in the size of groups under the leadership of individuals or councils, and the ways in which leaders' aspirations are controlled by those around them. In many West African societies patrilineal descent is the foremost principle according to which groups are organized. The typical village community may consist of two or more *maximal lineages*; that is, two or more of the largest groups sharing a genealogy which links them through their fathers, fathers' fathers etc., to a common male ancestor. Alternatively, a single lineage may occupy several communities; the size of both lineages and settlements is variable. Whatever the precise correlation between community and lineage, each lineage is divided into progressively smaller segments as one comes down the generations in the genealogy, the minimal segment being the living children of one man and his wives. Women born into the lineage leave it on marriage and the men find their wives from other lineages. The following diagrams should help to explain these processes to non-anthropologists.

The basic components on a kinship diagram consist of males and females linked by marriage and parenthood.

a) A man marries a woman... b) they have a son and a daughter.

c) Over successive generations, families like this intermarry:

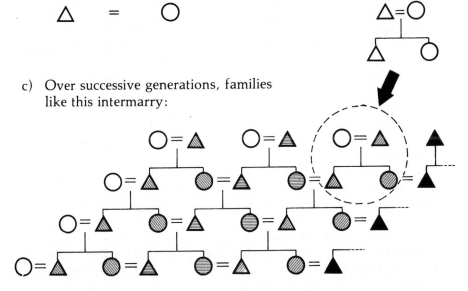

d) and within this pattern four lines of patrilineal descent can be recognized, designated thus: i: ii: iii: iv: ...
Everybody belongs to *one* descent group only; the group of their father. Only sons transmit this membership to their children.

e) In reality, some families have many sons, others many daughters, and so descent groups fluctuate in size. The fortunes of one group might proceed as follows:

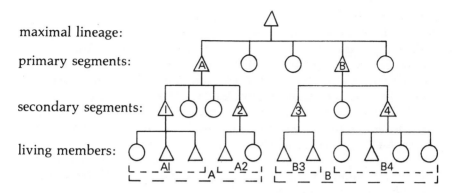

maximal lineage:

primary segments:

secondary segments:

living members:

f) Branches within the lineage are called *segments*. Each segment at
    a higher level (A + B) contains lower level segments (1, 2, 3, 4).

Frequently, several lineages whose members live close together
consider that they are all linked by common patrilineal descent of
some unspecified form at a point further back in the past. This larger
kind of group can (following Fortes) be termed a *clan*.

In 'acephalous' or 'headless' societies based on lineage groups,
there are leaders within the lineage, but the totality of lineages
sharing a common political purpose do not have a single supreme
ruler. Rather, it is local leaders, heads of a cluster of close kin, who
have most power. Leaders of maximal lineages frequently have less
real authority and fewer prerogatives than those with authority over
a component segment.

The Lega belong to this class of society. In Chapter 1, Lega
concepts of art and aesthetics were cited. Here we will consider the
more mundane question of how art objects are owned and used in the
political life of the Lega. Two institutions are fundamental to Lega
politics: patrilineal descent and the ritual cult organization known as
the *Bwami*.

The largest patrilineal descent group is called by Biebuyck the clan,
but since the Lega 'clan' traces its descent from a named ancestor at a
depth of about ten generations from its living members (Biebuyck,
1973:44) it will be referred to here as a 'maximal lineage'. These
descent groups are linked into wider units on the basis of putative
common descent (22) and such wider groupings could better be
termed clans. Three levels of segmentation are recognized and named
by the Lega: primary segments are traced from one generation below
the founding ancestor of the maximal lineage, and, within these,
secondary and then tertiary segments are also recognized. Each
village is generally occupied by men from a single primary segment,

with their wives and children. The whole segment may collectively occupy adjacent villages.

Bwami (see page 8ff.) controls both the rise of political leaders, and the ownership of art objects. The two functions are closely related. Art is integrally concerned with the values and status of leadership: art objects give the ideals of good leadership tangible expression, and ownership or custodianship of the objects is conferred on people who have been admitted to a certain level in the association. Even though the Lega are a chiefless people, they do not therefore reproduce the picture painted by Firth of an egalitarian community in which everyone has equal access to art. There are a number of grades within the cult, but only certain of the older people are admitted to the higher levels. Membership becomes progressively more exclusive as one moves up the hierarchy, and it is from the higher levels that lineage heads are chosen.

Advancing through *Bwami* is a process of education in the values of Lega authority. The initiate has acquired *izu*, deep insight and wisdom, rather than *kizio*, simple knowledge. 'An individual proves he has *izu* by not being quarrelsome, adulterous, violent, ostentatious or meddlesome. A man of *izu* brings *ibonga*, smoothness of social relationships at all levels and in all circumstances' (Biebuyck: 1973:128). A man demonstrates his distinction by building up a large kinship group, marrying many wives, having many children, attracting other kin and keeping the group together by commanding respect, enforcing the law and having a strong character. He also shows it in his enjoyment of the dances, songs and displays of objects at *Bwami* ceremonies, his rivalry with others for honour and power, his success at climbing through levels of initiation and in his economic prosperity (130-1).

These values are expressed in proverb. 'The little fish of the *mwami* [*Bwami* member] is an *nkamba* fish; in deep pools, that is where it used to swim' — a proverb which, Biebuyck records, was said of himself as he became admitted to the deeper levels of knowledge held by the *Bwami*. 'The hammer that remains with the children shatters the *nkoko* shell' is an aphorism which conveys the alternative situation: if left to uninitiated individuals, the land will be ruined (xx-xxi).

The fashion in which art objects express the values of *Bwami* is exemplified in Biebuyck's account of the well-polished, four-legged *kisumbi* stool carried by initiates. The legs of the chair are acknowledged to represent the segments of a lineage. The seat and base are referred to as two opposed heads, an image of the character Mr Many-Heads who exemplifies the wisdom, perspicacity and ·equitableness of high initiates. The polished surface of the stool provides an image of the transformation worked on an individual as he passes through initiation: 'The chair was bad, *bukenga* leaves have been made me shine around the eyes' (186). Sometimes the polished, four-legged stool is contrasted with the unpolished *nkeka* chair made from a forked aerial tree root, on which people rest: 'He who talks behind my back has given me an *nkeka* chair and other oddities that harm me' (186-7).

Popular control of leaders and their ownership of the prestige-giving art objects is exercised indirectly. It is in the manner of this control, rather than in the actual pattern of ownership, that the acephalous society differs most fundamentally from West African states. Those who achieve higher grades in the *Bwami* do so only because they are provided with much of the wealth they need to finance the initiation ceremony by members of their own lineage. Willingness to provide this wealth signifies acceptance of the aspiring elder's suitability for admission to a more privileged position. At the same time, senior initiates must be satisfied that the new candidate to their grade possesses the desired qualities. Rather than a limited number of lines of descent establishing a perpetual prerogative to provide positions of leadership, as occurs in centralized chiefdoms, privileged access to authority and wealth is thus something temporarily conferred by the community on a respected elder.

Accession to high status within the *Bwami* operates according to a fashion documented by Fortes (1940) in one of the original, and classic studies of leadership in an acephalous West African society; the case of the type of lineage head called *na'am* among the Tallensi of northern Ghana.

The basic grades of the Lega *Bwami* association are listed below.

1 *Bwali* (circumcision) is a prerequisite for joining the association. It is the occasion for systematic instruction in the values and behaviour expected of members of the cult. Men are circumcised between the ages of 12 and 20.
2 *Kongabulumbu* is the lowest grade.
3 *Kasilembo* is a short rite which gives those who pass through it greater knowledge in the lore of the association. It is not a distinct grade.
4 *Ngandu* is the highest grade in some communities, although not those most discussed by Biebuyck, where it has been supplanted by *yananio* and *kindi*.

   Bombwa is the equivalent grade for women. A man who has reached the *ngandu* grade has one of his wives pass through *bombwa*.

5 *Yananio* is a higher level within which are two sub-grades:
   musagi wa yananio and then *lutumbo lwa yananio*.
   Bulonda is the grade for women equivalent to *yananio*.
6 *Kindi* is the most senior grade, and has within it three subgrades.
   The lowest ranking is *kyogo kya kindi*, followed by *musagi wa
   kindi* and then *lutumbo lwa kindi*.
   Bunyamwa is the equivalent grade for women, providing a
   kindi man with an initiated wife.

In the view of the rather complicated proliferation of terms, this
list will probably have to be referred to in the course of the following
account.

Biebuyck gives an example which illustrates the restrictive nature
of admission to higher grades, describing the progress of one man's
eleven sons. The father had reached *musagi*, the second grade within
kindi. Eight of his sons entered the association. Three never rose
above the first grade, *kongabulumbu*. One reached the intermediate
grade, *ngandu*. Two climbed as far as the upper grade within
yananio and two achieved *kindi*, one stopping at *kyogo kya kindi*,
one passing on to *lutumbo lwa kindi*. Of the three sons who did not
enter the association two died while young and one migrated early in
life to a European town (88).

The highest political office among the Lega is that of *nenekisi*, the
head of the primary lineage segment. His dependants are likely to be
distributed between more than one village, and include 'distantly
related agnatic kinsmen and close or distant cognates and in-laws'
(these are the additional dependants a leader can attract). The group
of related villages under a *nenekisi* is a fairly independent unit
politically, having 'far-reaching autonomy in the ritual, political and
economic sphere' (47). Biebuyck translates the term *nenekisi*, 'Master
of the Land', 'because the word *kisi* encompasses ... everything that
is good of its kind and has utility: the country, the land, the people,
the animals, children, wives, relatives, wealth, wisdom, initiatory
experience' (131-2). The position of *neneski* can only be achieved
through *Bwami*, since it is conferred on members of the highest
(*kindi*) or middle (*ngandu*) grades alone. The *nenekisi*'s role is that of
arbitrator within his group and representative of it to outsiders. He
consults with a body of elders. Those who go against the elders'
judgement are subjected to a 'mystical sanction' which, more
practically, requires them to pay heavy fines and perform resource-
consuming rituals to exonerate themselves.

The kind of flux which might be exhibited in the life of such a
society was well illustrated by another classic study of a chiefless
society in West Africa, the Tiv. The Tiv live in northern Nigeria. As

in Tallensi and Lega society, patrilineal descent is one of the major principles organizing social groups. In Tiv society however age-grading is also attributed an important role. Men within a particular age set will help each other even when they belong to different lineage segments. This is an instance of different institutional matrices in what are, in gross terms, similar societies. It is true that the *Bwami* shows some resemblance to an age-grading system, but in the *Bwami* association, a progressively smaller proportion of people advance to successive levels.

The only 'formal office' among the Tiv, according to the Bohannans, is that of compound head; a man whose authority would extend over a few closely related families. All older men may, however, be attributed the status of *Elder*. To qualify as an elder one must have the strength of personality which is interpreted as control of the magical force called *tsav*. Elders come together periodically in an assembly whose primary role is to restrain individual aggrandizement. Tiv are aggressively egalitarian and take active steps to prevent the emergence of too great differences in wealth or power. Particularly vulnerable is the 'man of prestige', 'a man whose wealth, generosity and astuteness gave him a certain influence over people and formerly allowed the purchase of slaves and thus the formation of a "gang" to furnish safe-conduct to those strangers who paid tribute and to rob those who did not. These men, then, had (before the colonial period) a certain measure of physical force and material wealth at their command. Unless they were also elders, however, they were ultimately controllable by the powers of witchcraft and magic lying within the hands of that gerontocracy' (54). Whatever cultural efficacy one attributes to magic or witchcraft, it is clear that physical sanctions were also used in political confrontations.

'Talent, power, luck, wealth and strong character' are seen as symptoms of the possession of the force called *tsav*. *Tsav* is the currency through which calculations of equality are made. According to Tiv ideology everyone should have equal amounts of *tsav*, and anyone who has more than his fair share is held to have stolen it from his lineage-mates. Leadership is thus a two-edged affair. A man of influence can bring prestige to his lineage segment and he can materially help his fellow members. Bohannan (1958) shows neatly how the totally segmentary structure of Tiv political organization tends to engender processes which counteract a leader's extension of his influence beyond even the minimal level. If a man wishes to lead a larger segment of Tiv society he must inevitably at times favour parts of that larger segment equivalent to his own set of patrikin, and his own immediate kin will inevitably consider that they are being used — and suffering — in consequence. They will accuse him of witchcraft; the theft, in other words, of their *tsav* for his personal ends. As a result, whatever the benefits a leader may bring the lineage segment, 'its other members fear him and try to whittle him down to their level'. Most significantly, 'Tiv egalitarianism is manifest in the *physical damage done to the possessions of an outstanding man*' (55; my emphasis). If the egalitarian nature of Tiv society persists it would seem rash to attribute this solely to restraints imposed willy-nilly by environment or technology, or even to an irrational belief in witchcraft. The Tiv consciously hold an ideology of egalitarianism which, regardless of ideas about the efficacy of witchcraft, they take active steps to enforce.

Bwami, the distribution of wealth and art objects

Biebuyck's opinion is that '*Bwami* cannot be used to build up personal power and wealth' (135) but on the other hand he also writes that the cult 'is like a big corporation that produces wealth, distributes and redistributes it, invests and reinvests it, and provides economic incentive' (67). In the light of these remarks it is necessary to break down one's discussion of the association according to three questions: Who produces the wealth? Who distributes it? Who receives it?

Since much of the wealth created appears to circulate within the higher grades, the mechanism by which people are admitted to these grades is crucial. Birth order is one; in the example of the eleven brothers cited above, the one who reached *lutumbo lwa kindi* was senior by birth to the one who only reached the lowest grade in *kindi*. A father may also invite his son to join, if the younger man exhibits the desired qualities of character and respect. Once in receipt of such an invitation, the potential candidate needs the support of his kin, because among the Tallensi the labour and organization of his own household would be insufficient to accumulate all the necessary goods for him to realize the ceremony. Kin look for the following properties in a man seeking their support: that his seniority in the lineage is appropriate to the position he is seeking; that he is patient, pious and not verbose. Only when he has found the necessary backing can he hope to recruit the tutors and sponsors he needs to guide him through the ceremony. They too are kinsmen and they must belong to the grade to which he is seeking admission, or to a higher one. The distribution of goods and the making of arrangements before the ceremony are long and difficult, so advice from one or more tutors is absolutely necessary, yet no one will take on such a task unless they are sure of the candidate's worthiness. Throughout the ceremony the candidate must display 'humility, restraint, detachment and willingness to co-operate' (90). 'The general principle', comments Biebuyck, 'may be formulated as follows: the higher a man wants to move in *Bwami*, the more kinship support and the more wealth he needs, the more virtue he has to display, the more guidance and counselling he needs' (86).

The fact that admissions to the progressively more exclusive higher grades are of concern to a wider and wider community is neatly expressed in the size of the group which participates in the initiation. *Kongambulumbu* initiations are generally organized by a single tertiary segment, or by two or three such segments of different lineages, linked by territorial proximity or matrilateral ties of one to another (91-2). Admission to *yananio* may be controlled by a primary lineage segment, while admission to *kindi* might require the collaboration of more than one primary segment within a maximal lineage. Even where a single primary segment has the authority to act autonomously in admission to a higher grade it would still invite members of the appropriate grade, from equivalent segments within or beyond its own maximal lineage, to participate. Each ritual community owns a basket (fig. 12) containing the objects which are produced during the initiation ceremony: the natural and manufactured items, and art objects, discussed in the previous chapter (see page 8). Thus *kongambulumbu* baskets might be owned by teritary segments, *yananio* baskets by primary segments.

Figure 12 Lega (Central Africa): contents of initiation basket. Carvings and natural objects grouped together. (a) and (b) Wooden animal figurines, (c) and (e) Skulls of chimpanzee and young wild boar, (d) Unidentified figurine, (f) and (g) Wooden human figurines, (h) and (i) Sceptre-like objects made of elephant bone. *After Biebuyck*

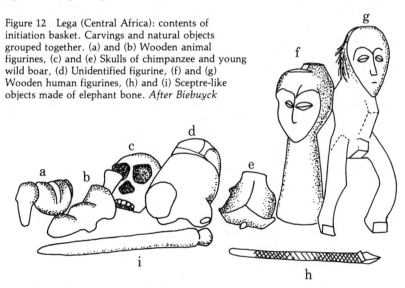

Actual guardianship of the basket is the prerogative of the most recently initiated member within the ritual community, and living members have a considerable knowledge of the history of their baskets' guardians. One instance is cited of a community organizing local admissions into the highest subgrade of *kindi*; in this instance the community coincided with a maximal lineage comprising four primary segments. Only four members of the grade were alive at the time of Biebuyck's fieldwork, but the names of forty-two members were remembered, together with the exact order in which each had succeeded to guardianship of the basket. It has passed 'in a totally unpredictable line' between members of the component segments, demonstrating how they were able to act as an undifferentiated group (89). As soon as the newly admitted candidate receives custodianship of the basket, he must distribute the goods he had accumulated for admission.

Ownership or guardianship of art objects is thus one important way in which such valued items figure in the characteristic patterns of interaction in Lega society. Some works of art are owned individually, some collectively — in which case they have an individual guardian. They are kept in the hut of the owner/guardian's senior wife who herself has high rank in the association, and they must not be approached by non- or low-ranking initiates. If the house where ceremonial objects are kept were destroyed by fire then the owner/guardian must make amends by inducting a kinsman into the *Bwami*. The owner or keeper of works of art does not readily bring them to an initiation ceremony, but 'only after he has repeatedly been informed about the good intentions of the gathering and well-rewarded in advance' (166). In addition to being a source of wealth and influence for their owner or keeper, art objects confer prestige. They are kept only by men of high rank. Members of the highest grades (*kindi*) are subject to no limitations on how many they may own or hold in trust until an appropriate successor is admitted to the requisite rank. Individual figures are awarded to a man by virtue of his appointment to specific roles in the *Bwami*, but only senior *kindi* can expect to achieve such a position: accession is demonstration of their achievement. As they are transmitted from owner to owner through the lineage or ritual community, valued art objects come to represent the continuity of the social group itself. They are called '*kasina*, the pleasant memory of something or somebody good, as if they were some kind of daimonion upholding the virtues of the great people of the past' (171).

Certain important carvings (large masks (fig. 13) and human figures made of old, patinated ivory, or certain wooden sculptures),

Figure 13 Lega (Central Africa): bone mask reserved for members of *kindi* grade in *Bwami. After Biebuyck*

are held by senior *kindi* on behalf of a broad ritual community comprising a maximal lineage or even several such lineages linked by ties of clanship. These figures must be present at an initiation held by the community for the ritual to be valid, but again their keeper does not go when first called: 'The candidate and his tutors, advisers and kinsmen must show deep piety and strong allegiance to the power of the symbols in order to be successful in their aspirations'. Any attempt to hold a higher initiation without such an object would be an act of rebellion that would lead to a serious (ritual) sanction. In this way those with established authority can control the rise of younger men to positions of wealth and prestige and ensure that traditional values are upheld. They do this through their control of art objects which validate the ceremony at which people are admitted to higher grades.

The fact that ownership of the objects is a source of wealth is not, Biebuyck writes, generally mentioned, except in the comment that the objects are ' "like the clapping of elephant ears" by which insects are caught' (173). The reference, he explains, is to the fact that the candidate must pay large sums of money to see the art objects, to learn about them and to receive possession or custodianship of them.

The obligations of the candidate are thus an important consideration. They throw light on the way that wealth is distributed through *Bwami*. It requires, writes Biebuyck, a tremendous effort for the candidate to accumulate the goods he needs to pass through an initiation. The length of time it will take him depends on the grade to which he is seeking admission. In the higher levels he also has the

The Anthropology of Art

responsibility of constructing the buildings required to accommodate the participants and provide a focus for the ceremony. Biebuyck divides the goods he requires into two categories. The first consists of perishable items which are consumed on the spot: lavish meals are eaten throughout the ceremony. Each participant has the right to put aside a small part of what he receives to send or take back to his relatives. The second category consists of durable items which participants must take back to their communities and redistribute. Shell money, salt and oil are the principle commodities involved. Shell money is used to buy salt and oil, ivory carvings and iron work from blacksmiths. It is also used in marriage exchanges (an important point) and can be reinvested in seeking admission to higher grades in *Bwami*.

Biebuyck provides as an example the case of a man seeking admission to the highest grade of *kindi*. Such a person is already wealthy, has many wives and children, some of whom are themselves married, and he has already participated in many initiation ceremonies held for admission to lower ranks. He has goods which he has produced himself and set aside for his entry to *kindi*: shell money, oil and salt which are 'the products of his own labour *and the labour of his wives and children*'. This underlines the significance of marriage transactions, for in any economy where people produce more than they require for their own subsistence and that of their immediate dependants, the head of a productive unit is likely to be able to deploy surplus production to his own ends. Even though it will be insufficient to buy him high status in the *Bwami*, in the kind of society we are looking at, a man who has more wives has more surplus at his disposal, once he, his wives and children have provided for their own subsistence needs. This enhances his prestige and does make him relatively wealthy. Other goods held by the *kindi* candidate have been acquired in the distributions made at other ceremonies he attended, or have been received in marriage payments for his daughters.

The candidate also receives help from a variety of categories of kin. His close agnates: his father, if he is alive, his brothers and brothers' sons and, in Biebuyck's example, his father's brother's son, all provide shell money. Men from his primary, secondary and tertiary lineage segments demonstrate their support for his candidacy by helping to construct the houses required, to hunt for game eaten at the feasts, to collect firewood and water and to provide bags of money for distribution at the ceremony. The agnates of those of the candidate's wives who were going through the ceremony with him helped, as did his sisters' husbands, his mother's brothers and his 'sisters' sons. All this illustrates the extent of the candidate's dependence on others' willingness to sponsor him. Biebuyck argues that the fact a man with few close relatives can still gain entry to the higher grades demonstrates that moral worth, not personal wealth, is the ultimate factor governing a man's rise in status (122).

Before the ceremony starts, special inspectors drawn from among the existing *kindi* visit the candidate to verify that he has collected the necessary wealth but the candidate does not, if he is intelligent and cautious, reveal the full extent of his accumulation.

Most of the goods which a candidate accepts from supporting kin impose on him an obligation to return equivalent goods at a later stage. But he has, in the meantime, used what he originally received to place himself in a position where he will have access to the necessary wealth. Biebuyck details the nature of the reciprocal obligations involved in supporting a candidate for initiation (118-22). The higher the grade, the greater the wealth required. The candidate is under an obligation to invite as many people as possible belonging to the grade to which he seeks entry. 'Failure to invite the proper initiates', writes Biebuyck, 'is equated in Lega thinking with "war", that is, with strained relationships that may result in retaliation. Also, the obligation to admit and to share with unexpected arrivals at the ceremonies is made clear'. Clearly, the candidate's distribution is substantial: 'Coming to the village of the candidate to take all his goods, the initiates compare themselves to ... poison that kills off all the fishes' (122). One of the duties of the candidate's tutor is 'to keep in check the sometimes playfully extravagant demands of the other initiates' (93). The candidate consoles himself with the thought that at future ceremonies he will be on the receiving side and 'I will be merciless in asking' (123).

In one sense, it appears, a man's very candidacy endows him with useful wealth. If he is prudent he keeps back some of the goods he has accumulated, to pay fines he may incur by transgressing taboos during the ceremony or to make presentations to unexpected arrivals. He is likely, nonetheless, to have a quantity of valuables left over. One man, whose admission to *kindi* was charted by Biebuyck, 'was able to realize the following projects shortly after his initiation: to marry an additional wife, to provide one of his sons with a first wife, to help provide an additional wife for each of the other two sons, and to give a classificatory maternal uncle a substantial amount of goods so that he could also complete his admission to *kindi*' (118). No mean achievement, especially in view of the fact already noted that it is the size of one's household which contributes — through its productive activities — to the level of one's personal wealth! A further substantial point is that on acceding to the status of *kindi*, a man sets up his own village. He is accompanied by wives, children, married sons, brothers and other kin — cognates or affines — whom he attracts as a personal following. When his initiation is complete he receives small gifts from the dependants who have settled with him as expressions of their allegiance and respect.

Genealogical fictions

It is clear, despite the principle that the village is occupied by a lineage segment, that the actual composition of a community is more heterogeneous. Several of the more interesting studies of West African societies have documented this divergence of ideal and practice. Biebuyck himself writes that the maximal lineages of the Lega 'frequently have a partly fictive unilineal structure' (44); that is, the descent groups incorporate people who, although treated politically as members of the group, are not in fact descended patrilineally from the group's ancestor. This dynamic aspect of politics, in which allegiances shift and realign partly in response to the popularity of leaders, was documented among the Tiv by the Bohannans. It is worth looking at some of their data to illustrate how realignments may become established.

Bohannan's analysis is more concerned with the mechanisms by which such imbalances in the size of groups are ironed out than with how they arise. Some lower-level segments may grow in size at the expense of others through purely demographic factors (perhaps one family has many daughters and another many sons) or, of more political significance, perhaps groups of strangers or dissident groups from other lineage segments are attracted to live with certain compound heads. Where the Bohannans stress the role of such adjustments in restoring equilibrium to the society, one of the most interesting aspects of Biebuyck's account is that it shows rather how the attraction of dependent families may enhance a respected leader's position once he has been admitted to the *kindi*. Members of incorporated segments cannot normally become village headmen and are deprived of other organizational roles.

The pattern of leadership among the Tiv is clearly germane to the processes of realignment among segments although the tendency to 'return to equilibrium' which Bohannan stresses must impose a limit on any man's ability to collect a personal following. In Biebuyck's account the fluidity of lineage-based societies can more clearly be seen to work to the advantage of an ambitious man although Biebuyck too is careful to stress how greatly a man's ambition is kept in check by the fellow-members of his society.

Realization of ideals concerning leadership

Unless one were to take an entirely materialist view of Lega society a second contribution made by art objects to patterns of interaction must be recognized. Biebuyck repeatedly stresses that wealth is needed to climb through the grades and repeatedly demonstrates that members of higher grades have greater access to wealth. However he also frequently underlines the importance of conforming to Lega society's principles of good leadership, to gain the support crucial to admission to a higher grade: support which must often come from less initiated kinsmen in the form of goods and from existing members of the grade to which admission is sought in the form of sponsorship, tuition and provision of the celebrated art objects whose presence is needed for the initiation to proceed. Biebuyck quotes a Lega proverb: 'Bwami is bought; greatness in Bwami is not bought' (91). Although Bwami is deliberately organized as a political institution facilitating the control of politics, economics, religion, art and the general social life of the people, the primary theme of the association is the pursuit of wisdom and moral excellence. Its social functions, Biebuyck insists, derive from this achievement. *It is in the display, dramatization and explanation of natural and art objects and proverbs during initiation that Lega ideals are communicated.* 'The seeds that scatter when the mbala pod falls from the tree are a reminder that the lineage disintegrates when it is torn by disputes. The sharpness of porcupine quills reminds an initiate that his heart should not be so "sharp" (quick-tempered) as they are' (145). A carving of a bird portrays 'Kakulikuli, the tattler', representing 'an old man of the lineage who is supposed to give advice and orders in the village, but who alienates his people because of excessive talking'. A two-headed carving represents 'Kamukobania, the Divider'. Kamukobania held a drinking party to which he invited people who were enemies with one another. Among them was a senior initiate in Bwami who should have known better than to attend. Once the drink had taken its effect, he 'underwent a sad fate, as everyone does who goes to meddle elsewhere' (both 202). 'On the one hand', writes Biebuyck again, 'concrete objects help to clarify the intricate, abstract notions of the (moral) code. On the other hand, the objects themselves demand interpretation, since their form does not reveal what they are and what they mean'. They are, rather, objects which act as reminders of the elements contained in 'the enormous amount of memorizing, of aphorisms and of actions, required by the initiations'; they are 'reminders (kalolesia) of things to be done or not to be done and mnemonic devices (kakengelezio)' (170). The way in which communication is achieved through the use of art objects will be the subject of the next chapter.

An achieved role in the *Bwami* of great importance is that of preceptor. The preceptor is a senior member of the association who gains his role by personal skill, although often acquiring the role from a kinsman. He leads initiations at all levels, determining the sequence of dances, leading the performance and displaying the objects. He knows hundreds of proverbs and can interpret them all in words, movements and the display of objects. His rewards are 'the hearts of all animals distributed and a large amount of shell money in addition to sharing in regular distributions as incumbent of a certain grade. Some art objects ... are owned exclusively by preceptors' (102). The candidate watches and learns what is displayed to him and through his willingness humbly to accept the teaching demonstrates his qualifications for admission to the grade.

The political role of the *Bwami* association is summed up in Biebuyck's statement that before it was broken up by the colonial administration of the Congo, it organized Lega resistance against slave raiding, against the Belgian colonizers and prevented the introduction of new religious cults, both anti-sorcery cults devised by other African cultures and Islam and Christianity (67). The segmentary tendencies of the lineage system were countered by the organization of bodies of elders drawn from different villages, lineages and clans on the basis of the common membership of *Bwami* and their support for its principles. Hence white administrators came to oppose it. One, 'although conceding that "only those were admitted whose wisdom and probity were recognized", concluded that "this social and moral institution is, in reality, only a vulgar exploitation of the native. Its power must be destroyed" ' (61). Another wrote that *Bwami* was 'detrimental, first, to our occupation, and second, for the evolution of the population toward a better state' (62).

ART IN TRADITIONAL KINGDOMS

The second half of this chapter will examine the role of art objects in Oyo and Benin, two traditional kingdoms that now lie in southern Nigeria. The political institutions of these kingdoms will be compared and contrasted with those of the chiefless societies already discussed, as will the corresponding status of art objects.

On turning to look at the political life of centralized societies we find quite a different settlement pattern. The country of the Yoruba is dotted with towns, whose population at the beginning of the nineteenth century may have approached 100,000 in the larger instances, while 20,000, according to Morton-Williams (1960:363), would not have been uncommon for a pre-colonial town. In Benin, settlements contained up to 4,000 inhabitants, while the capital city of Benin had a population of 54,000 in the mid twentieth century. Each Yoruba city ruled the surrounding countryside, across which were scattered farming villages and sometimes other towns which had developed in parallel with, or as an offshoot from, the capital. Benin, too, administered farming villages. Corresponding to this more concentrated pattern of settlement, we no longer see autonomous lineages managing their own clusters of compounds; special administrative and decision-making roles within the state have been allocated to certain lineages. These politically unique groups are related to one another through a pattern of checks and balances that contribute to the ordered running of the polity. In conjunction with such political specialization, specialized traditions of exclusive production, use and ownership of art objects have developed to provide badges of office, vehicles for administration and exclusively owned treasures.

Cult art in Oyo

For several centuries prior to the intrusion of the British, the western half of Yoruba country had been united into a single kingdom under the town of Oyo, to which the other towns of the region owed allegiance as dependent political units. Morton-Williams describes the political and cult organization within the town of Oyo (1960, 1964). In Oyo cosmology, the civilized world and the ordered way of life that went with it lay suspended between the Sky and the uninhabited, uncultivated bush, the Earth. Both Sky and Earth were the realms of spirit beings, but beings in some senses opposed to one another. The Sky was the kingdom of the supreme God, *Olorun Olodumare*, who ruled it and its inhabitants the *orisha* spirits. The orisha were sometimes presented as his children, sometimes as subordinate rulers, like the rulers of towns dependent on Oyo. The earth was ruled by a female spirit, *Onile*. She was thought to be coeval with Olorun, the Supreme Deity, and in some ways perhaps even more powerful. According to one story Heaven and Earth once went hunting together but all they caught was a small rat, over which they began to fight. Failing to have her way, Earth refused to allow the crops to grow and caused a famine until all the orisha went to Olorun and persuaded him to yield (cited in Williams, 1964:140). Onile has control of the spirits of the dead, and also bush spirits called *irunmole*: 'travelling from town to town through the bush one becomes aware of the nearness of the Earth Goddess's domain and the presence of irunmole when the branches of trees stir and the leaves rustle, although no wind blows, or a dry tree spontaneously catches fire' (Morton-Williams, 1964:146).

The structure of authority in Oyo is built on a balance between three political bodies. In all cases the key offices are vested in certain lineages. Central to the system is the position of king, or *Alafin*. The king is chosen from a limited number of royal lineages, elected by a body of hereditary chiefs resident in the capital (see also Willett in Fraser and Cole, 1972:210-11). Like the supreme deity Olorun, the Alafin is a secluded ruler who has subordinate officials to manage the daily running of his kingdom: Olorun has the orisha, and the Alafin an elaborate palace organization. Palace officials judge in disputes between subjects or vassal rulers, act as the king's spokesman at public festivals, represent him in battle, collect tribute and tolls imposed on trade goods. The second of the three bodies consists of the *Oyo Misi*; a council of elders drawn from non-royal lineages resident in the wards of the capital. They meet daily in the house of their leader and having discussed the day's affairs go to advise the king on the administration of the state. Once a year the Oyo Misi hold a festival at which their leader carries out divination to determine whether the king is fit to continue ruling. If the answer is unfavourable the king is ordered to commit suicide. The Oyo Misi thus clearly occupy a dominant political position in the structure of the state, but their power is checked by the third body, the one of particular interest to us, the *Ogboni*.

The Ogboni is a cult group whose lodge stands within the palace grounds. There are two principle offices within the cult, the *Oluwo* (chief priest) and *Apena* (speaker). Both were selected from specific lineages, the election being carried out by members of the lineage with the right to fill the office, but their candidate had to be confirmed by other members of the association (Williams, 1964:140). Within the association were two grades, the *children* and the *owners of the secret*. According to Morton-Williams, 'the Ogboni was recruited from free Yoruba on a basis of age, presumed wisdom and some prominence in secular or religious life' (1964:253). Members of the junior grade are not admitted to meetings of the senior members, and bound to secrecy should they learn anything of the senior members' discussions. It was, comments Morton-Williams, more of a potential than a real state of membership. Junior members were drawn from the lineages of senior members rather than from society at large, as was the case with *Bwami*, but even then only certain of them, evidently, became admitted to the secret of the cult and received the pair of cast brass figures which was the sign of initiation. Senior members watched the juniors carefully to discover who was a suitable candidate for admission. To be admitted to the senior grade a candidate had to be old enough to have adult children.

In certain respects there is a clear parallel between the senior grade of the Ogboni and the senior ranks of the *Bwami* association among the Lega. The former, 'Yoruba assert, are the wisest members of the community' (Morton-Williams, 1960:365). They are elders who have achieved their status in life and consider that they are above the manipulation of spirits and appeals to luck or misfortune that characterize younger men's preoccupation with the supernatural. They match the depiction of the *kindi* quoted by Biebuyck, 'the *kindi* are said to be unifiers, men of love, men of peace. They are men with a heart; compared to them, all others are like "shoulderbags with a mouth but with no heart" ' (in Fraser and Cole, 1972:12). Beyond this, however, the two associations diverge, both in their relation to cosmology and in their political roles.

The Ogboni cult was integrated into the administration of the state by virtue of two administrative roles: as a mediator between the king and the Oyo Misi, and as the judicial body which policed disputes and punished bloodshed. The Oyo Misi were obliged to join the Ogboni cult, which made them subject to its sanctions, but were prevented from office-holding in the cult, which deprived them of the ability to control it. Once every sixteen days, after their session with the king, the Oyo Misi were required to attend a meeting in the Ogboni cult lodge. It was an important occasion, writes Morton-Williams, for private discussion: men could talk for once without fear of being overheard and without the need to make a display of support for the particular whims of their personal followers. On the other hand, the fact that the Oyo Misi's personal retainers remained outside left the councillors somewhat exposed to the influence of regular members of the cult. Discussions were held in secret, and majority decisions were binding on all who attended; participants were not even permitted to reveal that there had been disagreement. The Ogboni priests had to be present at a king's funeral, and so the Oyo Misi could not order the king's suicide without the Ogboni soon learning of the fact. To the populace at large the Ogboni cult thus appeared wholly on the king's side in the balance of power within the state; but the king himself was not allowed to attend its meetings. During the annual ceremony when the leader of the Oyo Misi divined to determine whether the king was fit to continue his rule, the king was making sacrifices in the Ogboni cult lodge to see if the Earth supported him; yet when cult members met every sixteen days the king could only send a representative, a woman who reported back to him what had been discussed.

In its judicial role, the Ogboni occupied itself with punishing bloodshed, which was an offence against the Earth. If blood were shed in a fight, the *Apena* (speaker) learned of it and sent a messenger carrying a linked pair of brass figures called the *edan* (fig. 14). The messenger laid the *edan* on the ground where the bloodshed took place, and the participants in the dispute were then required to return to the spot and make themselves known. They travelled to the Ogboni lodge, where the Apena called senior members of the cult together and conducted a hearing. If one party to the dispute was obviously lying, he was made to submit to an ordeal. In every case, the disputants were both required to pay a fine, and provide animals for a sacrifice of atonement. To suggest the power of the Ogboni, Morton-Williams contrasts the Yoruba with the Bini, the inhabitants of the neighbouring State of Benin: 'Yoruba quarrels are far less likely to entail bloodshed than those in many parts of Africa — among their neighbours the Bini, for a conspicuous example — and the force of the Ogboni sanction may well explain this' (1960:366).

The Ogboni could also be called in to mediate in disputes between citizens of the capital, to prevent quarrels becoming too embracing or malicious. If the Apena considered the dispute serious enough he would again have the *edan* sent out, and the offender was required to pay heavy fines in the form of both money and animals. Finally, the Ogboni resolved disputes between its own members: where one admitted an accusation against him were true, the Apena tried to restore harmony. If the accused persisted in denying his guilt, he had to swear his innocence in front of the *edan*: an ordeal which would kill him if his oath were false.

In addition to specialization of its political role, the Ogboni cult differed from the *Bwami* in its cosmological foundations. Where the *Bwami* drew its inspiration from an ethos shared with the population at large, and simply admitted initiates to progressively richer and deeper interpretation of a common body of precepts, the Ogboni possesses a unique religious basis which sets it quite apart from the beliefs of the population at large. Unlike the *Bwami* (Biebuyck, 1973:91), the Ogboni is a secret association. The existence of more than one cult within a West African society is certainly not unique; the Tallensi (for instance) possess both an ancestor and an earth cult. The difference is that it is the fact of its ritual devotion to the Earth that constitutes the Ogboni's *secret* (Morton-Williams, 1960:362, 364). Whereas all Tallensi participate in both cults, only certain of the Oyo Yoruba are admitted to the Ogboni. This is a clear expression of the transformation in the structure of interaction which distinguishes centralized from acephalous political systems.

The Oyo Yoruba have an ancestor cult: the ancestors of a lineage are concerned for the health and fertility of their descendants, and they can be angered by the moral failings of their living kinsmen. The head of the lineage makes offerings at the graves of the group's ancestors. The most important group of cults for those who do not belong to the Ogboni appears to be those associated with the orisha. This fact is itself of political significance, because the orisha cults cut across lineage boundaries and fall, indirectly, under the control of the Oyo Misi (see Morton-Williams, 1964:253). The orisha have, as noted above, taken over the daily running of spiritual affairs from the Supreme Deity Olorun Olodumare. No one knows how many orisha there are, but 'conventional numbers' put it at 201, 401 or 16,000 (op. cit.:246). Fortunately, the orisha are ranked in hierarchies beneath a few principal spirits: Shango the god of lightning, Sopono the god of smallpox, etc. Morton-Williams states that people tend to join the cult of the orisha whose personality is supposed most to resemble their own (1964:246). Although an individual is expected to attend and contribute to the rites of the orisha worshipped by his parents, he does not join either parent's cult unless the orisha in question indicates, through divination or some extraordinary experience, that he should. The orisha cults are concerned with the manipulation and placation of the spirits; they attempt to reverse the spirits' malign or capricious influence on people's careers.

Members of the Ogboni cult stand opposed to this view of religion. Its senior members are recruited from those old enough to have achieved standing in the community and who have therefore grown beyond the desire to manipulate and influence the orisha. The symbolism of the cult is full of references to the number three, and this sets it apart from the symbolism of public life or the orisha cults, where two and four are the numbers most often alluded to: two expresses duality and four completeness and perfection. To offer three objects to an orisha at a ritual, or to a guest during a secular ceremony, is an insult that invites retaliation. In divination the world is represented with four cardinal points, each guarded by an orisha, and each Yoruba town has (conceptually, at least) four gates. The Ogboni cult members also make references to the left hand. They salute each other and the Earth by bringing their clenched fists together three times, with the left uppermost and the thumb concealed in the palm of the hand. The gesture of concealing the thumb, argues Morton-Williams, shows that one can no more hide one's secrets from an Ogboni cult member than pretend one's thumb is not there. Because Ogboni initiates have passed through one or another of the orisha cults and learned their fundamental principles, they tend to become dissatisfied, seeing the orisha ritual as a simple technique for obtaining magical power. Most important, senior members of the Ogboni cult reject the notion that the Trickster god can of his own volition mislead a man or disrupt social relationships. In keeping with their judicial role, they maintain that only human agencies provoke quarrels: witches who kill children, kings who rule badly. Morton-Williams further suggests that their emphasis on the left hand is representative of their refusal to blame extra-human agencies: 'they cannot reject one side of themselves, but must accept the unclean'. Ogboni cult members look to the Earth to provide a form of immutability behind the disorder of events.

Plate 3 Yoruba brass casting from Nigeria of *edan* figure for Ogboni cult: two heads on one rod. *British Museum*

How is this distinctive outlook on life realized in the cult's art objects? It is expressed both in the details of representation on cult figures and, according to Denis Williams, in their underlying style. Ogboni cult figures are further distinguished by the material with which they are manufactured: while much Yoruba sculpture is executed in wood, most Ogboni figures are cast in brass (Williams,

Figure 16 Yoruba wooden carving (West Africa): Eru-Ogboni, the slave of Ogboni, devouring a deceiver. *After Morton-Williams*

Figure 14 Yoruba brass casting (West Africa): a pair of *edan* figures from the Ogboni cult. *After Morton-Williams*

Figure 15 Yoruba brass casting (West Africa): *Ajagbo*, the female spirit of the Ogboni cult. *After Morton-Williams*

139; Morton-Williams, 1960:plate 11c). The meaning of the word *edan*, the name for the figures produced after bloodshed or serious dispute, is probably 'anthropomorphic brass ritual staff' (Morton-Williams, *op. cit.*:369). The *edan* consists of a pair of representations; a naked man and a naked woman, each mounted on a short spike and linked to each other by a chain (fig. 14). They are said to represent male and female members of the cult in an act of worship. The *edan* is the only Ogboni sculpture ever seen by the general public. Despite the fact that it constitutes a paired figure, 'The Ogboni express their metaphysical conceptions in the simple statement ... "Two Ogboni, it becomes three" ... The third element seems to be the mystery, the shared secret, itself. The union of the male and the female in the *edan* image', Morton-Williams argues (*op. cit.*:373), 'symbolizes this putting two together to make a third'. Typically, *edan* figures are shown making the Ogboni salute, the left hand above the right, with the thumbs concealed. During the initiation of senior members of the cult, the candidate has a cord on which three cowries are threaded, tied around his left wrist so tightly that it leaves a permanent scar. This is removed after three days. *Edan* figures may be shown wearing a bead bracelet on their left wrist. There are other figures which are not revealed to the public. One is the female figure, *Ajagbo* (fig. 15). She is brought out to subject quarrelling members to an ordeal, and more often when an unknown member of the lodge is suspected of having broken the cult's rules. In such a case, members arrive at the lodge for their next sixteenth-day meeting to find the priests have produced the carving. Sacrifices are made, and all members required to drink from a bowl containing the juice of forest snails. The body of the guilty member will swell and he will die within a few days. A third sculpture is associated with the requirement that all members subscribe to the majority's decision after debate. This figure, *Ikuku-oro* or *Aiwo-oro*, is brought out after the majority's wish has been determined, and laid on the ground with some broken kola nuts. A human sacrifice is then offered over the figure, and members required to eat the kola. Morton-Williams writes that this practice was well-known to the Ogboni members with whom he discussed the cult. 'The Yoruba were not a blood-thirsty people', he comments, 'and I am satisfied that [the sacrifice] would be regarded as a compelling sanction even in political issues' (*op. cit.*:370). Williams notes that *Ajagbo* and *Ikuku-oro* always carried some object identified with Ogboni ritual: the executioner's club, the staff carried by office-holders, a ceremonial fan, a dish or a wooden ladle used at initiation (143, 147). Both authors comment on the aggressive sexuality of Ogboni figures, a detail which Williams (143) interprets as a reference to the fertility of the Earth while Morton-Williams (370) views it rather as an expression of the spirits' ferocity.

Williams offers a characterization of the style of Ogboni cult figures which sets them apart from the art of the orisha. While orisha figures are full of movement, depict details linking them with everyday life and are often subject to experiment and innovation in design, the art of the Ogboni is unchanging, rigid and lacking in lively detail. This contrast he links with the figures' cosmological background. Orisha figures are never worshipped as spirits, Williams argues, while Ogboni figures are so worshipped. In a phrase which reminds one of Carpenter's study of Eskimo carving, Williams translates the brass-smith's title *akedanwaive* as 'he who brings the *edan* to earth' (143). The man, that is, who gives the spirit tangible form. Ogboni figures are seen as the vehicles of spiritual power. Orisha carvings therefore 'relate to the actual and the concrete, while the latter [the sculpture of the Ogboni] relates to the world of spirit and of being' (139). The brass caster is subject to careful scrutiny of his product. Prescriptions surround the caster's role. He must be an older man. His task is said to give him spiritual power but at the same time to render him less fertile. Williams interprets this as a characterization of the requirement that he should be experienced in Ogboni cosmology and ritual, and therefore an older man whose own children are grown-up.

The casting of brass figures is itself surrounded by numerous rituals. These accompany the technical process in which the figure is first moulded in clay. Wax is then set over the clay, and details of representation built up on its surface in solid wax. The whole is then set in an outer frame of clay and the wax removed by the firing of the mould. Molten brass can then be poured into the vacant area left by removal of the wax, and the outer layer of clay broken off. The figure is left to cool for six days before removing it; the inner foundation of clay is left within the brass. From a sociological point of view, the most important control on figures' conformity with tradition is the right of the Apena to reject castings which he feels lack the necessary form: 'In his hands finally lies the control of the rectitude of the image, which he may reject for any of a number of reasons, such as incorrect rendering of cult insignia, failure to represent certain characteristics of the spirit, or on technical grounds as being simply not up to standard' (Williams, 144; but see also his comments on 151). It is the Apena's duty also to appoint Ogboni brass-smiths; determining whether a man's son will be allowed to follow his father's profession. The art of the Ogboni cult is thus in many ways bound up with the political institution for which it is manufactured.

Royal art in Benin

The art tradition which existed to provide the kings of Benin with public insignia of office provides an interesting case study to set beside that of the Ogboni cult in Oyo. In both instances there is some exclusivity over the control of materials and the recruitment of artists, and in both an iconography whose details of representation make specific references to the social status of those who use the objects. But where Williams sees a continuity of traditional forms upheld by the Apena, Fagg (1970) claims a gradual change in the style of courtly art objects which, he argues, corresponds to the decline of the king's secular power. All three aspects of the tradition further illustrate the links between art and social interaction.

The pre-colonial State of Benin occupied an area of some 8,000 square miles. It lay close to the area controlled by Oyo, situated in the tropical rain forest belt to the west of the Niger delta and the territory of the delta groups such as the Kalabari. During the sixteenth century, the era of its greatest expansion, Benin's control extended into the delta and beyond the western boundary of modern Nigeria. Both Benin and Oyo have oral traditions of links with the older Yoruba kingdom of Ife.

Benin itself, the capital city, is divided into two sections by a broad street. On the smaller side lives the king, the *Oba*. He is surrounded by his court and the palace chiefs, who act as administrative officials beneath his control. The other part of the city is controlled by the town chiefs, a body of elders comparable to the *Oyo misi* in the checks that they impose on the king's free reign. Like the Alafin of Oyo the Oba was not (by the time the kingdom's independence was destroyed by the British) intimately concerned with the daily running of his state; this task fell rather to the town chiefs. (Bradbury, 1957, is the key reference for details of the political structure of the kingdom.) Each Oba was believed to be a divine person, the vehicle for the powers which established the fortunes of the kingdom. His supernatural powers required elaborate ritual for their preservation, and by the end of the nineteenth century the performance of these rituals occupied much of his time. It was the function of royal art works to express the symbolism of these ceremonies.

Many rites were performed in public, and provided an opportunity for the display of the art objects. The Oba performed two rituals which, although also carried out by others, assumed particular significance when executed by him. In Benin culture, ritual reference to the *hand* signified the power of personal achievement. Warriors, and wealthy and high-ranking members of the kingdom, performed rituals towards their hands. For the king's worship of his hand, special brass altars were cast. The *head* was also the object of ritual activities: attention to the head was concerned with securing good fortune. All Bini people from time to time make sacrifices to their heads, but the Oba's particular cult was concerned with ensuring good fortune for the entire kingdom. No altars were made for this rite, because it was towards the king's own head (as a symbol of the kingdom) rather than a representation of it, that the ritual was directed. Fagg suggests that 'the annual sacrifice to the king's head can be regarded as the central rite of his divine kingship' (Fagg:20).

The mystical powers attributed to the Oba, the manner in which participants in ceremonies dressed and decorated themselves, and the power of the kingdom in warfare are also recorded in brass plaques manufactured for the palace.

Plate 4   Benin ivory mask from West Africa, worn by king on his hip. The mask depicts a coral bead collar and a fringe of Portuguese heads. *Metropolitan Museum of New York*

Craft guilds are situated on both sides of the city's main street. Each guild occupies one or more of the 40 wards into which the city is divided. Production of craft goods was controlled by the Oba, who rewarded craftsmen with gifts, slaves and money. The art of Benin was a royal art, produced for the king, not the people. Blacksmiths occupied four or five wards, manufacturing tools and weapons, lamps and personal ornaments for royal use. Only the king could own ivory carvings, and these were made for him. Brass casting was carried out in yet another ward, using the lost wax technique outlined above in discussion of Ogboni cult figures.

Whenever an elephant was killed within the kingdom one tusk had to be presented to the Oba, and the other offered to him for sale. Fagg (op. cit.) considers that the latter option was rarely exercised, but a major consequence of the Oba's prerogative over ivory was probably the access it gave him to the goods introduced by European traders, one of whose aims was to obtain ivory. From a comparative point of view, it is interesting to note that among the Lega it was members of the highest grades of the *Bwami* association who had the exclusive right to own ivory objects (Biebuyck, 1972:15). In Benin, the Oba wore ivory ornaments. The modern Oba carries ivory masks upon his belt (plate 4), wears carved ivory bracelets around his wrists, and carries a double bell carved from ivory and struck with an ivory rod (Fagg, op. cit.:24).

The Oba's monopoly over the use of brass castings was absolute, and in the past the artists' work was displayed in the many courtyards of the royal palace. The palace standing in 1897, when Benin was defeated by the British, contained thirteen courts, each given over to the worship of a deceased king. Earlier records suggest that previously the palace had occupied almost half the capital, with many more yards. A British traveller who visited the palace in 1668 describes a series of long rectangular galleries, of which the largest stood on wooden pillars 'from top to bottom covered in cast copper, on which are engraved the pictures of their war exploits and battles' (cited in Forman and Dark, 1960:21). By 1702, however, these plaques appear to have been taken down for protection during a period of civil war, and they were evidently kept in storage until unearthed by the British soldiers who arrived in 1897 and removed them to England.

Benin artists utilized a number of iconographic conventions to portray the institution and superhuman attributes of kingship. In some cases the Oba is shown on brass plaques with mudfish in the place of legs (fig. 17). The heads of the fish curve upwards on either side of his body. Sometimes he is shown gripping in each hand a leopard, an animal only he could sacrifice. The animals' bodies are

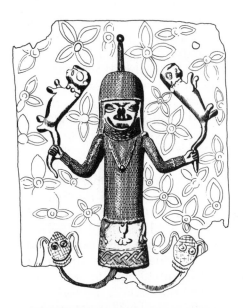

Figure 17 Benin brass casting (West Africa): plaque showing Oba with legs as mudfish, gripping leopards by the tail. *After Fagg*

Plate 5 Benin brass from West Africa: plaque depicting king swinging leopards by the tail, with mudfish at the king's waist. *British Museum*

Plate 6 Benin brass: plaque showing a Portuguese warrior. *Schwartz Collection, British Museum*

73

swung upward on either side of the Oba's head. The leopard, writes Fagg, is a common symbol of chiefship in West Africa (*op. cit.*:10): its strength, courage, ferocity and cunning being appropriate traits. The Bini craftsmen repeatedly used the leopard in their imagery: it appears on masks worn on the hip or the waist (plate 5); water vessels are made in the shape of leopards, and there is a famous pair of free-standing leopard figures carved from ivory (Fagg, plate 5). The significance of the mudfish is less clear. The explanation apparently favoured in modern Benin is that the motif originated when a past king was stricken by paralysis in both legs. In order to provide some explanation for his misfortune, the Oba announced that he had been transformed into Olokun, God of the Sea. The mudfish is the emblem of Olokun, the Sea God. Fagg prefers the idea that this manner of portraying the king was related to the importance of trade with European expeditions. The Portuguese came by sea. They brought the coral used in the Oba's decorations, and a local tradition claims that a past Oba wrestled with Olokun to obtain these decorations. Perhaps, comments Fagg, this alludes to some hard bargaining with Portuguese merchants (22). The Portuguese soon established good relations with the Bini, setting up a trading post, providing soldiers who fought in the Oba's army with European weapons, and introducing missionaries. A number of cast brass figures made in Benin depict these soldiers in their armour (Fagg, plate 23). The association of the Oba with the god of the sea could therefore be a reference to the greater power which Portuguese contact conferred on him.

The history of Benin art has been subject to considerable discussion. In part this has concerned itself with the sources of motifs and techniques, in part with their development within the context of Benin culture. Fraser has traced motifs he considers to be comparable to that of the Oba swinging the pair of leopards about his head to the Ancient Near East and Egypt, where he assigns the type of composition an antiquity dating back to 3,000 B.C. (Fraser, 1972:263). The fish-legged figure is compared by Fraser to numerous Mediaeval and Renaissance representations, but he considers it to be most closely paralleled by similar motifs belonging to Etruscan and Eastern Roman art traditions dating between them from 300 B.C. to 300 A.D. (282-3). His opinion is that both modes of representing the Oba reached Benin by a presumably lengthy process of diffusion. Many anthropologists would tend to reject such speculation as irrelevant to the role of art in Benin culture and, particularly in the heyday of Radcliffe-Brown and Malinowski, stress rather the need to see such traits (regardless of their origin) as components in an on-going way of life more amenable to direct study. The fact that the fish-legged figure may have come to represent the value of overseas trade to the Oba would be the important consideration. It should not be forgotten, however, that the formulation of appropriate motifs, or modes of representation, is a critical aspect of any art tradition. *If the evidence is reliable*, the origin and evolution of motifs is therefore a legitimate, and separate field of study.

What has probably been a major factor in debasing such studies in the eyes of anthropologists has been its use to detract from instances of genuine independent invention, such as the separate evolution of the centralized state in West Africa. Attempts to dismiss Benin's brass casting tradition as a practice introduced to them by the Portuguese is another. The first direct European contact with Benin was made by the Portuguese in 1485. Portuguese influence continued up to 1660, after which they were supplanted by the Dutch. Forman and Dark have argued that since the Portuguese are themselves skilfully portrayed in a characteristically African style in brass castings known to date from the fifteenth century, indigenous Bini casting techniques would have had to develop at an implausibly rapid rate had the Portuguese themselves introduced the technology (*op. cit.*:10). Ivory carvings made by the Bini specifically for Portuguese purchasers appear to show the deliberate incorporation of European motifs and styles, modifying indigenous modes of representation (see Fagg:46), while carvings and castings made for local use show characteristically indigenous stylistic traits. More telling is Willett's statement that: 'the earliest European visitors to Benin in 1485 recorded that the Oni of Ife used to send a staff, a pectoral cross, and a hat, all made of brass, to confirm each succeeding king of Benin in office' (Willett, 1972:221).

There are nonetheless some striking instances of indirect contact between Europe and West Africa. Fagg presents a fascinating discussion of a particular form of brass casting found in Benin, which he terms (on the basis of its European parallels) the *aquamanile* (fig. 18). Each time that the Oba is about to emerge from his palace to perform a major public ceremony associated with his divine kingship, his hands are ritually washed by a palace official. The vessel in which the water is carried is cast in the form of an animal and constructed in such a way that it is filled through a hinged lid upon the head, while the water is poured out through holes in the animal's nostrils. Animals depicted include the leopard (Fagg, plate 14), the ram and the baboon. Fagg argues that these artifacts derive directly from a Mediaeval European model. Aquamaniles constructed in an identical fashion were common in Mediaeval Europe — they were characteristic of German and Frankish culture — but evidently ceased to be produced in Europe about a hundred

Figure 18   Benin brass casting (West Africa): 'aquamanile' in form of leopard. *After Fagg*

years before the appearance of the earliest examples in Benin. Fagg proposes two ways in which the objects may have been brought to Benin: by diffusion across the Sahara in Mediaeval times, or through the agency of Portuguese traders who might, at a later date, have brought already antique examples to Bini territory. It is interesting to note, apropos of the former possibility, that Fagg also reproduces a photograph of a brass jug discovered in 1896 in the Ashanti State, now part of Ghana, which had been manufactured for King Richard II of England at about 1400 A.D. It is surrounded by an inscription and has his badges cast upon it (51).

At the beginning of the present century British collectors, who enquired about the art objects they were appropriating from Benin, were told that the Bini had acquired their casting techniques from the town of Ife; the centre to which both Benin and the Oyo Yoruba trace their cultural origins. Benin and Ife are separated by a distance of about a hundred and ten miles. Bradbury, Forman and Fagg all accept the historical value of this tradition. It is also supported by Willett (e.g. 1972:218), who has excavated at and around Ife. When the Obas of Benin died their heads were, traditionally, taken to Ife for burial. Excavation at the spot where burial is said to have taken place revealed a small piece of Benin brass work, and other material radio-carbon dated to between 1000 and 1200 A.D. Fraser, however, points out that *motifs* in the art of Benin do not necessarily have parallels in Ife sculpture (*op. cit.*:262), and it is clearly important to distinguish between styles of representation and techniques used to realize them.

What early Benin brasses do appear to share with those from Ife is a type of style generally termed 'naturalistic': a style which encourages the depiction of individualizing features, such that one feels the figures must be portraits of real people, and the reproduction of the actual proportions of the human face (fig. 19). A general discussion of style will be reserved for Chapter 4, but Fagg traces in the history of Benin brass casting a development which art historians have sometimes viewed as part of a universal cyclical process. He divides Benin brasses into three periods of manufacture, the first of which covers a span of two hundred years and ends in the sixteenth century. To this phase he assigns the most 'naturalistic' of the castings. His reasons for doing so are first, that the Bini themselves commonly state them to be the earliest and, secondly, that their naturalism links them most closely to the art excavated at Ife. Fagg's second period begins in the sixteenth century and continues for 150 years. Characteristic of this period are brass representations of the Oba's head constructed as accessories to altars which commemorated past kings. The cast heads were constructed so as to support — to judge from later examples — carved ivory tusks. During this period free-standing brass castings were also manufactured: messengers, warriors riding or on foot, and the Portuguese soldiers who were lending support to the king. In this period, too, the brass wall-plaques depicted in relief the king's battles, his palace officials and his own person in the characteristic poses described above. But Fagg finds a change in the style of representation, particularly in the cast heads destined for the Obas' altars. The heads become heavier, details become more standardized and diverge more from the actual proportions of the human head:

Figure 19   Benin brass casting (West Africa): 'Early Period' head of Queen. *After Fagg*

Figure 20   Benin brass casting (West Africa): 'Middle Period' head. *After Fagg*

cheeks are inflated, eyes enlarged, noses become more angular. The third and most recent phase is characterized, according to Fagg, by more flamboyant but less carefully manufactured works. The Oba's head becomes covered with the symbols of his office, and his face almost disappears behind the mounting rows of neck-rings which rise over his jaw (fig. 20). Rather than portraits of individual rulers, the aim of the style appears to be depictions of the importance of the position itself. Permitting himself a value-judgement, Fagg writes: 'the anti-humanistic emphasis on ornament ... breaks through all restraints and eventually attains levels of absurdity not otherwise found in Africa before the rise of the modern export trade' (*op. cit.*:18).

He proposes a sociological explanation for the development he has traced. The brass heads were constructed as public expressions of the Oba's position, exhibited as they were in the shrines which stood in palace courtyards (see Fagg, plate 11). The decline in their quality, he argues, corresponds to a decline in the real power of the Oba himself. The increased emphasis upon regalia at the expense of the king's personal character 'may be regarded as a kind of frenzied over-compensation' for the decline in real power (18). It is not clear whether Fagg is referring to the decline of Benin as a state, or to the Oba's personal loss of administrative responsibilities (if indeed he ever had such power) to the councillor chiefs.

There is a certain danger in constructing such an evolutionary process according to what is implicitly a universal tendency in art styles, because it displaces the need to verify whether such tendencies are indeed universal. Fraser (*op. cit.*:262) expresses some doubt about the reliability of oral tradition for assigning relative dates to Benin castings; presumably because such sequences might themselves be the product of an indigenous model of stylistic evolution. It must be pointed out that Fagg is able to assign approximate dates to a number of pieces by virtue of their subject matter — Portuguese soldiers at one end of the continuum, and recently-deceased kings at the other. But even if Fagg is correct there may be alternative explanations for the change of style. Perhaps what is given expression is the passage of the Oba's position from a charismatic one, in which precedures were ill-defined and personal initiatives admired, to a bureaucratic status where all the Oba's actions are governed by procedural rules that he follows simply as the present incumbent of that office. Weber (who devised this model of political development) would certainly not have considered this a decline (see Weber, 1947).

Whatever the explanation, it is important to note that Fagg has taken a major initiative in looking not only at a transformation that may have occurred in Benin politics, but also at the possibility of related changes in an art tradition.

Conclusion

It would be unsatisfactory to leave this comparison of related African societies without discussing why social systems built on what seems to be a common cultural base vary so widely. A number of explanations have been put forward for the region of Africa from which this chapter's examples have been taken. Stevenson (1968), like Durkheim (1947), has argued that increased population density promotes the formation of a centralized state, although Durkheim was careful to point out that density of social interaction was more important than the sheer density of people. Differences in the richness of the natural environment also offer tempting hypotheses, but Forde was surely correct to argue that the environment *permits* social systems of a certain level of complexity to develop without compelling them to do so (Forde, 1948).

According to Bohannan, the environment of the Tiv is at its richest along the rivers on its northern and southern margins. Population density, however, ranges from 25 people per square mile along the Benue River in the north, to 550 per square mile in the south, so there is by no means a perfect correlation here. In the north, where the population is at its lowest, age-sets are absent. Have age-sets emerged as a response to greater population density, or is the dispersed population of the north due to the absence of age-sets? Only age-sets have the right to use force to defend their members against others' witchcraft. Bohannan comments: 'It is not without significance that in the north of Tivland ... the manifestation of serious witchcraft within the lineage leads to panic — sometimes to the dissolution of the community. The protecting role of the age-set is an important factor in the continued existence of Tiv communities' (*op. cit.*:56).

A comparison of neighbouring systems within a single district may show some to be more viable than others or, at least, to be better able to impose their own political structure on neighbours because in warfare they can bring more force to bear at a given point. Not only might chiefless societies succumb to centralized states, Sahlins (1961) argued in an interesting essay that chiefless societies may differ among themselves in their predatory tendencies. He noted the Bohannans' statement that the Tiv differed from their neighbours in having a comprehensive patrilineal genealogy which could unite them against external enemies, and cited the historical evidence that they are expanding at the expense of neighbours with shallower maximal lineages. He put forward the same argument for the success of the Nuer cattle-herdsmen of East Africa in assimilating neighbouring groups to their own political system. Implicit in Sahlins' argument is the suggestion that the Tiv and Nuer came from somewhere else to find their victims occupying the spot they wanted. Two more recent essays (Newcomer, 1972 and Southall, 1976) have argued that the many similarities between Nuer culture and that of their neighbours and victims imply a common origin, and these writers have therefore examined possible causes of the cultures' subsequent differentiation.

If Sahlins is correct about the efficacy of a unifying genealogy and if Bohannan is correct to assign such power of social control to Tiv age-sets, there would be good reason to attribute an important role to political institutions *per se*. The emergence or demise of a single institution might affect the whole quality of interaction in a social system. Terray, in an unconventional Marxist analysis, makes such a claim for one West African society. As a Marxist he tends to assign primary causal power to the production economy, but also like some other recent Marxist writers, Terray (1972) stresses that a 'mode of production' includes a set of economic activities, a political structure regulating access to resources exploited and produced, and an ideological scheme which provides a justification for the economic and political relations with which it is linked. His proposition is illustrated by an examination of Meillassoux's work on the Guro. The Guro combine agriculture with hunting, and in Terray's opinion the two activities belong to separate modes of production, with their own resources, tools, techniques and rights over produce. Agriculture is practised by lineage segments, but hunting by the community as a whole, using large nets. Meillassoux saw net hunting as the primary 'integrating social factor' in the organization of the village: the community could divide only if the two resulting sections would be large enough independently to carry out their own hunting expeditions. The recent disappearance of net hunting from some communities greatly weakened the stability of the village, the setting within which other social activities were conducted. Little has likewise argued for the crucial role of a single institution, resembling the *Bwami* cult of the Lega, in the political systems of Liberia and Sierra Leone. He points out that while it may be relatively easy for a centralized state to impose its domination on others, conditions may make it much harder to preserve that domination if a crucial institution were absent. 'It was quite possible for a warrior chief of resource, backed by a competent band of followers, to win one or two quick victories and thus overcome a whole chiefdom within a short space of time. To keep it permanently under control was another matter. Should war break out afresh, his communications with the area were likely to be impeded not only by forests and rivers but by the presence of fortified towns on the route' (1966b:65-6). Little discusses the role that the *Poro*, an association of the same type as the *Bwami*, may have played in stabilizing the structure of the state.

Like the *Bwami*, the *Poro* of Sierra Leone appears to have been the main organizing institution in a society with sometimes only localized leadership. It regulated the harvesting of palm fruit, the leaving of land under fallow and the times when rivers could be fished. It also fixed market prices and co-ordinated warfare, including a revolt against the British colonial forces in 1898 (Little, 1966a:350). It punished witchcraft and murder. As with the *Bwami*, initiation to the junior grade was almost universal. One could not marry unless initiated, and initiation was the major occasion for impressing on people the values upheld by the association. The *Poro*, like the *Bwami*, contained a number of ranks and, as with the *Bwami*, only certain members rose to high positions. Accession to higher rank brought the right to 'take charge of the society's paraphernalia, including such things as drums, masks, initiation knives, etc.' (359). Little argues that the rulers of major chiefdoms in the region were able to subordinate the *Poro* to their own government, and use *Poro* lodges in outlying areas as a means of controlling local leaders' aspirations. From the perspective of *Bwami*, the *Poro* was (if Little is correct) subverted to the cause of a single, central authority.

It would be a mistake to argue that centralized states develop because they are inherently 'better for people' than uncentralized societies, and therefore accepted with pleasure by the bulk of those who become subject to them. Sahlins' paper on the Tiv and Nuer was written within an explicit social evolutionary framework based on the proposition that human societies tend through an internal momentum to develop in stages of progressively increasing complexity: from the band of hunter-gatherers like the Australian Aborigines, to the (chiefless) tribe of societies like the Lega or Tiv, then to the chiefdom and finally to the state. While it is undeniable that some such a progression is implied, where states have developed, in the archaeological record anthropologists suspicious of the implication that our own society is altogether better (i.e. more evolved) than others have frequently pointed out that the complexity of one's political structure is not necessarily an index of the sophistication of one's religion or the efficiency of one's food production. In his more recent work Sahlins himself emphasizes his rejection of the idea that comprehensive progress follows complexity of political relations. It may be only a minority who profit. Marx used to illustrate his criticism of capitalist society with the proposition that an independent farmer or artisan would need to work for only six hours a day to supply his own wants, even if he had to barter some of his own goods for those of other independent producers. If the factory worker of the Industrial Revolution worked for longer each day — and he did, of course — without achieving more than a subsistence wage, it was because any labour he exerted after the notional six hours became the *surplus* appropriated by his employer. Sahlins adopts a similar standpoint in his concept of the *domestic mode of production* (see for example his reference to Marx in Sahlins, 1974:83), and adds to this the discovery that a population of hunter-gatherers probably expend *less* time gaining their subsistence than a population of peasant farmers. Data on the hunting and gathering activities of an Aboriginal group in Arnhem Land (Northern Australia) demonstrated that they expended only *four to five* hours a day supporting themselves, while similar observations on a Kalahari Bushman group proved that: 'One man's labour in hunting and gathering will support four or five people.

Taken at face value, Bushman food collecting is more efficient than (or, rather, as efficient as) French farming in the period up to' World War II, when more than 20 per cent of the population were engaged in feeding the rest' (*op. cit.*:17, 21).

Sahlins argued that it is typical of small-scale societies that their members do not fully-exploit the productive potential of their economy. Whether they are farmers, pastoralists or hunter-gatherers, 'labour power is under-used, technological means are not fully engaged, natural resources are left untapped' (41). This is not to say that their technology is deficient, but rather that there is comparatively little political pressure on them to produce a surplus over the subsistence needs of the household economy. His *Domestic Mode* expresses an ideal in which the household does support only itself, an ideal which he sets in opposition to the variable ability, in practice, of political leaders to extract a surplus which they turn to their own ends: warfare, ceremony or the patronage of technological activities. 'Everywhere the petty anarchy of domestic production is counterpoised by larger forces and greater organization ... that join one house to another and submit all to a general interest' (95).

The variable organizational power of political leaders can be expressed at two levels. In certain societies, leaders rise and fall through their own skill at production and exchange, being displaced by younger men as old age weakens their abilities, without the social structure itself being modified. The New Guinea highlands provide prototypical examples of this kind of system, but there are probably elements of it in Lega, Tallensi and Tiv society too. The household itself is not immune to exploitation from within in such a society. In the chiefless agricultural societies of West Africa a man's use of the productive efforts of his own household may be an important tool in his political activities. His inability to control the resources of other households, except by indebting them through the loan of part of his own produce, or attracting their voluntary support, makes him largely dependent on the backing of kinsmen and vulnerable to their disapproval if he transgresses the norms. Terray has some interesting observations to make on this in his discussion of the Guro. The technology of such a society is relatively simple and requires little effort to maintain or replace. One of Marx's main themes in his analysis of capitalism was that a relatively large proportion of labour was expended in producing machinery into which the capitalist invested the surplus wealth he had extracted from his workers. This source of control over productive resources is absent from societies like the traditional Guro, Lega, etc. Nor is there a shortage of land. Human labour itself, as Meillassoux pointed out, becomes the major productive resource. Guro elders appropriate for themselves the right to allocate women in marriage and so make the young dependent on them. But not only do the young themselves in due course succeed to the position of elder (so that there are no social classes), a young man who is deprived too long of a wife can remove himself to the settlement of a more sympathetic kinsman. Terray says of his own fieldwork in a neighbouring society: 'I could list many instances among the Dida where elders fell from office because of their "greed" or "egoism" ' (*op. cit.*:170). Clearly, this is a similar situation to that of the Lega and Tiv. At another level, although the transition may not in practice be clearly perceptible, transformations in the political *structure* of a society may be attendant on changes in the work-loads placed on its members, so that the control of political leaders is partially removed from the hands of society at large. The extraction of an undue surplus of labour can in fact precipitate political change when people revolt against the burden imposed by a centralized chiefship, but the revolt now appears to be co-ordinated by other potential leaders from the existing chief's class. Viewed over a long period, the basic procedures of government in certain social systems may set up a cyclic process. Sahlins interprets Polynesian traditions in these terms. Chiefs seek to enhance their power by extracting a greater surplus from their dependants and by further conquest, while dependent leaders revolt and fragment the chiefdom when the chief's demands grow excessive. The analysis of Highland Burma by Friedman cited above (Friedman, 1975) provides a detailed analysis of the processes that might be involved in such cyclic development.

The most striking aspect of a comparison between the chiefless societies and kingdoms discussed in this chapter is the number of features they share. All (with the possible exception of the Lega) are essentially agricultural. All possess patrilineal descent groups, religious cults and a system of assigning seniority by age. They differ specifically in the distribution of power. In one category political leaders are distributed evenly through the population, and do not occupy hereditary positions. Lacking a specialized administrative hierarchy, exclusive access to large quantities of valuable resources or armed force, they are vulnerable to the pressures of their communities at large, encouraging them to obey the tenets of good leadership. The other category exhibits a concentration of political power at a capital city. Administrative and political authority is the particular possession of certain exclusive lineage groups, within which the major checks and balances on the king's actions are confined.

Little is explicit in portraying the cyclic development of chiefdoms in the region dominated by the *Poro*. The general history of West Africa likewise supports a theory that individual kingdoms suffer a cyclic development, as the earlier dominance of Ife over Oyo and Benin documents. It is possible that certain environments preclude the concentration of political and economic resources in one local area, and that Lega and Tiv societies, for instance, may never have undergone the transformations required to produce a centralized state. On the other hand, it is clear that all societies discussed here realize and sustain their current political systems by consciously-operated procedures, allowing but controlling the scope for political competition.

In those examined in detail, art objects have been seen to play a major role in the patterns of interaction which bring the political systems to life. Further than that, the ideas which gain tangible expression in art objects appear to be something more than a passive reflection *of* the political system; they are rather philosophical reflections *on* the nature of political authority and its place in the world.

3
Art and visual communication

The theme of the previous chapter has been that art has a crucial role
to play in social life, an argument illustrated by the specific case of
leadership in some African societies. Here art communicated
concepts of good leadership and took part in the rituals during which
such concepts were brought to bear on social life. The concluding
section of Chapter 1 cited Lienhardt's and Tambiah's analyses of the
conceptualizing and mnemonic functions of ritual. The examples of
art and leadership in West Africa show how art objects can parallel
these functions in another medium of expression. Biebuyck makes
explicit reference to the mnemonic function (*kakengelezio*) of Lega
carvings while the sculptures of Benin kingship realize in their
imagery the king's superhuman properties and those of the Ogboni
cult the members' distinctive world-view. Now that the social
context of art in some traditionally non-literate cultures has been
described, the present chapter will focus on *how* a tradition of artistic
representation can in itself provide a systematically organized mode
of expression at the heart of social interaction. To interpret art in this
way is certainly not a new approach. In his classic analysis of religion
among the Australian Aborigines, Durkheim wrote: 'without
symbols, social sentiments could have only a precarious existence ...
social life, in all its aspects and at every period of its history, is made
possible only by a vast symbolism' (1915:231). Durkheim was
thinking primarily of ritual rather than art but, as the ceremonies
surrounding African leadership show, and as Durkheim himself
recognized, art and ritual can form complementary media in this
respect. The first chapter mentioned the value of Durkheim's
demonstration that 'primitive' religion could be viewed as more than
superstition, but criticized his view that the forces conceptualized in
religion exist solely in society. As Morphy writes in one of the studies
this chapter will discuss, 'Durkheim over-simplifies matters by
focusing on a single source of real power, the moral force of society'
(Morphy, 1977:333).

Australian religion

According to Durkheim, totemism, the term by which he
characterized Australian Aboriginal religion, was made possible by

an organized method of classifying the animal and natural world. Black cockatoo and white cockatoo were two birds, similar in many ways but strikingly different in the colour of their feathers. Sun and moon were two comparable celestial bodies which appeared alternately, with day and night. Durkheim argued that when a culture possessed such a structured classification, its component concepts could be used as 'badges' for social groups. The dual oppositions quoted by Durkheim would be most appropriate to the division of society into two moieties (one moiety is Black Cockatoo, the other White...), but Lévi-Strauss developed his predecessor's idea into a model for totemism in a society of small descent groups, expressing totemic relationships in the following way:

> descent group A *is to* group B *is to* group C
> *as* kangaroo *is to* emu *is to* goanna (Lévi-Strauss, 1966)

To each totem in the scheme of classification corresponds a particular social group within the tribe. For Durkheim, celebration of the totemic ancestor in ritual became a reaffirmation of the group's identity within the wider society. Lévi-Strauss saw each group's responsibility to perform ritual to increase the numbers of its totem species as an expression of the several groups' inter-dependence on one another in social life, expressed also in the exchange of women between them in marriage.

At least two criticisms may be made of this theory of totemism. The first is the simplistic notion that each social group has an exclusive relationship with a single animal species. The ancestral beings who combined the attributes of man and animal often travelled vast distances through the Australian bush, traversing the territory of a number of social groups. While each group has the responsibility to carry out ceremonies at sites visited by those ancestors within its own country, there will be several groups sharing a single ancestral track. In many Aboriginal cultures, moreover, what distinguishes a group is the distinctive *collection* of tracks that traverse its territory. A number of different ancestral tracks pass through each territory, and each group has a unique combination of 'totems', even though each separately is shared with other groups. Morphy (*op. cit.*) shows how this more complex situation operates in the politics of Aboriginal social life. As is the case with African descent groups, the membership of Aboriginal clans may grow or shrink. In response, some groups split into two, while others amalgamate to preserve their numbers. Each new group emerges in possession of a territory that gives it a new, and distinctive combination of ancestral tracks, even though no new totems are created.

The second, and more central criticism of the Durkheimian theory concerns the alleged social origin of religion. Aboriginal religion appears on the contrary to *integrate* moral and political aspects of the social world with the animal and plant domain and with the physical world of creeks and hills. To suppose that there is one order of experience among all these which the others 'symbolize' is to miss the point that it is in revealing a common order behind all of them that religion gains its conceptual value.

This is the position Lévi-Strauss himself has taken in more recent work on South American mythology. Morphy illustrates the point with his material on the Yolngu speakers of North-east Arnhem Land. One instance of the complex links that exist between different domains of experience in Yolngu culture is provided by the imagery of funerals expressed in ritual and painting. The imagery of Yolngu bark paintings depicting burial is described in Morphy, 1977c. The Yolngu first leave the dead body to decompose. During the final funeral ceremony relatives of the dead person have the task of stripping decayed flesh from the skeleton before its bones are put into a hollow log coffin. Those allotted this task are, not surprisingly, held to be contaminated by their work. A long, narrow oval shape (a 'sand sculpture') is constructed on the ground, with banks of sand. Inside this is dug a hole representing the clan's major waterhole. The people who prepare the skeleton eat inside the sand sculpture and

Plate 7   Yolngu bark painting, North-east Arnhem Land, Australia: mortuary ceremony with sand sculpture. Note fish at centre of sculpture. Photograph by Dr H. Morphy

bury uneaten scraps beneath it. In due course crabs and gulls unearth the scraps and disperse them. 'That fish', said a senior man, referring to the food, 'is really dead Yolngu' (239). When left-overs are buried 'that is like burying the body in the ground'. The scavenging crabs and gulls are mourners stripping the corpse of flesh. The long oval of the sand sculpture is the boat in which the dead person's spirit travels to the afterworld — but it is also a copy of the clan ancestor's first sand sculpture which survives as topographical features (such as hills and springs) in the clan's territory. Spirits of the dead return to their clan waterhole where they live like little fish until the wife of a clan member, swimming in the water, becomes impregnated — and the spirit is reborn. When Yolngu depict mortuary ceremonies in bark painting (plate 7), Morphy writes, their explanations of these paintings constantly move between the various realms of meaning the ceremony evokes. But paintings are frequently more than depictions, since they are held often to embody ritual power, and this was a point recognized by Durkheim.

ART AND EXPRESSION

Whatever the limitations of his theory, Durkheim brilliantly perceived the importance of art objects in the totemic system. In his view the cohesiveness of the social group was given visible expression in depictions of the totemic species on sacred objects which the group possessed. Lévi-Strauss argues that the economic importance or spectacular appearance of totemic species is less important than the cognitive value they acquire through incorporation into the totemic scheme. Durkheim earlier made the same point: objects selected as totems 'are frequently insignificant... so it is not the intrinsic nature of the thing whose name the clan bears that marks it out to become the object of a cult' (205), rather it is its ability to function as a 'badge' of the group. From this, he developed the argument that: 'It is the figurative representations of this plant or animal [on ceremonial objects]... which have the greatest sanctity', because it is these which provide the tangible expression of the group's place in society, 'personified and represented to the imagination under the visible form of the [picture of the] animal or vegetable which serves as a totem' (206). Hence, he believed, the depictions acquired a sense of power. Durkheim has some relevant remarks to make of the abstract style of much Central Australian Aboriginal art. It is a style based largely on geometric forms: circles, arcs and straight lines. The style, Durkheim argued, is not primarily intended to convey faithfully naturalistic depictions of the animal or plant, but to provide visible markers of the concept of a totemic relationship. 'The facts prove that if the Australian is so strongly inclined to represent his totem, it is not to have a portrait of it before his eyes... it is merely because he feels the need of representing the idea which he forms of it by means of material and external signs, no matter what these signs may be' (127).

Morphy shows that the Yolngu talk about the representational quality of paintings. Each clan has a particular design which marks out its paintings from those of other clans. This consists of a series of semi-circles, or elongated diamonds, which are repeated in the painting. It is seen as depicting a totemic ancestor. The clan design is also painted on members' bodies on ceremonial occasions. Such a design is described as likan. The word likan, writes Morphy, has connotations of 'connectedness'. It is also used of an elbow, the branch of a tree joining the trunk, or a bay between two headlands. It is further used to describe the special names for the clan's sacred objects (187). Alternatively, paintings are sometimes described as the spirit or shade of the ancestral being they depict, and also as bones: 'in this sense the designs are the bones of the clan. They are expressions of its continuity with wanggar (creation) time and of its continuity into the future' (190). It is this ability to provide a material link with concepts that makes paintings valuable.

One of the most appreciated qualities of sacred paintings among the Yolngu is the shimmering finish they are given by the delicate addition of fine, cross-hatched lines. Before this cross-hatching has been applied, writes Morphy, the component figures look dull and the structure of the painting is difficult to discern. After, the painting 'attains a shimmering brilliance' and its components stand out. As Forge reported of the Abelam, there is here a close correspondence between aesthetic judgement and the perception of power in a painting. The two main criteria by which a painting is judged are the correctness of its design (a semantic question) and 'its brightness and the firmness of its lines... the ability to do cross-hatching is used as the main criterion for artistic skill' (186). The startling clarity of such paintings is seen as an expression of the power they contain. Morphy argues that if the Yolngu attribute power to a painting it is not because they identify the representation with the spirits it depicts but because paintings possess an inherent power to express. As he puts it: 'The artistic system itself is powerful because of the ways in which it encodes meaning' (334). Paintings have the ability to isolate different aspects of the Yolngu world-view according to the way in which a cosmological theme is depicted, and this allows them to be used in diverse contexts — the grief of funerals, the well-being of initiation; public and private ceremony. They also play the political role

Durkheim attributed to sacred objects by codifying the separateness of clans from one another, and the links of each with its territory. During the disputes that precede the splitting of a clan, they are powerful vehicles for stating the claims of component segments. In recent years they have also been used to express Aboriginal land-rights to white Australians. In other words paintings gain their power not from the ideas they express, but from their ability to express them — their capacity to communicate. This idea is not very far from the theory of communication that Durkheim implies in his analysis of Aboriginal religion.

Art and language

As was noted during discussion of Wollheim's view of art, Saussure's theory about how communication works in language attaches just as much importance to the tangible vehicles of expression as to the ideas they convey. Saussure's formulation of his theory took place shortly after the publication of Durkheim's study of totemism. It gives a more concise statement of principles that Durkheim himself had already recognized.

Saussure was primarily interested in the connection between words and their meanings. During the nineteenth century linguists had been prone to imagine that language began through the use of sounds which imitated the objects or actions they denoted. Saussure, like the Functionalists in anthropology, rejected this speculative approach. Not only was there no record of these hypothetical onomatopoeic languages, even if they once existed they could not explain the operation of modern speech, in which, as Saussure stressed, there is no intrinsic connection between the sounds of a word and the objects or actions to which it refers.

Saussure argued rather that sounds are associated with meanings by cultural convention. A language consists of two major components:

(a) the division of experience into an ordered set of mental constructs,

(b) the conventional association of each such construct with a specific set of verbal sounds.

The individual *sign* consisted of one unit from each component series: a selection of sounds, the spoken *signifier*, and a corresponding concept, the *signified*. The meaning of a word derives not from any onomatopoeic association with something in the real world, but from its place in the total system of signs making up the language. Like the totemic designs of Durkheim, each unit of sound signified a particular mental construct, and the corpus of signs constituted a *language* corresponding, in a sense, to the totemic classification. In Saussure's terms, the paintings and carvings which appear on totemic objects, and which represent the group's totemic species, are *signifiers*, while the sense of the social group's internal unity within the wider society is the real *signified* concept. The actual totemic animal which is, in a sense, what the design represents, is less important than the place occupied by the concept of that species as a component in the totemic system.

According to Barthes (1967:23), Saussure had been influenced by Durkheim's work, although the analogy with Durkheim's totemic system is not stated in his *Course in General Linguistics* (1959). The closeness of the two men's views is nonetheless striking. One of the most deceptive aspects of the art of other cultures is its ability to be read by us as representational. The arbitrary association between the signifiers of spoken language and the objects they may denote apparently distinguishes language from art, tempting us to assume that while we could not understand African speech without learning the appropriate language, we might be able to understand the art of that language's speakers. Unfortunately, much has been made, by those who find themselves frustrated in such attempts at understanding, of the failure of art in other cultures to appear to us sufficiently naturalistic, a mode of criticism that will be examined in the following chapter. It is undeniable that many art styles gain much of their interest from the way that they play, in a regular fashion, with the visual qualities of the objects they depict. On the other hand, it is fascinating to discover that Durkheim, far from considering the geometric style of central Australian art detracted from its communicative value, was led — precisely by the highly geometric nature of designs on sacred objects — to believe their representational quality was irrelevant to their expressive function: 'The meaning of the figures thus obtained is so arbitrary that a single design may have two different meanings for the men of different totems' (127). The excellent research carried out by Nancy Munn (e.g. Munn:1973) shows that despite this fact the designs are still in an important way representational, but Durkheim's misunderstanding does draw him even closer to Saussure. Indeed, he added a footnote saying: 'It cannot be doubted that these designs and paintings also have an aesthetic character; here is the first form of art. Since they are also, and even above all, a written language, it follows that the origins of design and those of writing are one: it even becomes clear that man commenced designing, not so much to fix upon wood or stone beautiful forms which charm the senses, as to *translate his thought into matter*' (127n, my emphasis).

Durkheim and Saussure would probably have nonetheless agreed that the structure of a language is considerably richer than the totemic systems envisaged by Durkheim. And, perhaps even more importantly, the individuals who share a common language use it, according to rules of grammar, to create an enormous variety of individual statements whose meaning depends on the choice of words and their combination in particular sequences in speech. The only kind of 'statement' possible in Durkheim's totemic system would be that in which each clan celebrates its particular totemic affiliation — and it is doubtful whether that deserves to be considered 'speech' in Saussure's terms, because it simply abstracts a single 'sign' from the totemic system and does not combine that sign with others. The rigour of Saussure's analysis and the tremendous success of its application in the study of language has resulted in a reversal of the earlier situation, because anthropologists now look to linguists for a model according to which they can analyse non-verbal modes of communication. So, for instance, Leach has written: 'the relation between speech and ritual deserves close attention... speech is a form of ritual; non-verbal ritual is simply a signal system of a different, less specialized kind' (1966:404).

Lévi-Strauss, who is very largely responsible for showing how revealing analyses of culture based on linguistic methods can be, has also discussed how art can be understood as a system of signs, like language in some respects but not in others. In his main discussion of the parallels between art and language (1960), he seems nonetheless to make two basic mistakes.

The first of these is to blame the failure of art objects to be completely naturalistic on poor technique. 'In the arts which we call primitive', he writes, 'there is always a disparity between the technical means at the artist's disposal and the resistance of the materials he fashions, which prevents him from making the work of art a simple facsimile. He is thus constrained to *signify* the object he portrays' (1960:65-6). In taking this view he confuses the object portrayed with the mental construct which is the true signified component of a work of art. All representational art objects, he argues, unlike linguistic signifiers, *do* resemble the objects they portray, but this leads him to a false equation: 'The particular character of the language of art is that there is always a very profound homology between the structure of the signified and the structure of the signifier' (96). A *signified* cannot be a material object; it must be a mental construct.

His second major mistake is to overlook the possibility of art having anything comparable to a grammar. He echoes a Durkheimian view of society when he correctly points out: 'language is a collective phenomenon, it is a characteristic of the collectivity and exists only by virtue of the collectivity'; but he deduces from that, that 'as much as an element of individualization intrudes into artistic production so, necessarily and automatically, the semantic (meaningful) function of the work tends to disappear' (66). If we suppose that art traditions lie somewhere between Durkheim's simplified account of totemism and the real complexity of language itself, then we ought to ask if any possibilities exist for meaningful, but individual statements by those who create works of art within these traditions.

The examples discussed in this chapter are divided into two sets. The first set will illustrate how meanings are attributed to elements of design in small-scale societies. An examination of motifs, or meaningful units, in such art traditions shows that, far from a faithful naturalism being their major characteristic, the significance of many designs relies largely on mental structures peculiar to the culture which uses them. In some cases the tangible elements of meaning are simply colours: a fairly generalized level of representation. The first section will demonstrate this through three examples. The final example from the first set begins to illustrate how *composition* may involve a visual grammar. The second set of examples will show in more detail how the way in which motifs are combined in the composition of an art work may contain information about the relationships between the ideas these motifs stand for.

VISUAL SIGNIFIERS

The Kalabari are village-dwellers of the Niger delta. Their sculpture has already been mentioned in the discussion of aesthetics, above. Each of their villages is peopled by the members of once-autonomous lineages brought together by powerful men during a former period of warfare, and this dichotomy between village and lineage is alluded to in their cosmology. The Kalabari consider the world to have been created by a supreme being, beneath whom are the three classes of spiritual being represented in sculpture: the lineage ancestors, the water spirits (fig. 7) who live outside society in the delta and are responsible for anti-social or innovative behaviour in humans, and the village heroes. In accordance with his theory of religion, Horton describes their cosmology as a theory the Kalabari use to 'classify, interpret and manipulate all significant events in the world about them' (1965:7). Although its form is related to the social conditions of the Kalabari it is not, Horton insists, a mere reflection of them, but something which influences the way people think about their institutions and hence something which plays an important part in determining what those institutions actually are' (8). People worship a spirit to influence him, making offerings and singing songs of praise to his material realization, the sculpture. A rather complex set of attributes show which kind of spirit is depicted by each particular carving.

The heroes stand between ancestors and water spirits: they came from the delta or the sea but lived with men to teach them the valuable institutions that unite the several lineages of the settlement into a single community. The duality of the heroes' attributes is expressed in the imagery of carving. Heroes and ancestors are best carved from a particular wood said only to grow in human settlements, while water spirits are represented in mangrove wood. Neither hero nor ancestor figures are shown associated with the fishing implements and aquatic animals figuring in the iconography of water spirit sculptures. On the other hand, only ancestors are depicted with backbones (plate 8), so here the heroes are classed with water spirits. One Kalabari man told Horton: 'The heroes and water spirits are not people. We do not see them. They stay in the breeze. So we cannot carve their sculptures by comparing them with people.' Again, while ancestors are painted in monochrome brown paint representing human skin, both heroes and water spirits are painted in white or polychrome. Heroes are unique in one respect; they wear a type of conical hat called the *sansum*. Horton says its origin is obscure. The elements of Kalabari design and their significance are shown in the accompanying figure (fig. 21).

The connections between carvings and the spirits they represent are established by a variety of associations characteristic of Kalabari culture. The places of the various spirits are expressed through the association of the materials used with swamp or village and the location of their shrines, through the classification of certain animals as swamp animals and their opposition to people, the inhabitants of the village; and through the depiction of implements used in specific settings. It is the people, animals and implements that are represented pictorially, but it is cultural concepts about their place in the world that give them meaning. One bird, for instance, which actually 'frequents houses and settlements' is seen by the Kalabari as the messenger of creatures living in the delta (33).

The relationship between visual signifiers and the concepts of spiritual forces is more complex than in the Durkheim/Lévi-Strauss model of totemism. Not only does it combine pictorial representations with non- or loosely-representational qualities like the materials used and the colour of pigments; neither is there a one-

Plate 8 Kalabari sculpture from Nigeria: ancestor figures on screen. *British Museum*

to-one relationship between each element of the sculpture and a single class of spirits. Some signifying elements (such as the absence of a backbone) characterize two classes and therefore make more generalized statements about the spirit's place in the cosmology.

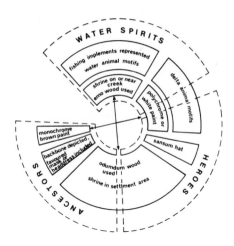

Figure 21 Kalabari design motifs and their significance, from Nigeria. *Adapted from Horton*

When this is the case, the exact class a spirit belongs to could only be discovered by looking at other elements of the carving. In some cases there are opposed pairs of traits, such as *brown* versus *polychrome or white* paint, one or other of which must be included. In other instances, such as that of the water spirits' fishing implements, there is no complementary artefact for inclusion in carvings of the other classes of spirit (see fig. 21).

Horton writes that not all motifs indicative of a particular class of spirits are found on a single carving. 'Hence', he comments, 'there is the possibility of considerable sculptural variation from cult to cult within a given category of spirits' (*op. cit.*, 36n). This is not exactly an instance of visual grammar, but it does illustrate the fallacy of Lévi-Strauss' sweeping judgement about individualization.

Humphrey's essays on the Buryat (1971, 1973) are also helpful demonstrations of the complexity of visual expression in art. Humphrey discusses analogies between language and a tradition of producing pictures called *ongon*, used in ritual. The Buryat are a Mongolian-speaking people living on the shores of Lake Baikal in south-east Siberia. They are a chiefless society whose traditional way of life was one of cattle herding, entailing long seasonal or migratory journeys. Cattle play an important role in their religious symbolism. Both a spirit and the material object in which it is incarnated are called *ongon*: a bull or a shaman can house a spirit, so too can pictorial representations which all Buryat adults used to construct from a variety of materials such as silk, wood, metal, animal skins, feathers and paint (fig. 22). These pictorial *ongon*, like Kalabari sculptures, provide a physical home for the appropriate spirit and hence have power to bring luck in hunting, to assist in childbirth, to prevent cattle disease, depending on the spirit which is represented.

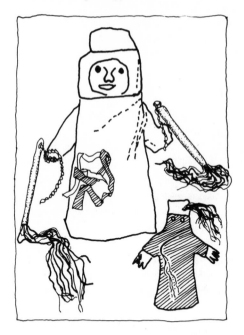

Figure 22   Buryat *ongon* (south-east Siberia): the Husband and Wife *ongon*. *After Humphrey*

There is a special way of depicting each spirit using standard materials and designs and hence like a language, Humphrey writes, the practice of making *ongon* constitutes a system of communication which 'conveys a great many complex ideas with rather few elements, ordered by specific rules' (1971:271).

The meaning of items used in the construction of an *ongon* depends on their place in Buryat culture. The connections between signified and signifier range from pictorial representations of the depicted object to conventional associations, as in the use of colour to denote compass direction: a white ribbon signifies south-west (a point of seniority, purity and maleness) while a black one signifies the opposed point, north-east; red signifies north-west (associated with hunting) and yellow south-east (associated with procreation). There may be alternative but equally acceptable ways of signifying a single concept. These have different degrees of visual resemblance to, or *motivation* by, members of the class of objects represented. The mental construct 'human being' may be depicted by a human stick figure or simply by a tuft of red silk representing 'hair' (remember the cross of parasol wood substituted for an animal carving by the Lega, see page 9). As was the case with Kalabari sculpture, there is a recognized pattern for representing each Buryat spirit and all realizations falling within these constraints are equally valid (1971:273).

In our culture we perhaps tend too much to equate conscious thought with thought we can express in words. A number of anthropologists have experienced the inability of people in small-scale societies to explain in words what their art means (e.g. Forge among the Abelam; Forge, 1967), and have been tempted as a result to interpret the art as purely formal, or as expressive of the subconscious, a realm of thought to which, given our exposure to Freudian psychology, we tend to attribute a fairly limited range of ideas. One of the valuable points made by Humphrey is that although *ongons* 'say' a lot about how spirits are thought of, they do so independently of language. There are special ritual forms of verse describing spirits' characteristics and there are formal narratives relating the myths about the spirits' adventures, but some concepts expressed in *ongons* may not be translatable into speech, even though the concepts are complex and analytical. Humphrey illustrates her point by showing the elaboration of ideas about purity and impurity, and about hunting and procreation, conveyed by *ongon*. Among the animal skins used to construct *ongons* are those of the goat and polecat.

The 'purity' of the goat is related to:	*The 'impurity' of the polecat is related to:*
the hide being tanned; the animal being a mountain beast which lives above ground, and has hooves.	the raw, untreated nature of the skin; the animal being a lowland creature which burrows, and has claws.

Hunting and procreation form a second opposed pair of concepts.

Ongons *associated with hunting:*	Ongons *associated with procreation:*
are hung inside the house, on a north-west wall.	are hung outside the house, on a south-east wall.

One general point which these examples make clear is that few cognitive schemes are as simplistic as the totemic model that has a series of terms such as 'social groups' equated with a second series of mental categories such as 'animal species'. Even that model of cognition depends on the culture drawing an analogy between two sets of ideas, but the Buryat culture Humphrey describes builds a much more elaborate system of correspondences, analogies and hierarchies in its thought. The Buryat examples are very like the classificatory schemes discussed by Lévi-Strauss in *La Pensée Sauvage* (1966). Kelly (1963) has discussed the general process of building and comparing mental categories in our own culture, including the question of personal variation (see Layton, 1971, for an account of non-verbal communication, using some of Kelly's ideas, in a French village). From the complexity of Buryat imagery stems another important observation of Humphrey, that in constructing *ongon* the Buryat 'use an already existing evaluation and classification of objects [in Buryat culture] in order to signify, just as poetry and myth use an existing language to create a further statement' (1971:289). The same point is made by the authors of the third and last example. This is a study of visual communication in a culture which relies heavily on non-pictorial elements of colour and design; the Stratherns' work on *Self-Decoration in Mount Hagen* (Strathern, 1972).

Mount Hagen lies in the east central New Guinea Highlands, some 150 miles south-east of the Sepik. The inhabitants of the Hagen area have developed body-decoration as their major art form, producing designs for festivals, funerals and warfare. Like Humphrey, the Stratherns write that as with 'any other art form, self-decoration carries its own symbolic load, and transmits messages that are not exactly replicated in other media' (171-2). In other words, there may be no way of explaining, in Hagen speech, the exact significance of some visual messages conveyed by decorating the body.

Highland New Guinea society exemplifies the kind of leadership developed to a lesser extent among the Lega and Tiv in West Africa. In highland New Guinea there is no permanent, single office of village head, but rather a status of 'Big Man' to which people can aspire. One community may have none, or two or more at any particular moment. Big Men organize productive activities in their own households and among those of kin who support, or are indebted to them. The success with which they achieve this co-ordination is expressed in ceremonies at which the products of their gardening economy are exchanged. There is competition to see which group can produce most. Warfare, arising from attempts to annexe neighbouring communities' gardens or raid their livestock, was also common. Allies in war cemented their relationship by exchanging women in marriage.

Mount Hagen is one of these societies: the small descent groups led by Big Men are constantly competing for temporary advantages over one another. The principal field for this competition is in a ceremonial exchange system called the *moka*, in which groups attempt to outdo one another in the wealth of pigs, food and valuables they present to each other, as the turn of each to be hosts at such a feast comes around. Exchange festivals proceed in a regular sequence: first minor exchanges between segments of a clan, then major exchanges when all clansmen assist one of their segments to feast members of another clan. Women have a special role to play in enhancing positive links between autonomous groups: not only are they exchanged in marriage; it is they who rear the pigs and tend the garden crops which form the substance of exchange at feasts. This role is dramatized in their ceremonial decoration. In the past, warfare provided a crucial complementary activity to ceremonial exchange: groups who did not exchange raided and carried out revenge killings on each other. The payment of pigs and shell valuables, in fact, was often treated as compensation paid to ex-enemies who were now ceremonial partners, for losses in warfare. Indemnity payments passed gradually into reciprocal exchanges and so two groups might be drawing together into a closer alliance. Equally, however, a clan nominally united in ceremonial transactions might be undergoing fission. Each ceremonial exchange had elements of alliance but also elements of rivalry, expressed in aggressive speeches, the competitively great size of presentations and the form of decorations worn. It is within this context of constantly changing inter-group relationships that Hagen self-decoration operates, and it operates partly to give tangible expression to the particular form of current relationships between groups. Despite its greater complexity this is therefore not a system completely unrelated to Durkheim's simple model of totemic ritual, but with the greater ambivalence of social relations goes more scope for individual 'statements' by component groups about their current positions. In the model of Aboriginal totemism it was possible for one social group to say, 'we are goanna men as you are kangaroo men' but, since the group inherits its totem from one generation to the next, their statement would have been very much a foregone conclusion. In the Hageners' case the statements are rather 'we are allies' or 'we are enemies', 'we are mourning' or 'we are celebrating'; statements which appear by no means so predictable, given the Hageners' way of life.

The social situations to which decoration relates include funerals, warfare, daily productive activities, trading visits, courting parties and ceremonial exchanges. Within the latter the status of the donor subclansmen, their wives, helping sub-clans and receivers are differentiated. To show that there is a self-contained system of visual communication in body-decoration it must be proved that there are enough signifying units for each social situation to be conveyed by a different unit of expression or by a unique set of such signifiers.

One element of Mount Hagen signification is colour, principally the colours red, white and black. It is clear, however, that three colours alone are not enough for one colour to stand only for a single situation out of the list given above: the same colour is going to have to reappear in several contexts. The Hageners sometimes appear for this reason to adopt 'ambiguous' attitudes towards the meaning of

Figure 23　New Guinea body-decoration: Hagen mourner —
negative decoration. *After Strathern*

colours and this raises the question as to whether colours have a
constant significance or whether they are analogous to the phonemes
(discrete elements of sound without constant meaning) of language.
In certain contexts for instance, Hagen men wear white clay to
signify health and attractiveness. They do this at exchange festivals
and here the clay represents shining pig fat, pigs being the major item
of value and exchange at such festivals. Here the clay is only one
component of the predominantly glossy decorations the men wear.
Hageners also wear white clay at funerals, where they combine it
with ashes (fig. 23). Now the clay signifies ill-health; a poor skin
condition. The clay, like the ashes, is viewed as a dull substance. In
both cases texture is as significant as colour.

The third set of signifying units (after colour and texture) extends
from careless to careful design. At one pole lies the form of body
covering used in funerals. Funerals, write the Stratherns (echoing
their informants), are the only major occasions at which 'decorations'
are inappropriate. Yet the appearance of the mourners is modified:
they tear off their wigs, pull out their hair and smear their bodies
with mud, clay and ashes.

The neutral position on this scale (that of minimal decoration)
corresponds to garden and household work. In such mundane tasks
men wear a bark belt with an old string apron in front and bundle of
leaves behind. The head may be uncovered. Women wear few
ornaments, less profusely dressed than at festive occasions. From this
point, we pass to the category labelled 'second-best decorations', a
degree of elaboration appropriate to two rather different contexts:
warfare and minor ceremonies (it is other elements of design which
distinguish between these). Few or no decorations are worn in minor

Figure 24   Hagen self-decoration (New Guinea):
'Second-best' decoration worn on visit to market.
After Strathern

skirmishes, but in major warfare participants wear red plumes of an inferior brownish shade and other feathers which might be worn when peacefully visiting other groups. The whole body is charcoaled. On his forehead the warrior wears wings of the *swiftlet*, a bird with the specific cultural quality of being a creature of ill-omen. This is evidently one of the diagnostic traits distinguishing war-decorations from other 'second-best' assemblages. A similar degree of decoration is appropriate to those who travel on trading expeditions. Men wear a wig covered by a knitted headdress and trimmed with grass, leaves and perhaps fur (fig. 24). Women wear pearl-shell pendants.

The most complex decorations accompany major exchanges. The donors are marked out by a special feather headdress, the *køi wal* (fig. 25). Recipients generally wear rather less elaborate designs resembling those worn by both donors and recipients at the minor exchanges preceding a major ceremony. The greater the differentiation in the composition of decorations between donors, recipients and helpers (allied clans or sub-clans), the greater the implied political distance separating these groups (*op. cit.*: 66-8, 82).

On this axis of progressive elaboration one thus finds several discrete elements of signification: the negative one of funerals, the neutral one of everyday work, then 'second-best' and 'best' designs. There is also a suggestion of continuous variation in the progressive differentiation of donors, receivers and helpers, even if donors also carry the specific marker of the *køi wal*. Continuous variation is not a characteristic of language at the level of phoneme and morpheme that concerned Saussure, although it does occur in (for instance)

Figure 25   Hagen self-decoration (New Guinea): 'Best' decoration worn at exchange festival. (a) Wife of helper, (b) Man wearing *køi wal* headdress. *After Strathern*

a

b

cartography, where the width of a river on the map varies in direct relation to its width on the ground.

The remaining axis, already mentioned apropos of white clay, is that embodying the single contrast between glossy and dull decorations. It is on the basis of this distinction that warfare is classed with funerals and differentiated from minor ceremonies of a positive kind. Just as dull muds and ashes are worn at funerals, in warfare the participants decorate themselves with dried grasses or banana leaves, or whitish-grey, non-glossy leaves of other kinds. When decorating themselves for a courting party or bridewealth transaction, on the other hand, the men choose fresh leaves and may grease their bodies so as to appear glossy. A glossy appearance is crucial at the major exchanges. There is an interesting parallel here with some of the elements in Kalabari sculpture. The specific quality of village heroes was portrayed through the use of images shared with water spirits or ancestors, and established only by the specific *combination* of elements of meaning unique to heroes. Hageners,

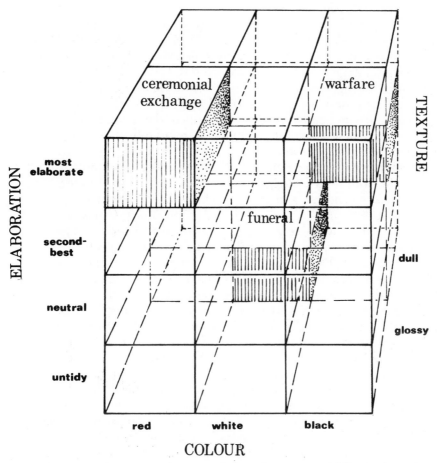

Figure 26 Hagen self-decoration (New Guinea): chart showing axes of differentiation and location of alternative compositions

however, are applying elements of design not to wooden carvings, but to their own bodies.

The system made up from the elements of Hagen body-decoration allows the signification of quite a large number of particular social positions. Each status is denoted by a combination of one element from each of the three axes. To illustrate the total number of positions that might be denoted in this way requires a three-dimensional grid: the three colours constituting one dimension, the two textures another and the four degrees of elaboration the third (see fig. 26).

The number of social positions that could possibly be represented seems to be 4 x 3 x 2 = 24: more, apparently, than the actual number — but some combinations such as *dull* + *red*..., may involve an internal contradiction, for red is exclusively the colour people wear at festivals to make themselves appear attractive. The Hageners recognize rules for the combination of elements of decoration so as to form a set appropriate to the context signified: 'People ... refer to ... the overall appearance of a dancer, and the way the different items of his attire *fit together* and *suit the occasion*' (11, my emphasis; see also 126). This sounds very like a visual grammar.

There are, nonetheless, some elements of decoration which are not subject to these rules, often (but not invariably) the case with the species of bird from which feathers are taken or the use of particular design motifs in face-painting. Here variation does not affect the 'meaning' of the total design; like personal intonation in speech, they are *not pertinent*, at a primary level, to the system of meaning.

Saussure defined *speech* as the selection of signs from out of the total set and their stringing together to form messages. Speech, he argued, was as individual as language (vocabulary and grammar) was collective. Despite Lévi-Strauss' comments and the fact that in Hagen self-decoration it is sub-groups, not individuals, who are here constructing messages, these messages still convey a significant amount of *information*; that is, those who observe a set of people wearing a particular form of self-decoration can learn from it status positions and intentions of which they might have been unaware before or, at least, the designs can reinforce and concretize what was suspected.

One of the most interesting possibilities raised by the Hagen material is that it may have features comparable to the rules of syntax in language. That is, that each composition with which an actor is decorated — each message — combines a number of discrete signifying units, some of which separately always mean the same thing. The Stratherns record that the black face-paint worn by the men denotes their identity with the group's ancestors (and hence their corporate power) in both warfare and ceremonial exchanges. Likewise, glossy decorations invariably signify health and positive social interaction while dull ones signify negative social occasions: two discrete signifiers thus combine to convey a composite message in both cases. The colour white, on the other hand, seems not to have a constant meaning.

Despite such tempting parallels with language it is important to note some crucial differences between the structure of this system of visual communication and that of language itself. If self-decoration is treated as an independent system, the number of messages which can be conveyed is vastly smaller than those possible in verbal communication, if only because there are fewer signifying units. But to what extent is it valid to abstract self-decoration from the universe of meanings of Hagen culture and treat it as an isolated system? Probably it should be treated as a sub-system within that wider field. Humphrey made this point with her analogy between *ongons* and poetry, as special cases of a more extensive mode of expression. Some writers would argue that culture imbues the appearance of every object it makes or uses with meaning. Lévi-Strauss saw this as characteristic of some small-scale societies in which, he wrote: 'each manufactured object, even the most utilitarian, is a kind of crystallization [*condensé*] of symbols accessible not only to the maker but to all the users.' Barthes, whom Humphrey cites, would maintain that the same is true of objects in our own culture (cf. Barthes, 1967:II): even the clothes we wear make statements about our intentions, our social class, the conditions we are expecting to encounter. Art and language may therefore express different, although perhaps overlapping components of the total organization of meanings in culture.

The Stratherns describe how some of the meanings conveyed in self-decoration depend on general cultural associations, when they are arguing against the temptation to assume that there is some *universal* 'language' of colour symbolism recognizable across cultures. There is a tree in the bush called the *kilt* tree, and the attractiveness of red decorations is linked with the qualities perceived in this tree. The situation was explained to them as follows: 'It is the brightness of the *kilt* tree's red flowers which attracts flocks of birds to it, and we attract women in the same way' (*op. cit.*:90). The cultural significance of pigs as a form of wealth and object of exchange determines the significance which the representation of white, glossy pig fat in body-decoration possesses. In Western culture on the other hand the pig, as a scavenger, assumes quite another symbolic significance. And white paint, as the Stratherns point out, can represent ill-health and mourning for the Hageners, when used in a different context.

As in many art styles a clear resemblance can be seen between portrayed objects and the motifs portraying them, so the connections between ideas characteristic of the symbolic systems of other cultures can often be appreciated. But the fact remains that the ideas associated are different from one another; it is an act of creative imagination that perceives a certain analogy between them, just as the development of an art style is achieved through analysis, not mimicry.

A comparison of neighbouring cultures exemplifies this. Gell's recent study of body-decoration in another New Guinea culture, the Umeda, gives a fascinating counterpoint to the Hagen case, particularly in its discussion of the imagery of colour. Like the

Hageners, the Umeda have a set of alternative 'compositions' for body-painting and the one a performer selects denotes his position in a complex scheme of alternative cultural status (Gell summarizes those occurring in a specific ritual, in his fig. 29, 1975:191). Black and red are seen to represent opposed sets of ideas (cf. *op. cit.*:308-29). Blackness corresponds to a 'terminal phase' of growth: old plants, senior men, smoked corpses, and also a peripheral position in the social group or animal world (typified by the flightless cassowary of the deep bush). Redness corresponds to a phase where growth is in progress: ripening young plants, boys undergoing initiation. In the fertility ritual Gell analyses, some participants, according to their status, paint themselves in pure black or pure red, while others place themselves in intermediate positions by adopting designs that mix colours in varying proportions. Gell also finds a contrast between careless and careful design, but here it is used as an expression of anarchic or controlled roles in the ritual drama (327).

Despite the representational qualities of art, these examples underline the importance of cultural convention in establishing meaning in systems of visual communication, showing there is here a very real analogy between visual and verbal expression. It is also clear that, as poetry is a special form of verbal communication, so peculiarly artistic forms of visual communication exist where many levels of meaning are conveyed by visual imagery. Is there any sense in which such visual symbolism is not also purely a matter of convention?

The cultural basis of imagery

White pigment seems to be exceptional in Hagen body-decoration in its lack of a constant signification, but this situation is not atypical of other cultural systems. Biebuyck depicts it as a central feature of Lega ritual, where the leader of a ceremony delights his audience by moving out from the object he handles into diverse realms of meaning: 'The striking and unexpected interpretations, along with the element of surprise, the festive mood, the poetic style, transform every dance and song, every display of objects, every rite and initiation, into a fascinating and entertaining experience' (1973:157). Note that in Lega ceremony both carved representations and real objects of everyday use appear side-by-side, illustrating vividly how art can be part of a wider system of meanings. Perhaps a useful parallel would be with a Braque collage in which actual newspaper headlines, or postage stamps, are incorporated. The essential point, according to the views of Gombrich (to which we will return in the following chapter), is not that the artist represents things because the real objects are unavailable to him, but because in transforming them through the medium of his chosen style he can say *more* about their cultural significance.

Fundamental to the success of the ceremonial leader's interpretations among the Lega must be some *motivation* in the appearance, or use, or behaviour of the object he manipulates. But Biebuyck maintains that the diversity of meanings revealed are in no way intrinsic to the object (the outside observer, from another culture, could not find them by examining the object himself), nor are the range of meanings equivalent; indeed, if they were, the richness of the experience would be cancelled. Rather, the aim seems to be to find unity in diversity, a skill very like that Aristotle admired in the poet — to reveal, through the use of metaphor, the similarity in dissimilars. Biebuyck's discussion of the hornbill beak illustrates the point. Two of the proverbs this object evokes are: 'The chick, the tender care of both father and mother' and 'Hornbill, the miserable one, has tried to imitate the call of animals'. These, Biebuyck explains, have the following implications: the first tells people that not even bad children should be neglected, while the second ridicules a man preparing for admission to *Bwami* but lacking the required wealth to support his claim (152). Because of its grotesque form, Biebuyck writes, the hornbill beak is preferably treated as a symbol of abnormal social situations. Others alluded to with the aid of the beak may be a man's failure to pass through initiation in his own descent group, or 'the inexplicable cause and moment of death'. Clearly these are very different kinds of abnormality and the skill of the ceremonial leader must lie in harnessing the hornbill beak to the purpose of revealing unexpected analogies between them. In other instances a single object may evoke opposed ideas. The spotted hide of the genet may be used as an image of 'bad kinship, here light coloured, here dark coloured' while on the other hand the spots may be pointed to, to remind someone that as the coat is stained, so they are affected by the deeds of their ancestors. Again, the hide may become a reference to the genet's behaviour; like the tutor who 'turns and sneaks behind the house' to verify the candidate's accumulated wealth, but also like the low-ranking member of *Bwami* who, although 'a clever catcher, cannot arrive where the hawk arrives' (146).

Biebuyck's portrait of Lega ritual symbolism contrasts markedly with Turner's account of ritual symbolism among the Ndembu of Zambia. Turner considers that the objects manipulated in Ndembu ritual have a permanent set of meanings. To explain the apparent diversity of ideas associated with them, he introduced the concept of 'situational relevance': certain of the concepts evoked by an object come to the fore in particular contexts, but the others remain subliminally perceived to give more complex, and ambiguous force to the ritual message. For Turner the most important ritual symbols among the Ndembu are those which unite disparate ideas ranging from, at one pole, 'ideological' concepts about the social order, to (at the other) 'sensory' concepts of bodily functions. One tree, with the peculiar property of exuding a white sap, evokes both continuity in the matrilineage and breast milk. Through the unifying power of such evocative objects, 'norms and values... become saturated with emotion, while the gross and basic emotions become ennobled through contact with social values' (1967:30). These *dominant* symbols, actualized in specific types of tree around which ritual occurs become, *because* they have constant significance, fixed reference points in cultural life. When, however, Turner illustrates their use in ritual, he argues that certain aspects of their meaning are suppressed, just as otherwise recognized social conflicts are put aside. The unity of the matrilineage, for instance, takes precedence over hostility between mothers and daughters. A rite to stop excessive flow of menstrual blood dramatizes the replacement of menstruation by pregnancy. A young specimen of the tree whose red sap represents blood is cut down and carved to represent a baby. But 'Ndembu red symbolism... nearly always has explicit reference to violence [and] to killing' (41). Implicit in the rite, he finds aggression towards the sick woman, in which she is covertly criticized for wasting her blood instead of playing the proper role of a married woman. Far from being deterred by admitted changes in meaning attributed to symbolic objects, Turner argues 'that discrepancy between *significata* is a quintessential property of the great symbolic dominants in all religions' (43).

There is one essay in which Turner comes closer to Biebuyck's vision of the creative exploration of new meanings in ritual imagery: his account of meeting a ritual expert called *Muchona*. He describes how Muchona taught him unsuspected and more complex meanings in Ndembu ritual: 'I had heard many other Ndembu interpret plant symbols before, but never so clearly and cogently as this'. When Muchona began to talk, Kasonda (Turner's companion) 'whispered to me, "he is just lying" ' (*op. cit.* 133), but Turner accepts the validity of many of Muchona's explanations as a general account of the meaning of Ndembu ritual. Nonetheless, he records that Muchona's elaborate accounts were not given in ritual; instead he sees their encounter as a unique event which stimulated both to explore Ndembu symbolism: 'he became as eager as myself to learn the hidden meanings of Ndembu beliefs and practices' (134).

The danger inherent in Turner's approach lies in coming to assume that meanings are intrinsic to the objects used in ritual, not there by conventional association. This error is particularly illustrated in his early essays on Ndembu colour symbolism where he argued, for instance, that the colour white embodied, for the Ndembu, purity, power, authority and deathlessness (cf. Turner, 1966:58-9) and in one essay found an analogy with the symbolism of Christ's resurrection from the tomb and Melville's symbolism in the character of Moby Dick (1962). Yet even in listing all the associations of white in Ndembu culture he finds 'ambivalence': whiteness also represents leprosy and the marsh lights that lead hunters to their death, and these in turn have connotations other than purity or deathlessness. 'My principle aim,' he concludes, 'is to show that in all three cases — Ndembu, Christian and American — Whiteness ... represents an attempt to grasp the ungraspable, to embody the invisible' (1962:91). When he later considers the symbolism of red and black he tells us of black that although it represents evil, sorcery and so on, it also represents death, which to the Ndembu is merely a passage from one form of existence to another, another initiation. And in discussing red he cites an Ndembu man who remarked: 'Red things belong to two categories, they act both for good and ill', adding, 'This statement well expresses the ambivalence of the red symbolism' (1966:60). It would seem that if the total spread of symbolic references even within Ndembu culture can only be summarized in terms of 'ambivalence' or 'the ungraspable', something must be wrong.

The Stratherns, writing with explicit reference to Turner's work, take the more satisfactory view that Hagen colour symbolism is determined by associations characteristic of usages and experiences in that culture, that context can modify meaning and that in certain cases (particularly with respect to the colour white) certain of the ideas symbolized in different contexts may be unconnected.

As is often the case, it is impossible to know how far the Lega and Ndembu differ in the constancy of symbolic values in their ritual, or in the creative imagery of their ritual experts; or to what extent the apparent differences result from different theoretical foci on the part of the anthropologists. What is needed is a more general approach which allows particular cultures the possibility of constant *versus* fluid approaches to the elaboration of symbolic values and draws attention to the conventionality of meaning. Gell has a useful phrase where he considers the relevance of Turner's work to Umeda colour symbolism: colours are not intrinsically meaningful, rather 'the intrinsic "colourfulness" of the world presents consciousness with an inchoate field which can be the object of an indefinite number of pattern-building exercises' (1975:310). Colour is particularly able 'to express underlying continuities between disparate domains' not because of some inbuilt meaning, but because so many things are coloured. Particular birds, particular trees, particular fish, acquire greater cultural significance than trees, fish or birds in general because the ways they are conceived exemplify certain complexes of ideas for which their colour provides a convenient focus.

It is true that occasionally many cultures appear to recognize similar symbolic equations, but where this is the case the reason seems to lie in the sharing of experiences which suggest parallels between different phenomena. Such common experience in no way denies the essential role of culture in codifying the parallels.

There are certain simple groups of traits, of which colour is one and parts of the body another, which every culture recognizes. Because bodily functions are common to mankind, and because colours can readily be associated with well-known natural phenomena such as night and day, different cultures, when they use these traits in a metaphorical fashion, often produce similar analogies. Hertz (1960) demonstrated this in the imagery attributed to 'left' and 'right'. He argued that in all societies the majority of people are right-handed. Culture, in organizing experience, often took this tendency and converted it to a simpler, absolute contrast: right is right and good, left is false and sinister. Van Gennep (1960) argued that the journey through a no-man's land between two tribal territories becomes a common image for changes in status, such as the passage from childhood to adulthood.

Behind these simple metaphors often lie complex hierarchies of analogy like those of the Buryat or Umeda, so that the simple images of 'right-handedness' or 'redness' evoke layers of meaning running through diverse areas of cultural experience. Here, the term symbolism is apt and the power to reveal such layers of meaning is integral to the distinctive qualities of art. But to the extent that such analogies are elaborated, it seems likely that the structures characteristic of different cultures will diverge. One should never be seduced by the recurrence of similar meanings attributed to 'redness' etc. into believing that these meanings are intrinsic to the object. That view seems directly comparable to the theory which believed language communicated through onomatopoeia. Onomatopoeia occurs in language, of course, or else the term would not have been coined; and the words with such a quality have their own appeal. The aptness of artistic imagery, likewise, derives from the revelation of perhaps unsuspected parallels of form or behaviour or context, but such 'natural meanings' are not integral to the way we express ourselves through cultural media, and one cannot therefore assume common images always retain the same meaning, either within a single culture or between cultures. It is the essence of cultures to construct patterns of meaning and social relevance out of the diverse phenomena of experience, and the variety of patterns so constructed show how creative a process this is.

In concluding this section, there are two important aspects of communication in art to be borne in mind. There is, first, a very real difference between the conventional signifying units of language and pictorial representations in art. We can often (although by no means always) start to identify what is portrayed in the art of cultures whose language we cannot speak because while the sounds have no necessary connection with the objects, concepts of which they denote, pictures do resemble what they portray. Our *idea* of this object, however, is unlikely to correspond exactly with that held by members of another culture. The objects which are portrayed in art are, secondly, themselves associated, by virtue of cultural experience, with more general and less readily apprehended phenomena. That is, the ideas signified by visual motifs themselves stand for other ideas. Taking these points in turn, one might first distinguish unmotivated signs in language, whether it be a vehicle for poetry or prose, from motivated, iconic signs in visual representation. In this respect, art possesses the same attributes as the graphic designs of trade marks, road signs etc. With respect to the second point, however, prosaic speech and mundane graphic design aim to evoke a single level of meaning, while art — like poetry — achieves its effect by giving tangible form to many layers of meaning at once.

COMPOSITION AND GRAMMAR

If it is accurate to talk about a grammar of visual expression in Hagen body-decoration, it is a simple kind of grammar which merely adds together several statements: ceremonial exchange is 'a positive social event of great value in which we wish to be attractive to our partners'; warfare is 'a negative event of moderate value in which we stress our solidarity against our opponents'. If more complex rules exist for the composing of alternative messages from a given set of motifs, or signs, they are likely to be found in pictorial compositions. Humphrey finds such a visual grammar in the construction of pictorial *ongons* among the Buryat. Shamans and animals can, like pictures, become possessed by a spirit. Humphrey argues that the specific virtue of pictorial *ongons* is their ability to convey ideas and make a statement about spiritual forces and their place in the world;

a simple manifestation of the spirit of a bull ancestor would be best realized by carrying out ritual to incarnate that spirit in a bull from the herd. A vital distinction is drawn between pictorial *ongon* and poetic narratives: the latter present ideas about spirits and their inter-relationships in a story which develops, as it is told, through time, while *ongon* express these ideas spatially in the composition of motifs (fig. 22). While listeners must wait for the story to unfold, the structure of an *ongon* can more immediately be taken in (Humphrey, 1973:19). Not that narrative and composition necessarily convey the same message; Humphrey also argues that the two media are each particularly apt to the expression of certain kinds of relationship recognized in Buryat religion. *Ongons* generally depict a single spirit's place in the cosmology while myth narrates a drama of interaction between spirits (1971:282). The cloth background, or 'canvas', on which the motifs of an *ongon* are sewn orients them in the structure of the Buryat world-view 'like a graph':

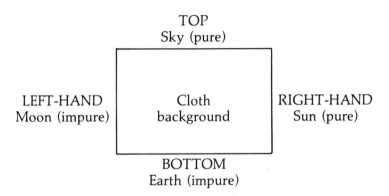

The position of motifs on the cloth thus says something about where they stand in the more general scheme of Buryat cosmology (1973:20).

Art in protodynastic Egypt

During the third century B.C. a writer named Manetho composed a history of Egypt for the reigning Pharaoh, Ptolemy II. Manetho was himself an Egyptian and he had access to lists of past pharaohs and records of the major events that occurred during their reigns. Manetho's history has since been lost, but while it existed it was quoted by a number of later classical historians and from their (more or less accurate) quotations it is possible to reconstruct the history of early Egypt. The first king whom Manetho mentioned was named Menes: he is said to have reigned for 62 years and to have founded the First Dynasty, succeeding a number of legendary leaders referred to as 'the spirits of the dead, the demigods' (Emery, 1961:255). Archaeological evidence indicates that the first dynasty was established around 3000 B.C.

A thousand years before, the area of the Nile Valley had been inhabited by village communities with a late-Neolithic material culture. These villages were situated on ground high enough to escape the annual floods of the Nile but it appears nevertheless that it was these late-Neolithic people who began the process of controlling the flood waters of the river by digging canals and constructing dykes (Stevenson-Smith, 1958:11). During this thousand-year period, fusion was occurring between neighbouring communities, leading to the establishment of political units which were to be forerunners of the *nomes*, or provinces, of historical Egypt. The latest phase of predynastic material culture, the Gerzean, extends into the political period of the earliest dynasties. The Gerzean was preceded by a different culture, the Amratian, which ended some time before 3800 B.C. (Trigger, 1968:64). Archaeology also suggests the emergence of social classes during the period leading to the dynasties: that an upper class is appearing which had privileged access to luxury goods like beads and amulets in lapis lazuli, gold and silver (66).

By the end of the predynastic period, the several political units of Egypt had been grouped into two kingdoms: one in the Nile Valley itself, one in the delta. The Nile Valley, the southern kingdom, was the kingdom of Upper Egypt. The delta, to the north, was the kingdom of Lower Egypt. These two kingdoms co-existed for a period of between 50 and 200 years, and it seems that their rulers were the demigods to whom Manetho referred. Both kingdoms appear to have been ruled by members of a single class who called themselves 'The Followers of Horus', and the two kingdoms fought each other for supremacy. Some evidence suggests that for a time the kingdom of the delta (Lower Egypt) defeated the southern one; but eventually it was the south that won, and with the establishment of rule by the king of Upper Egypt over the whole country, the First Dynasty begins. A new capital was built close to the border of Upper and Lower Egypt, at Memphis. This brings us up to 3000 B.C. (Emery, *op. cit.*:51), and the beginning of Manetho's history.

Art objects which date from successive phases of this period of late-Egyptian prehistory have been used to support various arguments about the course of events and the identity of the actors. The ancient capital of Upper Egypt (the eventually victorious kingdom) was Hieraconpolis. This was excavated by an

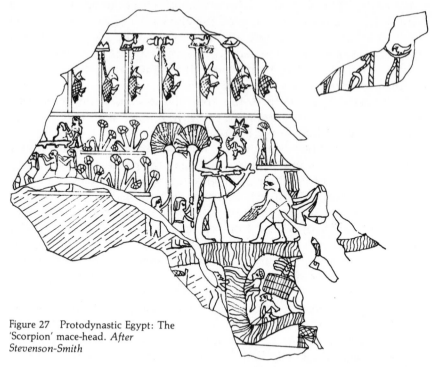

Figure 27 Protodynastic Egypt: The
'Scorpion' mace-head. *After
Stevenson-Smith*

archaeologist named Quibell in 1894. Quibell found evidence of two
predynastic or early dynastic kings here. His most important
discoveries were (a) the ceremonial mace-head of a king known as
King Scorpion, and (b) the ceremonial green schist palette of a ruler
whose name is interpreted as *Narmer* ('ceremonial' because neither is
assumed to have been constructed simply for its implied job as mace
or palette). Both objects depict warfare between the south and north
of Egypt. From the point of view of visual communication, the
significance of the pictorial statements lies in information about who
won an encounter whose conclusion may have hung in the balance.

The 'Scorpion' mace-head is shown here with the design on its
pear-shaped head unrolled into a flat band (fig. 27). The composition
shows a complex organization. In particular, two horizontal bands
serve to break up the design into three distinct 'registers'. The top
register shows a line of poles, each topped by a figure (some animal,
some not). From each of these poles hangs a bird with a crest at the
back of its head and a curved beak: the birds are evidently dead —
their heads are drooping. The figures on the tops of the poles have
been identified as the emblems of some of the *nomes* (provinces) in
Upper Egypt whereas, in historic times, the plover was frequently
used as a symbol of the common populace... (see Petrie, 1953:6).

Emery (*op. cit.*), Petrie, Gardiner (1966) and Stevenson-Smith (*op. cit.*) agree in interpreting the top register as a scene expressing the fact that the people of the delta have been defeated by the Southern Kingdom. The middle register shows a more complex scene. The central figure is a man wearing the crown of Upper Egypt: he stands with a pick in his hand. In front of him a smaller figure bows, and holds out a basket. On the other side of the scene, behind the king, stand two fan bearers, and two rows of even smaller figures, some of whom seem to be dancing in a line. The interpretation of this scene depends on inferring *three* kinds of referent from the actual, visual motifs to more general ideas. The identification of the hoe and basket, together with the fact that the king stands on a band hatched in such a way as to resemble later Egyptian conventions for showing water, is taken to mean that the king is opening a new irrigation canal. The relative size of the central figure, and the fact that he is wearing the southern crown, show that he is the king of Upper Egypt: to know *this* (unlike the case of the hoe and basket) one has to know what the specific conventions of royal costume were. Thirdly, there is a hieroglyph in the composition; a scorpion in front of the king's face. One assumes the scorpion is *not* suspended in the air and that it is rather a label identifying the king; hence the habit of referring to this figure as the Scorpion King. The rosette which appears over the scorpion is inferred to have the meaning it held in contemporary Mesopotamia, namely 'king' (Petrie, *op. cit.*:7). Emery (*op. cit.*) sums up the significance of the middle register as a scene portraying general rejoicing at the king's reorganization of the country following his victory.

Finally, we come to the lowest register. On what has been preserved of it, a smaller canal branches off from the one which defines the break between the middle and lower registers. Next to this two men are working, apparently at agricultural tasks. Emery concludes that 'the mace-head thus records victory, re-organization and peace' (43): three successive episodes which could be compared to a sequence of three sentences, each with an internal structure (see also Stevenson-Smith, 16; Gardiner, 402). However, even if the Scorpion King had achieved a victory over the delta kingdom of Lower Egypt, there is no indication on the mace-head that he claimed to *rule* both kingdoms. The earliest evidence of someone making this claim is the Narmer Palette.

The Narmer Palette (fig. 28) stands at the end of a long cultural tradition of palette manufacture. The production of palettes had been common during the Amratian, when they were cut from slate or schist and used for grinding malachite to be used as eye paint. Towards the end of the Gerzean a few appear with low relief

Obverse Side

Figure 28   Protodynastic Egypt: The Narmer Palette; both sides

Reverse Side

The Anthropology of Art

decoration occupying a small part of the surface. Finally, in the years immediately preceding the First Dynasty, elaborately decorated palettes were manufactured. A total of about twenty have been found, and they can be placed in an apparently temporal sequence which demonstrates progressive organization of the pictorial units into meaningful compositions.

One of the earlier of the palettes decorated with relief carving survived as a fragment depicting dead men 'lying on a battlefield, attacked by a lion'. There is, however, no indication of discrete registers on this fragment (even though it seems to include more than half the length of the total palette) and the figures are loosely distributed, as they might be in reality, upon the ground. On one side of the palette of King Narmer, in contrast, three distinct registers are marked out by horizontal lines. The top band contains two cows' heads (identified as the head of Hathor, an Egyptian goddess), and a hieroglyph between. The middle register depicts a man wearing the crown of Upper Egypt, who grasps a kneeling captive by the hair and is about to strike him with a mace. Above the captive a falcon grasps a human head (see Chapter 1 page 21). Behind the king stands a small servant figure. There are two more hieroglyphs, one over the servant, one behind the captive. In the bottom register two men, apparently lying dead, are each given a single sign over their right shoulder. These are assumed to indicate their home provinces.

On the other side of the palette there are four registers. One contains a rather complex scene. A large figure wears the crown of *Lower* Egypt, but the accompanying hieroglyphs identify him as the same man as that wearing, on the other side, Upper Egypt's crown. He is preceded by a smaller figure, identified by a further hieroglyph as a scribe. In front of the scribe walk four figures carrying standards surmounted by the emblems of the various *nomes*. The whole procession is advancing towards two rows of decapitated human figures, which lie horizontally with their arms bound and the severed heads placed between their feet. Above these corpses are small pictures of a door and a ship. The bottom register shows a bull standing with one foot on a fallen man, breaking open the fortified wall of a town with its horns.

There are three ways in which the archaeologist obtains clues as to what is represented in these scenes. First, from elements of style and iconography: that is, in the way that the figures are portrayed, and in the way that certain diagnostic features of the clothes they wear, implements they carry etc., give clues as to their identity. As an extension of this aspect, we can consider the symbolism of certain figures which appear on the palette, during historical times. Secondly: clues are provided by the inclusion of hieroglyphs — small pictures which can be said to 'intrude' upon the scene because they are not to be understood as part of a pictorial record of the events portrayed. Most interestingly, perhaps, the boundary between these two fields is not precise.

The most important element of style is perhaps the depiction of the king as a larger figure than his followers. In terms of iconography, the most important element is the depiction of the king wearing, on one side, the crown of Upper Egypt, on the other, that of Lower Egypt. This is the clue which has been inferred to reveal this king as the first to unite the two kingdoms: it makes him a contender for identification as Menes, the first king of Manetho's first dynasty. Other iconographic elements are details such as the sandals and water pot carried by the servant. The figures on the standards also provide clues as to who participated in the scenes depicted (i.e. the *nomes* of Upper Egypt). If we assume that the falcon and cow already had attributed to them the symbolic values they possessed during historic Egypt, then we can see them as motifs expressing the qualities of kingship: the falcon (Horus) was the deity of the ruling class, while Hathor, the cow deity, was his female counterpart (Emery, *op. cit.*:124). The Narmer Palette is the earliest object on which she is represented. In historic Egypt the bull was frequently used as a symbol of the king's power (Stevenson Smith, *op. cit.*:16), and so the bull breaking open the town wall can be seen as an allegorical vision of an attack directed by the king.

Strictly speaking, one distinguishes hieroglyphs from iconographic elements in that they stand precisely and unambiguously for words or syllables of spoken language: the practice of *labelling* pictorial representations in this way. persisted throughout Egyptian history. Nevertheless, hieroglyphs can be seen, historically, as an offshoot from pictorial representation: many depict the objects whose concepts they refer to (cf. Durkheim's remark about Australian Aboriginal art: 'the origins of design and those of writing are one'). Many other hieroglyphs, however, signified specific sounds in spoken language rather than specific ideas (fig. 29). These are called 'phonograms'. Reading the name of the king as *Narmer* depends on a phonetic interpretation of the hieroglyphic motifs of fish and chisel. Many hieroglyphs on the palette have nonetheless been construed as ideograms. Beside the man whom the king holds are two characters: *ua*, the top sign, means 'the sole one', and is interpreted to indicate he was an autocratic ruler. The lower sign, *she*, designates a lake, probably the Fayum, and is taken to denote the area over which the captive autocrat had ruled. In historic times, the papyrus shoot signified the number 1,000. Here, where six such shoots sprout from behind the head clasped by the royal falcon, the motif is taken to

The Anthropology of Art

Iconographic elements

White crown of Upper Egypt   Red crown of Lower Egypt

Alleged phonograms

'Mudfish' and 'Chisel' = 'Nar'/'Mer'

Alleged ideograms

'The sole one of the lake'   'Door' and 'Ship' = 'Port'

Six papyrus shoots = 6,000

Figure 29 Elements of protodynastic Egyptian design. Various sources: see authors cited in text

mean that the victorious king had taken 6,000 prisoners. On the other side, the door and ship above the decapitated victims are taken to signify a *port*, which had been captured.

The point to be made in conclusion, then, is that one 'reads' the palette by identifying first the characters portrayed, then the relationships between them. Hieroglyphics here play a role in the first, but *not* in the second, which are expressed purely in the spatial distribution of the characters. From one side of the palette we learn that the king conquered the ruler of a lake and took 6,000 captives; from the other that he slaughtered the inhabitants of a port and broke open the wall of a fortress, presumably capturing that also. Especially, it should be noted that the positions of characters could have been reversed, so as to change the total message *without* changing the meaning of individual characters: the ruler of the Fayum might have been holding the king of Upper Egypt by his forelock; the bull might have been subjugated by a man, rather than *vice versa*. Thus the pictorial relationships resemble those of grammar in language. The palette is deliberately divided into a series of separate visual statements, so that the horizontal lines of the registers determine the field within which relationships between motifs are to be inferred. This technique of visual expression seems to evolve during the course of protodynastic history.

Bark paintings from North-east Arnhem Land

The second example of visual 'grammar' comes from a living culture, which means there is a lot more information about the significance of paintings to the people who make and use them. The culture itself contrasts; many of the older artists grew up following a hunting and gathering way of life. They have since spent some of their lives living on settlements established by white Australians, but there is now a movement back to traditional land in the bush. The hunting and gathering economy, however, has partly been replaced by foodstuffs and implements supplied by the dominant European culture. One of the main reasons for the production of bark paintings today is their sale to Europeans for cash. Nonetheless, the designs painted on bark derive directly from the art tradition documented by white people who were the first to live with the Aboriginal communities earlier this century.

Some of the background to bark painting provided by Morphy has been discussed above. The significance of the organization of their compositions is to be found in the many corresponding levels of religious imagery. At one level, a bark painting can be a depiction of topography in a clan's estate. One of the essential features of Aboriginal religion is the idea that during the creation period the natural features of the country were made by the actions of ancestral heroes, who imprinted their bodies, their implements and actions on the ground. These marks survive as waterholes, mountain ridges etc., which are a proof of the ancestors' existence. Paintings which portray part of a clan's country are not 'maps' in the sense of scale reductions preserving relative compass bearings between natural features. This kind of organization is modified in order to emphasize conceptual relationships between the legendary events that, in the time of the ancestors, led to the landscape acquiring its present form (Morphy, 1977:284). The same paintings may also be seen as depictions of a current Yolngu custom, such as the mortuary rite referred to in the introduction to this chapter. Since the customs were codified by ancestral heroes the same scene can, at another level, be identified as the prototypical events in which ancestral beings established current practice. This change of focus is one way that young Yolngu people are introduced to the deeper aspects of their own religion (286). Because it was the drama acted out by the ancestors that led, at the same time, to social customs crystallizing in their present form, *and* to the creation of the landscape, the landscape provides a monument to the origin of social institutions. A single painting can thus simultaneously depict landscape, ancestral and present events (256). As youths grow older and are admitted to progressively deeper levels of knowledge, revelation frequently takes the form of uncovering further imagery, in narratives whose outlines they already know or paintings they have already seen. Heroes actions that seemed arbitrary become meaningful, and apparently unrelated aspects of social life or the environment prove to have been brought about by a single event in the creation period. Far from being 'fairy tales' the narratives and paintings constitute subtle reflections on the order of the world. In learning the levels of imagery men are entering an artistic system in the sense defined by Aristotle: a system of correspondences between orders of experience given expression in the landscape, in dance, song, narrative and painting. The specific question to be answered here is: how does the organization of a painted composition contribute to the realization of this system?

The preparation of a painting begins with the definition of its surface and frame. The surface to be painted (on a coffin, human body or bark) is defined by the application of a background colour of red ochre. The border of this area is then delimited. Major 'feature blocs' (see Morphy, 1977b:199-200) are then drawn up; the area enclosed by the border is subdivided into sections. Each of these will correspond to a discrete portion of the composition. Morphy gives as examples:

Example (i) (a) The upstream portion of a river
         (b) A fish-trap across the stream   } feature
         (c) The downstream portion of the river blocs

Example (ii) (a) Coastal sand dunes
(b) A ceremonial dance ground } feature
(c) Inland sand hills } blocs

We have seen that a fundamental element of art in small-scale societies is the production of many instances of 'the same painting', and Morphy writes that Yolngu clans each possess a number of repeatedly-produced painted compositions. Within each type, the definition of major feature blocs is constant, although the inclusion of particular motifs in the painting each time it is produced will vary. When given motifs appear, their location must fall within the appropriate feature bloc. Thus Narritjin, a member of the Manggalili clan which owns the painting-type that provides example (ii) above, told Morphy that fresh-water or land animals should only appear in feature bloc (c), while salt-water animals should be confined to bloc (a). Perhaps there is an analogy between Yolngu feature blocs and the registers of Protodynastic Egyptian art.

A major source of variation between individual realizations of a single Yolngu painting-type lies in the existence of two styles of representation (these will be examined in more detail in Chapter 4). One is a figurative style that depicts silhouette forms of men, animals, plants etc. The other is a geometric style similar to that Durkheim learned of from the work of Spencer and Gillen in Central Australia: here characters are depicted by means of simple geometric shapes, diamonds, circles, parallel lines. Its crucial characteristic is the ability of a single motif to represent *more than one thing at once* (see fig. 30ii). Because of its capacity to synthesize meanings the geometric style tends to predominate in paintings seen only by initiated men. Morphy quotes Narritjin again: 'If I were away from women the painting would be just the same but this possum, this bird [silhouette motifs] wouldn't be there, I would just put a number [geometric motif] for them' (1977:242). Use of the figurative style thus predisposes a painting towards one particular level of interpretation — it is a landscape, a scene from modern ceremonial life, etc. — while the geometric style facilitates the revelation of layers of correspondence between these specific alternatives.

Unfortunately, Aboriginal cultures have suffered from anthropologists who publish details of sacred paintings at a time when it was assumed these publications would not return to the Aboriginal community. Since the assumption has turned out to be false the following illustrations are necessarily incomplete. The general principles can, however, be shown in a series of paintings by artists of the Manggalili clan (Narritjin and his kinsmen), which refer to an episode in an ancestral drama.

In the creation period an ancestral being, described as a Guwark (a species of bird), travelled through the bush accompanied by a Possum ancestor (this narrative is summarized in Morphy, 1978:4-5 and Morphy, 1979). In the course of this journey they entered Manggalili territory. Each night, as they camped, the Guwark ate the fruit of a native cashew tree while the Possum climbed the tree, spinning string from his fur until the Guwark told him to stop. The fur string was handed out to those clans whose countries the ancestral being passed through. Each clan received a piece of a different length, and the Guwark thus determined this distinguishing feature of each clan. Emus travelled with the Guwark and Possum, drilling in the ground with their feet for water. Finally the party arrived at a salt lake enclosed by coastal sand dunes at a place called Djarrakpi. Here the Emus, in despair at failing to find fresh water, threw their spears into the sea. Fresh water bubbled up which today is exposed at low tide. The ancestors at Djarrakpi form the subject of a Manggalili painting-type, of which several instances are illustrated. The principal feature blocs in this series constitute three vertical bands:

(a) Coastal sand dunes.
(b) The lake at Djarrakpi.
(c) Inland sandhills.

The first painting (illustrated in Morphy, 1979) was executed by Banapana, one of Narritjin's sons (fig. 30i). It has a high proportion of figurative motifs. Two depictions of the Guwark face each other, eating fruit from a cashew tree placed between them. Below the cashew tree, two Emus search for fresh water. On either side, the Possum is shown climbing the Guwark's back as he spins his fur string. The string appears as lines on the Guwark's body. Although Narritjin first explained the painting to Morphy as a depiction of the ancestors' journey, he later used it as a representation of Djarrakpi, to outline the salient geographical features of the area. The Emus became the lake, the left-hand Guwark the sand dunes intervening between lake and sea, the right-hand Guwark low sand banks on the landward shore of the lake. The Possum-fur string of the Guwarks' bodies became gullies in the sandhills. Transverse lines across the Guwark bodies indicate the points between which he measured out the lengths of fur string given to other clans; and the strings impressed a visible record of themselves on the ground *in the form of the gullies* which, in the painting, the fur-string motif represented. The cashew tree indicates the location of a grove of these trees on the lake shore (see Morphy, 1979).

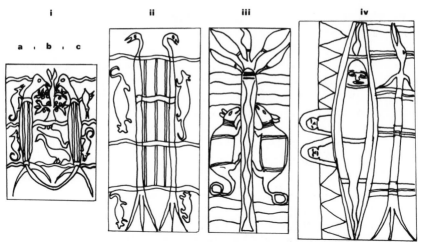

Figure 30 Bark paintings from Arnhem Land, Australia: four Manggalili paintings representing the landscape and mythology of Djarrakpi (Cape Shield). *After Morphy*

The second painting (Morphy's plate 59, 1979), is by Narritjin himself (fig. 30ii). It contains a higher proportion of geometric motifs. The Possums are still present, as are the Guwarks. The geometric design between the Guwarks' bodies represents, at the most concrete level, the water of the lake. In the third painting (Morphy, 1978 plate 4, fig. 30iii), two Possums climb a tree spinning their fur into lengths which they will hand to the Guwark.

Another painting (fig. 30iv) depicting events, and corresponding natural features at Djarrakpi (Morphy, 1978 plate 6), shows the central area — feature bloc (b) - as the body of an ancestral being. On one side stands the ancestral Guwark. His body is identified both with the lengths of Possum fur string and with the sandbank into which the string was transformed. On the other side are two representations of an ancestral woman who also features in the narrative (Morphy, 1978:6).

The structure of the painting not only defines the significance of placing motifs in positions relative to one another in a single composition; it also establishes correspondences between the motifs which are substituted for each other in different paintings. Saussure referred to comparable relationships in language as *syntagmatic* and *associative* (1959:124-7).

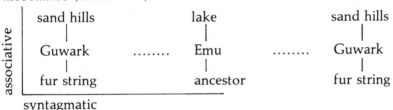

syntagmatic

Morphy argues that as Yolngu are taught by senior men successive interpretations of a single painting, and as they are shown successive versions of the same painting-type, they come intuitively to perceive this underlying structure (1977:276-7), just as one learns the grammar of one's language. To 'decode' particular paintings within the series that consist entirely of geometric motifs, he argues, the structure must already be known, otherwise there would be insufficient clues to the appropriate meaning of motifs occurring at specific places on the bark (272). The series of barks which realize each painting-type thus provide a vital means of expressing, and hence transmitting to successive generations, the understanding of the world which is contained in Yolngu religion.

The phrase 'series of barks' does not, I think, refer to a limited set of specific alternatives, but rather to an endless series of possible paintings which artists can create by using the grammar of the painting-type. The creativity of the artist is the only limiting factor. In the oral literature of the Yolngu, the painting-structure may well allow men like Narritjin to continue finding fresh images in the corresponding mythological themes. If the existence of such an underlying structure in religious and artistic imagery is a general phenomenon, it provides a way of synthesizing the apparently opposed views of Biebuyck and Turner on symbolism: yes, ceremonial experts among the Lega may creatively perceive new metaphors but, equally, they may be following an underlying structure in their culture's thought, such as Muchona was perhaps exploring in his conversations with Turner. Like Lévi-Strauss in South America, one could extend the imagery of Djarrakpi paintings by finding further implicit equations according to the logic explained by Morphy; although one might not reach the same conclusions as the Yolngu.

Symmetry and redundancy

Redundancy is a technical concept used in communication theory, where it complements the concept of *information*. The final section of this chapter considers the relevance of the concept to artistic expression. The quantity of information contained in a message is defined in terms of the extent to which it removes uncertainty from the mind of the person receiving it. For example, it was argued that people who participated in Hagen ritual received messages from the body decorations of other participants. At exchange ceremonies they can see who are the donors of the pigs, yams etc. that are presented, which actors are helping the donors, and also something about the degree of political separation between donors and their helpers. It was argued that, given the fluidity of political relations in the Mount Hagen area, people might have some real doubt about other people's status until they saw what decorations were being worn. Such a situation was contrasted with Durkheim's model of Australian totemism, in which each descent group possesses a unique totem which they transmit from father to son. In this case, the information conveyed by someone acting, or being decorated with a picture of his totem species, would be minimized by the fact that onlookers would, in all probability, already know which group he belonged to! Really, as we saw in the Yolngu case, Aboriginal art can communicate a considerable quantity of information, but it does so by making statements about political realignment during the splitting and regrouping of clans, and by teaching unsuspected correspondences between aspects of the world view to those who proceed through deeper and deeper levels of initiation.

Redundancy, in communication theory, is measured by the quantity of repetition in a message. If the information has already been put across, to repeat it is redundant. But the medium we use to communicate is always imperfect: background noise, or mechanical failure, may obliterate part of the message and so we repeat ourselves to make sure the person receiving it has understood. The less efficient the medium, the more redundancy must be introduced. Thus, face-to-face conversations are said generally to contain less repetition of information than discussions held by telephone.

Repetition is a feature of Aboriginal art and ritual, as it is of many comparable traditions in other cultures. Boas' analyses of rhythmic elaboration and variation in decorative art demonstrate the generality of the practice. Does this mean that art is a particularly inefficient form of communication? This cannot really be true, and I think I may have been wrong to have argued in an earlier paper (1970) that repetition in the ritual of North-east Arnhem Land introduced a high degree of redundancy into the rites. Yolngu bark paintings likewise repeat motifs: where there is one Guwark in the Manggalili narrative, in the bark paintings illustrated there are two, either facing each other or back-to-back. Where there is one Possum in the myth, depictions of him proliferate in the paintings.

One alternative reason for creating repetitive dance or musical rhythm is to bring about a hypnotic effect on the participants. A quite different reason is pointed out by Wollheim when he considers repetition in relation to aesthetics: 'the conditions in which a work of art gains in unity are the same as those in which redundancy is increased: for our awareness of a pattern is coincident with a large number of our expectations being realized' (1970:150). But should one even suppose that in complex art forms, at least, the sense of harmony or order experienced can be reduced to a predictable formula of repetitions? The pleasure gained probably derives from the judicious mixture of satisfaction and surprise that the artist evokes partly by matching expectations and partly by creating new forms. Wollheim continues: 'We may expect Mozart to treat a theme, or Van Dyck to order a mass of detail, in a particular way, but we could not formulate this in terms of past performances' (152). Art is not an extension of secular, prosaic communication, nor is it its opposite: it utilizes repetition and reformation to different ends.

When he explained why Yolngu bark paintings were not, in our sense of the word, topographic maps, Morphy argued that motifs representing natural features were distributed on the bark in such a way as to emphasize connections between the mythological events which created those natural features, rather than accurately to reproduce the features' relative location on the ground. Morphy's discussion of templates more than adequately demonstrates that the composition of a bark painting does work to express the structure of the Yolngu world-view, but it seems as if aesthetic considerations may also be present. The Guwarks in the examples illustrated are placed so that each is the mirror image of the other, while the relative dimensions of lake, coastal and inland sandhills acquire a symmetry that in reality they lack.

Ideally aesthetics and the intuition of metaphor may complement each other. Boas (*op. cit.*: 212-16) argues for the contrary case in one form of art among the North-west Coast Indians of North America: the highly-decorated blankets which used to be exchanged between groups. Normally, the motifs of these peoples' art, which depicted totemic animals, gave a clear expression of the owner's rank or group affiliation (Boas fig. 103). On the blankets, however, the elements from which the depictions of totemic animals were constructed became so fragmented that different people could construe them as representations of different species. Since the designs achieve an elaborate symmetry, Boas was inclined to see the desire for aesthetic harmony working against the composition's communicative value. It seems possible, on the other hand, that since the blankets were intended to be exchanged, it was appropriate for each group to be able to see in the designs a different totemic creature. Humphrey's analysis of Buryat verse demonstrates how the aesthetic balance of a poetic narrative can be used to enhance its power to communicate.

Humphrey maintains that the ritual language of Buryat verse is particularly adapted to expressing certain of the concepts, and relations between ideas, in Buryat culture. Certain formal techniques must be used in Buryat poetry: the construction of verse in couplets, the alliteration of sounds at the beginning of words, and the repetition of sounds in successive phrases to establish parallel or complementary meanings (1973:15, 21-33). Ritual consists of 'manipulating [these] structures to convey meaning' (19). The 'back' and 'front' vowels of Buryat phonetics are also used as allusions respectively to male and female qualities. Her examples suggest a comparison with the visual balance of Yolngu bark paintings.

Some of the features to which she refers can be seen in her translation of four lines from a wedding speech:

> From the wide silver sky
> Patrilineal-essence drawing out descended
> From the dark-blue silver sky
> Umbilical cord drawing out descended

The only non-repeated words, as she points out, are two pairs between which the hearer is invited to draw some correspondence:

> wide .... dark blue

> patrilineal-essence ...... umbilical cord

The first pair of lines utilize back vowels (male connotations) while the second are expressed with front vowels (female connotations). The umbilical cord is an image of descent through females, and complements patrilineal descent. In another performance of the same speech, reference to the umbilical cord was replaced by a description of the womb as something that 'gave form'.

Where successive lines are linked by partial repetition and *not* distinguished by the opposition of front and back vowels, she argues, an equivalence between them rather than complementary opposition is implied:

> Like barley-grain scattered
> Like spring-water poured out.

Another aspect of Buryat verse is the repeated use of a limited number of verb forms. In the wedding speech, where references are repeatedly made to a bull ancestor and the present bride-groom, the restricted number of verbs make it unclear which of the two is being referred to in specific statements, thus implying an identity between them. This identity is backed up by a formal conversation in which the groom's kin arrive at the bride's camp saying that they are looking for a 'little bull' who has escaped from their herd. The aesthetic qualities of Buryat ritual thus reveal a set of analogies passed over by everyday speech and implying equivalents not present in the everyday world.

The analysis that Jakobson and Lévi-Strauss carried out on one of Baudelaire's sonnets reveals a Western poet achieving a comparable integration of aesthetics and imagery, again underlining the fallacy of equating the relative sophistication of art with the complexity of the economic and political systems in which the artist lives out his life.

Conclusion

Chapter 1 showed why it was dangerous to define ritual in terms of what, when seen through scientific eyes, it lacks; because this leads to its being viewed as irrational or non-rational. There is a similar danger in trying to characterize the difference between scientific and artistic thought. The ubiquity of balanced rhythms and metaphor-like images, however, suggests artistic expression has a definite character. Both art and science, as Horton wrote of religion in small-scale societies, use models and both look for order, but the way in which they do this differs.

Scientific explanations do not infer conscious, moral entities behind the workings of natural phenomena, and they state the patterns they perceive in terms of abstract, general laws. The social, moral component which both art and religion find in the wider world is implied in Horton's argument that small-scale societies draw their conceptual models from experience of social life. It is also expressed in Beattie's response to Horton that 'Myth dramatizes the world, science analyses it'. It was probably this which led many writers after Durkheim to conclude that religion, ritual and art existed primarily to support the social order.

Expression through specific imagery rather than general propositions is exemplified by Morphy's discussion of templates in Yolngu painting (note that the Yolngu do not express the order of their world in terms of the abstract formula to which the template could also be reduced). Biebuyck described how the philosophy of *Bwami* was never codified in a few generalities, but had to be deduced through the thousands of specific proverbs and images in Lega culture. The point is also illustrated by two parallel studies of Balinese culture, one by Geertz of a ritual drama, the other by Bateson of a pen-and-ink drawing. Both argue that in the particular characters of the art a number of themes in Balinese culture gain succinct expression, expressed at their most general level as a tension between order and chaos. But while such a statement expresses the content of the art work in an empty generalization, the play and painting *epitomize* these themes, realizing and drawing them together in form and imagery. Thus Bateson argues 'that the style chosen, the actions of the figures and their distributions in the composition all express in specific images the interwoven contrast between the serene and the turbulent ... in the fields of sex, social organization and death' (1973:255). Geertz likewise proposes that 'sacred symbols function to synthesize a people's ethos' (1966:3) but later, after discussing the variety of identifications attributed to Rangda and Barong — the two opposed characters of the drama — he insists: 'it is in the direct encounter with the two figures in the context of the actual performance that the [Balinese] villager comes to know them as genuine realities' (34).

If aesthetics and imagery characterize the kind of order art reveals in, or imposes on the world, then it is worth asking if there are any other common ways of achieving this. Style, in figurative art, may be one of these, and it is to style we turn in the following chapter. This chapter has attempted first to demonstrate that behind the richness and diversity of cultural imagery lie some general principles of communication that are shared with language, but realized in forms peculiar to visual representation, while secondly, to illustrate how art lends particular qualities to visual communication, as it does to language.

4
Style

Style refers to the formal qualities of a work of art. A style is characterized by the range of subjects it depicts, by the regular shapes to which elements of these subjects are reduced, and by the manner that components of the art work are organized into a composition. Strictly speaking, style is not concerned with the meaning of elements or of the whole, which are rather the subject of iconography or visual grammar. A style may be identified at many levels of generality: that of the individual artist, that of a particular school and, in still more comprehensive terms, figurative styles may be distinguished from abstract ones. Shapiro has a useful discussion of style (1953) in which he draws on earlier writers' terms and categories. We will refer to his essay in the following paragraphs.

The previous chapter showed how classifying the diversity of experience into manageable units was fundamental to Durkheim's model of totemism, and how Durkheim's theory provides a basis for studying visual communication in art. The subject of this chapter revolves around the way that styles represent and structure the appearance of objects. From the infinite variety of forms, styles derive a limited range of motifs and compositions, not because of deficient technique, but again to provide an essential tool in our understanding of the world.

Techniques of execution do have a bearing on the appearance of an art object. Many authors who have written about the anthropology of art: Boas, Shapiro, Lévi-Strauss, contributors to Biebuyck's book *Tradition and Creativity*, have argued that the tools available to the artist in small-scale societies limit the forms his work can take (fig. 31a and b), but most are agreed that the phenomena of stylistic variation require more subtle explanation than technological limitations provide. Even among cultures using almost identical technical processes styles may vary widely. This is well-illustrated by the numerous styles evident in Australian Aboriginal art. Depictions of animals range from a simple portrayal of their footprints to complex renderings of their bodily form which include details of internal organs. Some pictures of humans show them lithe and full of movement, others are static and rigid (see fig. 32). The geometric art of Central Australia, whose characteristic forms are the circle, line and arc, appears in rock engravings, body paintings and sand

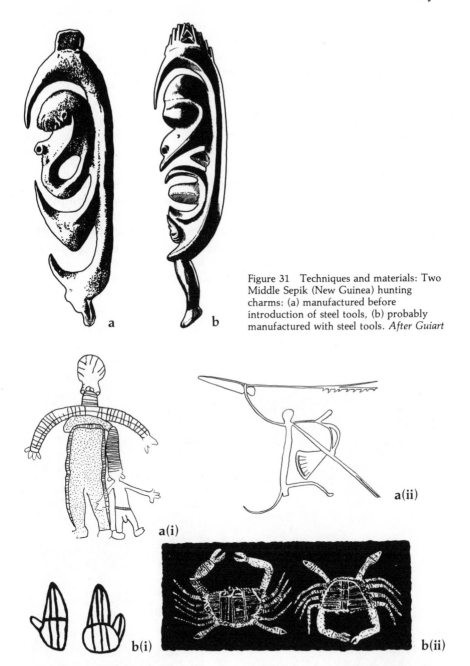

Figure 31 Techniques and materials: Two Middle Sepik (New Guinea) hunting charms: (a) manufactured before introduction of steel tools, (b) probably manufactured with steel tools. *After Guiart*

a(i)

a(ii)

b(i)

b(ii)

Figure 32 Variations in style: examples of Australian Aboriginal art: (a) i. Large female figure from rock shelter near Laura (Cape York), ii. Mimi figure from rock shelter in western Arnhem Land, (b) i. Animal footprints — kangaroo — from rock shelter near Laura, ii. Bark painting of two crabs from Groote Eylandt (eastern Arnhem Land)

sculptures executed with bird down or vegetable fibre. Techniques of execution do not obliterate the unity of style. Most telling are those instances where a single culture possesses more than one style. This allows one to pass beyond general hypotheses of technical or perceptual limitation, and instead examine cultural reasons for the development of particular styles. Later in the chapter we will consider a case from Aboriginal Australia and one from North American Indian culture which throw light on the motives that lead to the adoption of one or another stylistic convention where two or more are available to the artist.

The significance of the transformation of appearance into regular forms can be appreciated when one considers how fundamental it is to perception. An often-quoted example is that of the rainbow: a band of light refracted into a continuous gradation of wavelengths which we perceive as a series of discrete strips: red, orange, yellow etc. The relativity of these categories is suggested by the fact that other cultures do not necessarily acknowledge them. To the untrained observer, comment Segall *et al.*, 'it would probably come as a surprise to learn that our classification of the spectrum... is culturally arbitrary, and that persons in other cultures divide the spectrum quite differently' (1966: 37; see also *op. cit.*:38-48).

Plate 9 Aboriginal rock painting from Kimberley region, Western Australia: two styles of human figure (a) 'Bradshaw'-style figures on Mount Elizabeth Station. (b) From rock shelter in the Napier Range. Author's photographs

Plate 10   Two ways of depicting a human being in Australian Aboriginal rock carvings: (a) Outline silhouette from Sydney-Hawksbury area, West Head site, Lambert Peninsula. (b) Human footprints from Panaramitee, South Australia. Author's photographs

Paintings of the rainbow by members of our culture necessarily depend on our perception of it, even if they are unlikely to reproduce those perceptions with absolute precision.

Other cultures have different ways of dividing up the range of colour they experience. Forge writes that (although lacking terms applied exclusively to colour) the Abelam of New Guinea acknowledge four tints of paint among those they use to decorate their ceremonial houses: white, black, red and yellow. Other coloured substances are allocated to one or another of these categories, and treated as though they are substantially the same. Blue (introduced in the form of powder paint or Reckitts dye) is classed as a variety of black. Occasionally, as a result, 'both colours have been applied to the same object so that a patch that should be all black is half-black and half-blue with an irregular boundary totally meaningless in terms of the design, and indeed to my eyes completely ruining it. Painters... deny that there is any difference or that there is an inharmonious boundary' (1970:283).

The habit of perceiving continuous variation in terms of discrete categories is not a peculiarity of visual perception, or visual communication. It occurs just as much in the sounds utilized by spoken language. The sounds we hear as 'ba' and 'pa', for instance, have two components, one produced with the vocal cords, one with the lips. In making the ideal 'ba' sound we start to vibrate the vocal cords before releasing our pursed lips, while in the ideal 'pa' sound it is the lips that are released before the vocal cords start to vibrate. An apparatus for making such sounds artificially can, like a prism refracting the sun's rays, produce a continuous gradation between these positions. The apparatus demonstrates that if the lips are released first but there is only a very short delay before the vocal cords begin to vibrate, then English speakers will hear the sound as 'ba'. If the delay is greater than 25 milliseconds, our perception switches immediately to 'pa'. The gradation escapes us.

Such segmentation of experience is so general that one can readily suppose it is based on the way the mind works; that it is based on inbuilt, inherited tendencies. The question, as Lévi-Strauss pointed out in anthropology and Chomsky in linguistics, is whether *specific schemes* for sorting experience and organizing behaviour are ever inherited, or whether it is simply *basic methods* for developing such schemes that are so transmitted.

Cutting and Eimas, from whom the example of the sounds perceived as 'pa' and 'ba' was taken, seem to consider that this particular form of categorization is one based on human physiology. They carried out an experiment with infants aged between one and four months (described in Cutting and Eimas, 1975), and found that the infants they tested responded in a way that suggested they perceived the same distinctions as English-speaking adults. The two authors conclude that, since the infants were so young, their perception must derive entirely from an inbuilt mechanism and not incorporate learning that the difference between a 'ba' range and a 'pa' range of sounds is culturally significant among their elders and betters. They go on, however, to point out that other languages, such as Thai and Spanish, recognize different categories within the same continuum. 'English', they therefore conclude, 'is a much more reasonable language than Spanish' (1975:135), because it seems to make better use of distinctions infants recognize. As we have noted before, anthropologists react suspiciously to assertions that a speaker's own culture is inherently better than others with which he may be less familiar. Since Cutting and Eimas mention their belief that *unborn* children may already learn to recognize their mother's voice (127), might it be possible that learning conventional distinctions, aided by the intrinsic operations of the brain, can have begun a month after birth? We will be equally suspicious of theories that our art styles are intrinsically more comprehensible or truer to nature than those of other people, looking at them all instead as alternative systems built according to common procedures.

Rock (1974) provides some simple examples of how the mind categorizes complex visual data into an organized set of alternatives. A triangle can be altered in size, colour and various other ways without any change in its perceived shape. Turn a *square* through 45°, however, and it becomes a diamond. Is it because a different image is cast on the back of the eye? No, if one tilts one's head through 45° to look at a square stuck onto the wall, it still looks like a square. The perceived orientation of the square in the viewer's environment is clearly crucial, Rock concludes. He describes some factors which greatly influence how we perceive a shape, including his finding that people tested with made-up shapes possessing bilateral symmetry, found it impossible to recognize this symmetry unless the axis separating the two halves was vertical. A mirror-image reversal, however, had virtually no effect on the shape's perceived form. If they directly express the brain's cognitive processes, these results might throw some light on principles of harmonious composition in art.

How many of his findings do relate directly to the physiological mechanisms of the brain, and how much depends on the intervention of learning about the habits of one's culture, is not determined. Clearly, learning does greatly affect the specifics of perception. One of Rock's illustrations is an irregular shape (fig. 33) which, as he points out looks, when placed in one orientation, like a bearded face

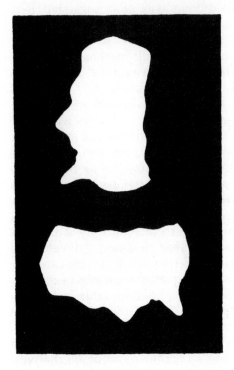

Figure 33   Map of United States/bearded face. *After Rock*

in profile, but in another like a map of the United States. What was the 'beard' becomes the 'Florida Peninsula'. Not only would one have to have learned what the United States looks like in bird's-eye view for this perception to strike a chord, but the fact that it becomes apparent only in one orientation must depend on the viewer having been reared in a culture where convention dictates that maps be drawn with north 'at the top of the page'. The shape which evokes the two alternative perceptions has little resemblance either to a face or to a map of the USA, which indicates that it is a mistake to equate graphic motifs with the forms of the models on which they are based. Nor does the shape actually change its form, when we assimilate it to the alternative mental categories 'bearded faces' or 'maps of the US', so neither should the graphic motif be equated with the image of it one forms in one's mind. Like the sounds of spoken language, the stylistic elements of visual representation must be allowed to stand on their own, separate from related phenomena.

The following discussion will begin by examining some general aspects of visual expression, then proceed to consider the bearing of these on specific artistic traditions.

Limits of the imitation of nature

In abstract or decorative art, the choice of style is probably determined primarily by aesthetic motives. There may be other impulses present. Shapiro, for instance, refers to style as a vehicle for 'communicating and fixing certain values of religious, social and moral life through the *emotional suggestiveness* of forms' (287, my emphasis), a suggestiveness which Bateson illustrates with his discussion of Balinese art and its complementary themes of chaos and serenity. Representational art, however, introduces a further element into style; that of devising means for depicting objects in the real world. This seductive correspondence between art and reality has fascinated many writers. For some, the most significant aspect is the artist's degree of technical skill in imitating his model, for others the degree to which the artist departs from his natural model may be treated as a symptom of his mental image of the world. Whichever view one adopts, representational art must be considered to possess a quality that interacts with the aesthetic and emotional qualities it shares with decorative and abstract art: a tension between fidelity to the natural model and its reduction to regular forms.

Naturalism, an apparently simple concept, frequently enters into discussions of representational styles. Shapiro opposes naturalistic to geometric styles while Löwy, whom he cites, opposes the term to 'conceptual representation'. A third opposition may be drawn between naturalism and schematization (see Ucko, 1977). The choice of terms says something about the reason the writer perceives behind an artist's departure from 'naturalism', but all, I think, are referring to a common tendency in the depiction of forms. Among the criteria selected by Löwy to characterize 'conceptual representation' are the following: the single forms are represented with regular, linear patterns; the shape and movement of figures and their parts are limited to a few, typical shapes; further, the parts of a figure are presented to the viewer in their broadest aspect. If several figures occur in the same composition there is a minimum of overlap, and depth and perspective are also minimized (see Shapiro, 301).

The first two criteria, as Gombrich demonstrates (1960) and as we have already suggested, refer to characteristics present in all styles. When one talks of 'naturalism' it is of a relative quality, meaning that a certain art tradition recognizes a wide variety of forms and compositions that correspond closely to certain aspects of forms found in nature. But what aspect does one select? There may be a number of conventions for reproducing things 'as they really are', some looking more familiar to us than others. There was a 'naive' artist living in Cornwall who is said always to have kept a bottle of sea water on a shelf in his studio. Whenever asked why the sea in his paintings was grey, he would point to the bottle to show how the water really was. Gombrich and Panofsky both show how revealing are cases of representation on a flat surface where, of necessity, some selection must be made from the many facets of three-dimensional models.

Löwy's second pair of criteria seem simply to be techniques for presenting a standardized motif to advantage. There is good reason to believe that the cultural context of an art work and its intended function may go part of the way towards explaining why particularly geometric or schematic styles are adopted. Gombrich takes this view in a discussion of the progressive refinement of trade marks in our own culture (1972). Like the road signs of the highway code, trade marks need to be readily identified and distinguished from one another. The shape they take represents an appropriate compromise between simplicity of form and recognizability as depictions of a class of objects in the real world (children crossing roads, locomotives approaching a level crossing), where the context demands simple and rapid communication.

Evaluation of styles

One of the most interesting, but also most problematic, aspects of analysing style is that the term can be used to pass judgements of relative value. It may be said of a particular artist that he 'has style', meaning that he has a particular skill in giving tangible expression to an aesthetic sense of rhythm and harmony, to the evocation of emotions or to the depiction of visual imagery. Thinking primarily of Classical Greek art, Shapiro writes: 'Some period styles impress us by their deeply persuasive, complete character, their special adequacy to their content; the collective creation of such as style... is a true achievement' (288). It is, however, difficult to pass such judgements on the work of other cultures unless one is sure of the goals they sought, or is content to confine oneself (as a professional artist might) to considering how alien styles bear upon our own particular cultural and personal standards. Panofsky's essay on *The History of the theory of human proportions as a reflection of the history of styles* (in Panofsky, 1955) provides a fascinating study of style and its cultural background.

'There is a great difference', wrote Panofsky, 'between the question: "What is the normal relationship between the length of the upper arm and the length of the entire body in a person standing quietly before me?" and the question: "How shall I scale the length of what corresponds to the upper arm, in relation to the length of what corresponds to the entire body, on my canvas or block of marble?" ' (83-4). He goes on to enumerate some of the differences: as the body moves, the relative proportions of its parts change; the artist necessarily views his subject foreshortened by perspective, and the audience's view of the artist's work may well itself be subject to foreshortening (Panofsky cites the case of sculptures placed above eye level). He discusses Classical Egyptian, Classical Greek, Gothic, Byzantine and Renaissance solutions to this dilemma; arguing that the ethos of the culture made a different compromise appropriate to each.

One manifestation of the failure to investigate an artist's reasons for adopting a certain style is the view, once widely held in the West, that the art styles of non-literate cultures reveal child-like attempts to portray nature accurately; attempts thwarted by ignorance, superstition or, worst of all, lack of intelligence. On the other hand, Shapiro cites the more recent, contrary view that any art style may be assessed in terms of the qualities and relationships of its component forms, and that perfect formal compositions may be achieved through the medium of any style. Critics who apply such criteria to the evaluation of representational art executed during former periods of Western history, Shapiro protests, also slight the artist by ignoring his attempts to develop a style that depicts his subject matter in the most appropriate fashion.

Leaving aside man's inherent tendency to ridicule other cultures, the problem derives in part from the fact that within both Western culture and other civilizations, developmental sequences of stylistic change can be traced that seem to show an oscillation, or a rise and fall, between on the one hand 'naturalism'; on the other 'schematization' or a 'geometric' style. The view that other cultures' art was primitive or child-like was at its height during the period of Victorian colonial expansion when, coincidentally perhaps, our culture favoured a kind of naturalism in its art. The artists who tipped the scale towards styles like Cubism had a very different opinion of exotic art. A parallel may be drawn here with changes in political theory. Weber's theory of political evolution contained an opposition between government followed for reasons of unthinking tradition (typified by alien cultures) and government followed because the participants perceived its inherent rationality (typified by our own bureaucracy). This view was later criticized by phenomenologists who pointed out that *rational* really meant *comprehensible to us*, making Weber's argument little better than a tautology. In Chapter 2, we suggested that Fagg ran the risk of a similar error when he judged recent Benin art to be inferior to its original forms because it had abandoned the naturalistic portraiture we admire in favour of conventional images of kingship.

Shapiro discusses various theories that have been proposed to account for the apparent oscillation of styles, and the extent to which they imply inevitable cultural processes. He tends to reject the concept of necessary evolution, although accepting the reality of the opposition between 'naturalistic' and 'geometric' styles. 'Study', he concludes, 'shows that both processes occur in history; there is little reason to regard either as more typical or more primitive. The geometric and naturalistic forms may arise independently in different contexts and co-exist with the same culture' (300).

STYLE AS AN ASPECT OF VISUAL EXPRESSION

To understand the value of a style it is important to distinguish between art objects and two other categories to which the material expressions of art might be related, but with which they should not be confused. Art objects are not the same as mental images, nor are they the same as the natural things they may depict. Style is manifest in the art object. How does it relate to the other two categories?

Correspondences between art and the world of objects

The apparent sameness of art and the objects it portrays is the illusion of Gombrich's *Art and Illusion* (1960). Boas (1955:78) anticipated Gombrich in the view that art does not aim to reproduce real objects in their entirety. Gombrich wonders whether our paintings, even those that now seem entirely naturalistic, will appear as unconvincing to future generations as Classical Egyptian paintings appear to us. If later artists had discovered more accurate means of representing the natural world, why was it that the Egyptians failed to discover these methods? Was it in part because they perceived the world in a different way, or was it because they looked for different things in what they saw? The view that art does seek to imitate reality has been given recent expression in the writing of Deregowski (1972, 1973). In a sense, Deregowski is a modern exponent of the Victorian opinions we mentioned above; in fact, he quotes from early missionary sources in support of his view that the art of small-scale societies is frequently the product of deficient skill, perception or intellect (1972:82). I have already made a detailed criticism of Deregowski's position (Layton, 1977), but since one of his papers has been reprinted in a collection to which this chapter will refer (Held, ed. 1974), some comments will also be made here.

The identity that Deregowski implies between art and nature is exemplified by his analogy between a painting and light falling on a screen. 'The veracity of a painting,' he writes, 'is the direct result of the extent to which light reflected from its surface approximates to the light which would be reflected from the depicted object... This very principle is embodied in those aids to drawing which rely on a translucent screen which intercepts reflected light and leaves the artist only the task of recording the pattern which the intercepted light makes' (1973:161). Deregowski proceeds to discuss the failure of members of other cultures to identify objects and scenes depicted in Western-style pictures, in terms of deficient perception among the viewers. One of the authors from whom he draws his evidence is Hudson, a South African who examined the ability of people to interpret Western graphic art. Hudson concluded that learning to understand pictures was closely bound up with literacy: those who lacked the opportunity to read magazines also lacked the opportunity to study the pictures in them and hence to learn their particular stylistic conventions. Hudson was particularly interested in the perception of depth in a two-dimensional representation. He found that 'White and Black school-going samples perceive depth more frequently in pictorial material than do illiterate Black samples and samples, both Black and White, which have terminated their school course and live in isolation from the dominant cultural norm' (Hudson, 1960:201). The presence of White people among the samples who failed to construe depth in the pictures has mysteriously disappeared in Deregowski's account, leaving us merely with the tribal Africans. Although he is willing to concede that 'some form of learning is required to recognize pictures' he constantly invites the reader to infer that failure to understand our graphic styles stems from a fundamental cognitive block. The irony of Deregowski's position is most apparent when he himself attempts to read the art of other cultures and here attributes his own failure to deficiencies not in his perception but in the artists' style.

Had Deregowski used one of the screens to which he refers, and traced the pattern of light reflected on its surface, he would no doubt have discovered the disturbing fact that when he moved, so would the pattern of light redistribute itself, although his traced lines remained fixed to the screen's surface. Had he tried to copy every detail of the intercepted light, no doubt he would also have discovered Gombrich's observation that 'The amount of information reaching us from the physical world is incalculably large, and the artist's medium is inevitably restricted and granular' (1960:182). Gregory, one of Deregowski's editors, makes the point forcefully: 'Pictures are the traditional material of perceptual research but all pictures are highly artificial and present special problems to the perceiving brain. In a sense pictures are impossible because they have a dual reality. They are seen both as patterns of lines lying on a flat background and as objects depicted in a quite different three-dimensional space' (1974:52).

The ability of the viewer to match a depiction with a real object under the right conditions despite the granularity of the depicting medium is well illustrated by Harmon. Harmon carried out an experiment to investigate how much information the brain required in order to identify representations of particular human faces. It is, however, crucial to note that the discrepancy between the appearance of the person's face and the appearance of its depiction by Harmon meant that the identification of one with the other could only be made under special conditions. The range of possible individuals from whom the viewer had to make his selection was fairly confined. In one test, Harmon refers to each viewer being given a list of 28 names, from which to select the names of the 14 persons depicted (104). In his account of another test he adds the crucial information that all 28 persons were known to those subjected to the identification tests (107).

Harmon used electronic processing methods to reduce the depiction of a person's face to a two-dimensional grid consisting of squares coloured in shades of grey. His images were made up of sixteen horizontal and sixteen vertical rows of squares, each coloured in one of eight or sixteen alternative shades. Examined closely, no configuration resembling a face is discernible, but as Harmon puts it, 'viewed from a distance of 30 to 40 picture diameters, faces are perceived or recognized'. Distance blurred the artificially precise edges of the squares and gave a better approximation to the original facial features. Under these conditions, Harmon found that, overall, people tested achieved a 48% success rate in identifying the faces depicted. When alignment of the grid over facial features was not arbitrary but arranged to give the best possible image, correct identification rose to 95%. According to his own calculation, the success rate scored by those carrying out the tests even under his restricted conditions could have been produced through random guessing 'only four times in a million trials'.

Clearly, these images are by any standards coarse grained and could scarcely be said to approximate to the pattern of light reflected from the original face. We are looking here at a case of recognition very like Rock's figure that resembled a map of the United States. Because representations of the model are well-known to the viewer, even a figure that resembles it only poorly can be assimilated to the representational category.

Such background knowledge seems to be crucial to the interpretation of much Australian Aboriginal art. The location of a painting in a certain cave for instance, will almost certainly also locate it in the context of a certain ancestral track, thus considerably narrowing its possible meanings to those with local knowledge. Macintosh gives an amusing account of how his own attempts to identify species and subjects among the figurative paintings in two rock shelters near Beswick, in Arnhem Land, were very different from those provided by the custodians of the caves. Comparing his private deductions with those provided by Lamderod, guardian of one of the shelters, Macintosh concluded 'without Lamderod I would have rated about 10 percent [correct answers] overall for interpretation' (1977:194). This experience led Macintosh to distinguish between four levels of understanding, of which the most elementary was to identify the forms represented by each motif, yet even that demanded one know: 'the minutiae of draftsmanship and the conventional norm for that region..., as for example to differentiate pademelon [sic: Paddy Melon] from rock wallaby, male from female, disincarnate spirit from spirits never incarnate, from people' (196). Beyond this lie levels of understanding which recall Panofsky's shift from iconography to iconology: an awareness of why paintings are placed in that particular shelter and how they are treated, an understanding of the significance of the depicted subjects and the shelter itself and, ultimately, of the religious philosophy they embody. 'At each level the key to unlock the schematization process is without doubt clear to the Aboriginal artist, but not to us'.

Gregory illustrates in a number of simple ways how the real world is more complex than its depictions, but how more 'naturalistic' styles can avoid some forms of ambiguity in representation.

Imagine a straight line of a given length drawn on a sheet of paper: this could represent a rod of a certain length placed at right-angles to the line of vision (see fig. 34). (Gregory instances the drawing of an ellipse to make the same point.) In the absence of further clues, such as linear perspective or a density gradient, it could equally represent rods of various lengths placed at an almost infinitely large number of angles to the line of vision, but in the same plane.

Increasing the quantity of visual information would, providing one knew how to interpret it, tend to reduce the ambiguity of the representation. For this reason, we associate 'naturalistic' art styles with such qualities of representation as apparent size differences, the overlap of certain components of the composition on others, density gradients, differences of shadow, linear and aerial perspective. Density gradients occur when a regularly textured surface recedes from the viewer: the apparent granularity of the texture decreases as

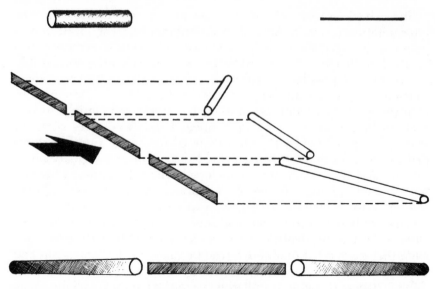

Figure 34   'Schematic' and 'naturalistic' depictions of rods

it moves further away. Harmon's procedure for viewing depicted faces from a distance, to eliminate perception of the sharp boundaries between the squares used in his depictions, illustrates the phenomenon. 'Linear perspective' describes the common experience that parallel lines like railway tracks or the sides of a road appear to lie closer together the further they are from the viewer. 'Aerial perspective' refers to the tendency for distant objects to appear bluer than those close to the observer: light travelling from the horizon has been more filtered than light reflected from close objects. All these qualities, it is noteworthy, are elements of style that Löwy and Shapiro excluded from 'geometric' or 'conceptual' representation. Many of them were also absent from the pictures Deregowski presented to his African subjects (see Layton, 1977:36).

It seems unlikely that even the most naturalistic of styles will always be comprehensible cross-culturally. Gregory argues that our ability correctly to identify depicted objects is also increased by the fact that 'fortunately for us the world of objects does not have infinite variety; there is usually a best bet, and we generally interpret our flat images more or less correctly in terms of the world of objects' (1974:52). Expressed in this fashion I think there might be some doubt about the proposition. It makes a more convincing argument to suppose that there is a finite population of objects, or situations, that are likely to be depicted in any tradition of artistic or graphic representation. The success of Harmon's experiment appears partly to depend on the finite set of known alternatives among faces that might be represented in his grids, but surely also on one's acquaintanceship with similar representations of faces in photographs. The success of the highly geometric or schematic motifs used in road signs depends on drivers' knowledge of the set of alternative messages from which each sign is drawn and his learning of the corpus of motifs. It is surely only in this way that ambiguity is avoided. A schematic or geometric style would appear to rest either on the desire to depict a limited number of alternatives or on a deliberate wish to create visual ambiguity. Given the inherent 'granularity' of the artist's medium, even 'naturalistic' styles can never completely escape this limitation.

Because of the poor resemblance and limited information contained in schematic representations, when the conditions necessary for identification are not circumscribed, they can become ambiguous, and are readily perceived as representations of several, alternative subjects. Gregory has written on this aspect of visual representation in our own culture (e.g. Gregory, 1966, 1973, 1974). Although he takes the view that 'the art of the draftsman and painter is, in large part, to make us accept just one out of the infinite set of possible interpretations of a figure' (1966:168), he argues that many of the optical illusions invented by our culture during the last hundred years derive their success from avoiding naturalism and instead providing insufficient information to allow the brain to decide between alternative interpretations of what they depict. Among these the classic instance is that of the Neckar cube. Figure 35a illustrates the perceptual dilemma: is corner (a) closest to the viewer, or corner (b)? Either interpretation is equally valid. Gombrich uses another long-established figure, the duck-rabbit illusion, to make some points about the artist's style and reality. The ambiguous figure (fig. 35b) can be viewed as either a duck's or a rabbit's head, depending on whether one considers it is facing to the left or the right. It is much harder, Gombrich comments, to be aware of the mental operations we perform to arrive at either interpretation. In neither case do we imagine it is a real head we are looking at; the shape resembles neither a duck nor a rabbit particularly closely. It is a question of how we interpret the clues provided and extrapolate from them. These clues, like those offered by the Neckar cube, are too meagre to allow us to be certain of either interpretation. In one case we ignore the small mark on the extreme right of the figure: for the 'rabbit' interpretation it becomes the animal's nose; for the 'duck' interpretation it is irrelevant. If we view the figure as a duck's head, then we interpret the two protrusions on the left as its beak; if we view the figure as a rabbit's head, these become its ears.

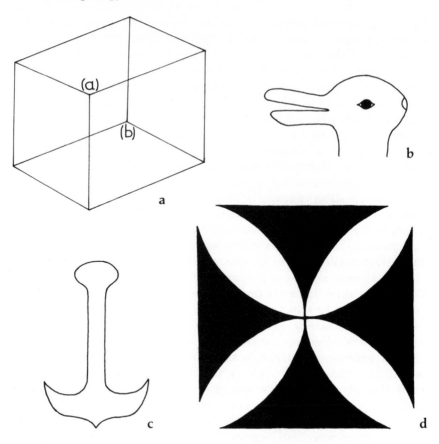

Figure 35   Ambiguous figures: (a) Neckar cube, (b) Duck-rabbit, (c) Pick axe-anchor, (d) Maltese Cross-white flower

The implication of this for the anthropology of art is clear: we have seen how fundamental a characteristic it is of cultures to select and organize experience into characteristic patterns of meaning and there is every reason to suppose that this will take place with form in the construction of artistic styles. To understand another culture's use of a style one would need to know the range of subjects depicted, the elements that have been abstracted from the 'incalculably large' information yielded by visual inspection, and the manner of organizing these elements into formal compositions.

For these reasons, it is not necessarily valid to infer that broadly similar styles are always adopted for the same purposes, and this also imposes a limit on the extent to which a style can be evaluated, against the effects it is imagined to be seeking, without knowledge of the specific cultural background. Modern children frequently produce drawings in which the background is left blank, and the

Upper Palaeolithic artists of Western Europe also depicted animals standing alone, without a scenic background yet, as Shapiro argues, if one were to infer that such a mode of representation was a universally primitive one, it would have to be borne in mind that it is a type of style also used for reasons of clarity in 'the most advanced scientific work' (309). Panofsky illustrates different ways of 'reading' the relationship between a figure and its ground, where the figure might be construed as suspended in mid-air: 'In a miniature of around 1000 (A.D.) "empty space" does not count as a real three-dimensional medium, as it does in a more realistic period, but serves as an abstract, unreal background' (1955:60).

Gombrich also provides an amusing example of how superficially similar styles may have different implications, contrasting what might be termed social and visual perspective, and implying that one culture failed to appreciate what another intended to represent. Since the Renaissance (at least), European artists have depicted the relative size of different figures in their work with the intention of signifying either that one figure is physically bigger than another, or that relative distance from the eye makes the nearer *appear* larger. As Firth points out (1951:175), many cultures utilize the relative size of figures in their art work to express their relative social standing: a chief is portrayed larger than his subjects. The Narmer Palette and Scorpion mace-head illustrate this usage (see pages 116-21). Gombrich provides the example of an Egyptian wall painting of 1300 B.C., in which the Egyptian army is depicted attacking a town in Canaan, 'the gigantic pharaoh confronting an enemy stronghold with its diminutive defenders begging for mercy'. This he compares with a Greek vase painting of the sixth century B.C., in which the Greek hero causes death and destruction among the Egyptians. The Greek artist, accustomed to (in our eyes) more 'naturalistic' conventions has evidently interpreted the classical Egyptian style as one of a battle between pygmies and a giant: 'The pictograph for a whole city becomes a real altar onto which two of the victims have climbed, and climbed in vain, stretching out their hands in comic despair. Many of the gestures of this vase could be matched in Egyptian reliefs, and yet their meaning is transformed: these men are no longer the anonymous tokens for a defeated tribe, they are individual people — [although] laughable, to be sure' (1960:115-16).

Split representation on the North-west Coast

One of the most strikingly exotic ways in which forms are created and organized is in split representation. Boas, who anticipated Gombrich's interpretation of style, made a special study of split

Plate 11   Wooden dance mask representing human face from North-west Coast, North America. *Belcher Collection, British Museum*

representation. By coincidence, it is also a stylistic technique that causes Deregowski particular problems of recognition. Overlooking the difficulty he himself documented, that members of other cultures experienced in interpreting Western-style line drawings, Deregowski complains, as though it were a specific limitation of split representation, that 'highly stylized art is not likely to be understood outside of its specific culture'. He sees the artists of the North-west Coast obliged to adopt special visual 'cues that compensate for the

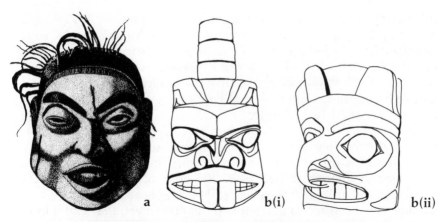

Figure 36   Masks from North-west Coast (North America): (a) 'Naturalistic' mask of dying warrior, (b) 'Totemic' carvings of (i) Beaver, Haida culture, (ii) Hawk, Tsimshian culture. *After Boas*

loss of communication value' (1972:88). Boas was, I think, right to propose the opposite position, that one reason for adopting split representation is precisely to aid visual communication. The point, however, is that it provides an alternative technique — when compared to our perspective drwings — for organizing motifs into a composition. The problem for a mind accustomed to the latter is perhaps like that Rock found in reading handwriting upside down: there are too many mental operations to be performed at once for it to be readily translated into our kind of art (Rock, *op. cit.*:77).

Split representation is a characteristic trait in the art of the North-west Coast of North America, and it was here that Boas studied it. A point of fundamental significance in the present context is that the Indian cultures of the North-west also possessed a style of sculpture which produced objects embodying what seems to us a considerable degree of realism: of faithfulness to a natural model in an idiom that satisfies our criteria of naturalistic style (fig. 36a and plate 11). Captain Cook experienced the difference between the two styles when he visited the area in the eighteenth century. Writing of the decorative style in which split representation appears he commented, 'The general design of these things is perfectly sufficient to convey a knowledge of the object they are intended to represent; but the carving is not executed with... nicety'. His opinion of carved human masks was considerably more favourable; he continued: 'The same, however, cannot be said of many of the human masks and heads; where they show themselves to be ingenious sculptors. They not only preserve with great exactness, the general character of their own faces, but finish the more minute parts with a degree of accuracy in proportion, and neatness in execution' (see Morphy, F., 1973:51 and Morphy, F., 1977:75). It happens that these human masks were intended by the Indian cultures to look realistic (fig. 36a). Boas described a carved head from the Kwakiutl, which was used in a ritual in which it was intended that the audience would believe a dancer had been decapitated, and Emmons, portrait carvings of the recently deceased (see Morphy, F., 1977).

Split representation entails depicting an animal figure as though its body had been split lengthwise and opened out. There are various ways in which this may be done. In some instances the animal is portrayed as though it had been cut open along the line of the backbone and unfolded: the chest and belly appear in the centre with the limbs bent inward so that left and right feet meet, the head split so as to join only at the nose and mouth (see fig. 37a). An alternative is to imagine the split made along a ventral line, unfolding the body so that the line of the back becomes the central focus. Boas illustrates this usage in the depiction of birds (see fig. 37b). A third variant takes the head as the midpoint displaying the left half of the body on one side and the right half on the other (fig. 38). Split representation is merely one of a number of related techniques characteristic of the style, all of which provide regular means of dismembering the body and arranging the parts to cover boxes, clubs, 'totem poles' etc.

Figure 37   Split representation from North-west Coast (North America): (a) Bear, Tsimshian culture, (b) Raven, Haida culture. *After Boas*

Essentially, the style provides a means of depicting animal species, but in a partly anthropomorphic fashion (figs. 36b i and ii and plates 12a and b). Morphy makes the point that the characters portrayed are ancestral, totemic beings which underwent transformations between human and animal form (1977:75). This is expressed in the manner they are represented; the figures appear part-human, but their animal nature is indicated by the inclusion of certain key, diagnostic traits drawn from the iconography of the tradition. The shark is signified by the representation of a tail in which one fork is longer than the other, a mouth whose corners are drawn down and vertical lines on the cheek to indicate gills. The beaver (fig. 36b i) is signified by the inclusion of two outsized incisor teeth within the mouth and by the presence of a scaly tail, often curved forward under the figure's feet. The hawk (fig. 36b ii) is designated by the depiction of a curved beak, bent back at the tip to enter the mouth or join the chin. The killer whale is characteristically indicated by the presence of a fin on the animal's back. Generally the head is elongated and a nostril placed high upon it. Such basic elements of iconography can be identified in the work of different, but neighbouring cultures.

RIGHT SIDE OF BODY   LEFT SIDE

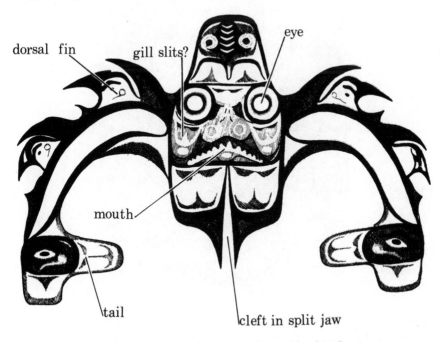

Figure 38   Split representation of shark, North-west Coast. *After Lévi-Strauss*

Plate 12 Totemic masks from North-west Coast, North America: (a) Wolf mask from Nootka culture. (b) Hawk-Sun mask from Kwakiutl culture. Note split representation of bird around margin. *British Museum*

Because these animals are totemic, identification of the species represented indicates the rank or descent group to which the art object's owner belongs. Yet it is often the case that not all diagnostic features would be clearly visible if one depicted the animal model from a single viewpoint. One of the functions of split representation is thus to provide an alternative vehicle for organizing the elements of iconography.

These elements consist of a finite body of alternative forms. As was the case with Harmon's coarse-grained pictures of faces, identifications of meaning are therefore made from among a predetermined set. Of course, Deregowski is in a sense correct to say that highly stylized art can only be understood within its cultural context, but we saw the same tension between imitation of nature and the reduction of motifs to a few regular forms in the styles of road signs and trade marks. It seems likely that this tension is in itself a major stimulus to artistic creation. Boas describes the creative variety of compositions that satisfy the need to include enough information for a carving or painting to be identified as the representation of a particular species. Very often the head of the carving is human in form (see figs. 36b i and ii); only certain key elements indicate that it is the representation of an animal. In a carved Haida headdress representing a squatting beaver, it is the two ears which appear above a quasi-human face that identify it as a non-human representation; the large incisors and scaly tail indicate it as specifically beaver. A painting from a Kwakiutl housefront depicting a beaver shows only the frontal view of a face with large incisors; beneath appear two feet and the characteristic tail, quite detached from the face and unconnected to any indication of a body. Similar instances are reproduced in illustrations of carvings of the hawk. One, by a Tsimshian artist, shows an apparently human head surmounted by two ears and with a beak-like nose whose end curves back into the animal's mouth. The mouth itself is quite separate from the beak and is filled with human-like teeth. A Haida face-painting representing the hawk consists simply of a large, hooked beak painted on the wearer's forehead.

Nor does it seem convincing to place all this art at the 'schematic' end of the representational continuum. One of the motives for adopting split representation seems to be the wish to portray as much as possible of 'what is really there'. Like twisted perspective, split representation is sometimes derided in our culture because it is assumed the artist has not carefully examined what the depicted object looks like from a single point of vision. But to do so is, I think, to define naturalism in too narrow a fashion, particularly since we know North-west Coast artists could produce realistic portrait masks.

157

In addition to its value in aiding visual communication, Boas finds two further distinct functions for split representation. The first embodies a quasi-evolutionary proposition that it developed in response to the forms of the objects decorated with the totemic animals. It is this aspect of his analysis that Deregowski picks up, but one does not need to express the proposition in an evolutionary idiom. Deregowski is quite right to question whether any record exists of the style's evolution towards the form it had in the nineteenth century.

One of the simplest demonstrations of the splitting of bodily form cited by Boas is that of a sea-creature (the 'sculpin') carved on the top of a wooden hat. Because the hat has to bear a series of rings indicating the wearer's social rank, the artist has opened up the back of the creature to leave a hole where the rings can be inserted. On bracelets the convention is carried further: the animal represented is carved as if it had been split from head to tail. The two halves are opened out so as to appear on opposite sides, occupying a semi-circle each, and meeting only at the head and tail. As Boas points out, there is generally a deep split down the centre of the head, so that this too must be interpreted as two side views, each portraying an eye, a nostril and half the mouth, joined by the nose and chin. On flat surfaces, component forms are sometimes organized as if such a bracelet had been cut through and bent out into a flat strip (see fig. 38). According to the evolutionary model used by some anthropologists at the turn of the century, the bracelet and hat might be interpreted as fossilized survivals recording earlier stages of the development that culminates in split representation on a two-dimensional surface. Deregowski may be right to detect such a gratuitous inference in Boas' presentation but this does not negate its value in linking the most dramatic of split representations with a continuum of other formal compositions belonging to the same culture.

Boas finally considers the aesthetic motive we have discussed in previous chapters. Some of the North-west Coast carvings and textiles with animal themes which he illustrates exhibit patterns of rhythm and symmetry as complex as any discussed in his chapter on *The Formal Element in Art*. He writes: 'Our consideration of the fixed formal elements found in this art prove that principles of geometric ornamental form may be recognized even in this highly developed symbolic art; and that it is not possible to assign to each and every element that is derived from animal motives a significant function, but that many of them are employed regardless of meaning, and used for purely ornamental purposes' (279).

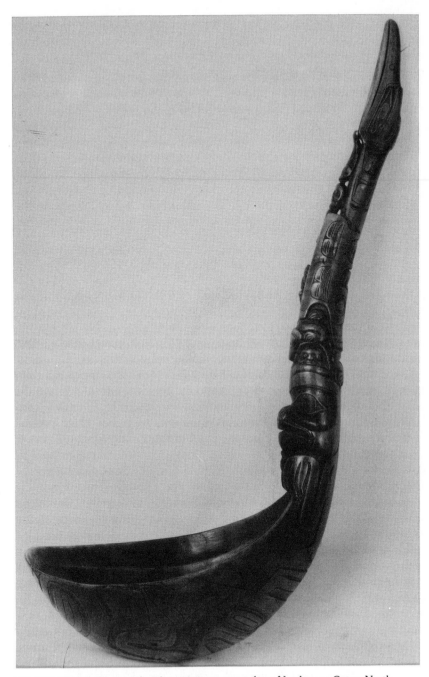

Plate 13   Horn ladle carved with totemic ornament from North-west Coast, North America. *Oldham Collection, British Museum*

Of the three reasons for adopting split representation that Boas proposes for the North-west Coast, it is the first to which he attaches greatest importance. The style, he writes,

> can be fully understood only as an integral part of the structure of the North-west Coast culture. The fundamental idea underlying the thoughts, feelings and activities of these tribes is the value of rank which gives title to the use of privileges, most of which find expression in artistic activities or in the use of art forms. Rank and social position bestow the privilege to use certain animal figures as paintings or carvings on the house front, on totem poles, on masks and on the utensils of everyday life... It is as though the heraldic idea had taken hold of the whole life and had permeated it with a feeling that social standing must be expressed at every step by heraldry (280).

CORRESPONDENCES BETWEEN STYLE AND MENTAL SCHEMATA

Having established that no art style seeks entirely to imitate nature, Gombrich (1960) proceeds to the observation that it is almost impossible to look at the duck-rabbit figure without imposing on it one or the other of the two interpretations. The same is true, he maintains, when one looks at the natural world: art teachers who try to instruct their pupils to copy nature discover that their pupils' difficulties arise not only from a technical inability to copy nature but also from an inability to see it (1960:10). What the would-be artist draws on his paper thus, in Gombrich's view, provides a mirror of his mental interpretation of the world. To illustrate his view further, he cites an experiment conducted by F. C. Bartlett, described in the book *Remembering* (1932). Bartlett showed the nonsense figure reproduced in fig. 35c to some of his students and asked them to draw it from memory. Some interpreted it as a pickaxe, and consequently reproduced it with pointed prongs. Others perceived it as an anchor, and misrepresented the circle at its upper end as a ring through which the anchor rope could be tied. The only student who correctly reproduced the original figure said he had seen it as a 'prehistoric battle-axe'. 'Maybe', comments Gombrich (who could perhaps conceive of prehistoric battle-axes looking like this), 'maybe he was trained in classifying such objects and was therefore able to portray the figure that happened to correspond to a schema with which he was familar' (64). The schema to which Gombrich here refers is a mental phenomenon; his argument leads him to the view that the artist can draw only what his mental schemata allow him to reproduce, something which may serve either a positive or a negative function: on the one hand the artist misses some of the real world's complexity but, on the other, he synthesizes the infinity of forms into regular patterns. To demonstrate the difficulty of escaping from the schemata one has established Gombrich reproduces some attempts at illustrating the rhinoceros executed during a time when this animal was quite unfamiliar to European artists (*op. cit.* 71-3).

Here, I think, Gombrich runs the risk of implying an identity between what the artist draws, and the mental image he forms of the world. Of course, if an artist regularly uses a certain style, one can assume he has a set of mental rules for reproducing motifs, but they are not necessarily the same as his mental images of the objects he depicts.

Gregory makes the interesting observation that the illusion induced by the Neckar cube demonstrates that one's mental perception is not the same as a graphic motif, nor the same as the image cast by that motif on the back of the eye. The drawing of the cube is unchanging, but one's perception of it constantly shifts, dependent on whether corner (a) or corner (b) is considered to be nearest to the eye (1974:48). According to the interpretation, certain faces of the cube must be construed as lying at the back, or at the front of the figure. One's mental interpretation of the motif is such that, according to Gregory: 'if we remove the cube's background... with each reversal in depth... whichever face appears to be the more distant appears to be the larger' (54) and yet, as he points out, there is no change occurring in either the drawing or the image it casts on the retina of the eye: particularly since 'It has been shown that depth reversal will readily occur without eye movement' (Attneave, 1974:95). The same is true of the duck-rabbit illusion, and other ambiguous configurations. A classic example developed by gestalt psychologists, who were interested in how the mind constructs configurations and applies them to recognition of real objects, is the figure-ground reversal illustrated by fig. 35d. Is it a black Maltese Cross on a white ground, or a white flower with four petals on a black ground? The artist M. C. Escher turned such illusions into powerful visual metaphors: according to what one construes as figures and what the background, in some of his etchings, angels stand out or are displaced by devils, birds by frogs and fish, black birds by white (cf. Escher, 1972, figures 11, 17 and 23). Escher provides his own commentary on the perceptual processes that such transitions demand (e.g. *op. cit.*: 11).

Attneave discusses a number of well-known illusions, including those cited here. He compares the switching between alternative perceptions to the opening and closing of a hinged trap door, such as one might find in a ceiling. The door rests in a stable position only when fully open or fully closed, but it can be switched from one position to the other, just as Gombrich described the shift from rabbit-interpretation to duck-interpretation without the possibility of holding the mind at a mid-point where both visions can be apprehended simultaneously. Sometimes, however one can see how the establishment of one alternative flows from the interpretation of certain components which contribute progressively to the weight that the alternative comes momentarily to possess: if certain lines are the ears of a rabbit, then the small mark must be its nose... Attneave terms this progression a 'locking-in process' (1974:94). It seems likely that when members of different cultures look at a particular work of art, they will form a different mental interpretation of it, according to how best its features may be 'locked in' to a familiar configuration.

An alternative view has been put forward by Goodnow, in her discussion of children's drawings. Rather than make the inference that children see the world in the way that they draw it, she argues that children develop techniques for drawing which are intended to solve certain problems of graphic representation. 'Children are often said to draw "what they see", "what they know", or "what is important to them",' she writes (1977:66), but each proposition 'is somehow unsatisfying... children must see more, know more or feel more than is displayed in their drawings'. Equally it is unsatisfying to have to fall back on unobservable mental phenomena if we are to understand the child's motives. On the other hand, 'the same sense of unease accompanies the idea that drawings may be considered as abstractions from "reality" ' and Goodnow proposes to use 'the term "schema"... *not* in the sense of an abstraction from a real object, but in the sense of a repeated shape, a "formula figure" that recurs over a number of drawings'. Her questions about children's style thus concern the form of the graphic motifs themselves: how are they built up and with what components? As with the child's early use of language, his or her early drawings consist of 'ringing the changes' on a limited set of motifs and of rules for recombining them. Goodnow neatly illustrates how children devise ways of solving problems of representation set for them. How does one draw someone picking up an object from the ground: elongate one arm on the 'person' motif, tilt the body forward or bend it at the knees? How does one complete a drawing like this:⊙? Does one depict a person lying on their side? Attach a vertical body and construe it as someone looking sideways? Add a third black dot in the upper right of the circle and construe the lower dot as a nose? Goodnow discusses some common elements of composition, reporting that all parts of a figure tend to be aligned along a common axis, and to exhibit symmetry of various kinds (70-1). These are features intrinsic to the motifs; while they draw on attributes of the real world and, perhaps, on cognitive processes hidden within the mind, they also have independent status as stylistic techniques.

In passing, Goodnow makes some comments on the lessons to be learned from her material in assessing Australian Aboriginal art. The art of adult Aboriginals is in no way child-like; rather it exhibits sophisticated solutions to some of the perhaps universal problems of representation that children encounter and reveal as they learn to draw. Different culturally established styles no doubt codify different techniques for resolving these problems. Panofsky demonstrates this clearly in his discussion of methods for formulating how to depict the human body (*op. cit.*).

It is at this point that it becomes necessary to consider the proposition that stylistic convention may not be an entirely negative thing. So far, if one followed Gombrich's argument, one might have the impression that the artist's store of schemata and techniques of composition somehow hold him back from improving his artistic technique. Yet neither Gombrich nor Boas would necessarily subscribe to such a view. Both consider that when the artist depicts his model in such a way as to analyse and structure it, he is performing a positive act which can contribute to our understanding of the model's cultural significance. The equation of style with mental perception is really a crude and misleading way of stating a genuine phenomenon: styles do embody some evidence about the ways in which cultures organize the world.

It is frequently culture that defines what are the 'characteristic' features of an object and one can suppose that artistic styles will be directed, at least in part, towards uncovering and revealing these in tangible form.

One can accept Gombrich's view that art works are not designed to reproduce in every detail some natural model — that, indeed, such a goal is unobtainable — but rather to isolate and present in a distinctive fashion those elements of the model that are significant to the artist and his audience. It is not necessary to pursue this line of reasoning to the extent of inferring that the artist and other members of his culture see the world the way they draw it. An anthropological analysis of art can make use of this insight by examining the styles current in some small-scale societies, and asking how these set out an interpretation of the world that is relevant to social interaction, religious belief, aesthetic impulse or technical exigency without resorting to theories of primitive mentality.

Geometric and figurative styles in North-east Arnhem Land

The second example demonstrating the co-existence of two styles in a single culture is taken from Northern Australia. Morphy's study of the use made of two alternative styles among the Yolngu of North-east Arnhem Land (Morphy, 1977) is particularly valuable because it is one of only two detailed analyses of style in Australian Aboriginal art, the other being Munn's (Munn, 1966, 1973 etc.). Morphy's discussion builds to some extent on that of Munn. They are agreed that one of the most important uses of a highly geometric style in the Australian context is to give visual expression to the transformations undergone by totemic ancestors. Munn considers the geometric style of the Walpiri of Central Australia to be representational, because of the cultural significance of similarities in form between the transformations each ancestor underwent; which the art reproduces. Legends relate, for instance, how the echidna (spiny ant-eater) was once a woman who was repeatedly speared for her misdeeds, and the visual resemblance between spears and the echidna's spines gives an added poignance to the narrative. Morphy differs in his interpretation of geometric art in North-east Arnhem Land, for reasons we will consider below.

When Munn carried out her research the only available material from North-east Arnhem Land documented the figurative style, overlooking the co-existence of a geometric one. This led Munn to contrast Central and Northern Australian art. Their typical styles, she argued, depended on different *visual categories*. A snake, tree or turtle motif among Yolngu art depicted a homogeneous category of subjects: different snakes perhaps, or several species of turtle; but not the enormous range a circle or line possesses in Walpiri art, whose representational value may include, in the first instance, a water hole, camp site or ancestor's body: in the second, a kangaroo tail, spear, track etc. Morphy shows her assessment of Yolngu art to have been based on insufficient data, but nonetheless finds in the co-existence of a figurative and a geometric style among the Yolngu, valuable insights into the relationship between style, thought and the real world.

Morphy refers to two representational systems in Yolngu art, distinguished by the different styles — figurative and geometric — on which they are built. Styles of the geometric class are put to two distinct uses, providing both an alternative means of portraying the scenes from legend which appear in figurative compositions, and also a series of background designs indicating to which clan a painting belongs. The anthropologist Thompson, who studied Yolngu art during the period of early White contact, recorded an indigenous classification of paintings closely related to the predominance of one or the other style of representation. In the 1930s, Thompson found depictions of ancestral themes were distinguished from *wakinngu*, decorative designs 'produced simply to make an object look attractive' (Morphy, *op. cit.*:217). Public aspects of sacred lore appeared in *garma* paintings depicting minor ancestral beings. *Garma* paintings had a large component of figurative representations. The geometric background indicating clan ownership could include only those clan designs not associated with sacred objects. Other sacred paintings were not revealed to women or children. Among these were three categories. One, *ngärrapuy*, appeared to Morphy to be almost indistinguishable from *garma* paintings. *Likanbuy*, the second, was characterized by a reduction in, or absence of, figurative motifs: clan designs and other geometric motifs predominated. *Bulgu*, the third, consisted entirely of outlined clan designs. *Likanbuy* paintings were the most highly valued and most restricted of access (217-24). Comparing paintings collected by Thompson with those for sale to tourists today, Morphy found that the craft shop now exhibits paintings indistinguishable from some of those in Thompson's *likanbuy* class. There are still paintings from which women and children are kept apart, but Morphy considers that these no longer always correspond to a class defined on stylistic criteria, because different clans have made different decisions about which paintings to sell. In some cases it is the meanings of designs, rather than the designs themselves, which are today restricted (237).

The reason for traditionally confining geometric motifs to secret paintings has been discussed in the previous chapter. The two styles, as Morphy puts it, 'signify meanings in different ways and... have different signifying potentials' (165). Geometric motifs have at once less visual resemblance with the things they portray, and more power to portray several things at once.

Following the tenets of structural linguistics, Morphy insists that to understand how the two styles work, 'the basic elements' of each system 'must initially be seen in terms of the ways in which they are contrasted and interact among themselves' before considering how the two systems of representation collectively complement each other within the wider artistic tradition. The two systems are based on different ways of categorizing experience and different ways of portraying classes of objects. This is what Munn described with her terms *meaning range* and *visual category* (Munn, 1966:936). Like Munn, Morphy refers to the component motifs from which each system is built up as schemata. In the figurative style there is a resemblance of form between the motif (or schema) and the class of objects it depicts: most are two-dimensional silhouettes. 'To those familiar with the code,' Morphy writes, 'the representation is intended to "look like" the object represented' (168). An important qualification, which demonstrates more clearly than anything that it is really mental categories that are signified, is the fact that some motifs depict imaginary beings from Yolngu cosmology. Here, writes Morphy, 'look like' should be read as 'is an acceptable representation of'. The portrayal is presumably based on regular transformations of objects in the real world such as quasi-human figures in which the relative dimensions of limbs and body are modified.

One of the primary purposes of figurative representation is to direct attention away from the symbolic equations of religious imagery by reducing the meaning of a painting to familiar ideas. Artists criticize or commend each others' paintings in the figurative style in terms of the likeness of motifs to specific depicted objects. In one example quoted by Morphy (fig. 39b), an artist was ridiculed because his painting of a water goanna looked too like a crocodile. According to other men present, the artist should not have drawn transverse lines on the animal's back because these looked too much like the scales on the crocodile's back. The water goanna should be depicted simply with a backbone running the length of its body

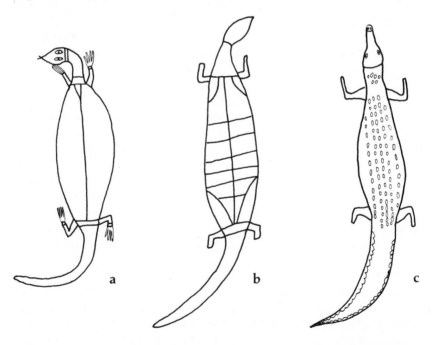

Figure 39   Yolngu figurative art (North-east Arnhem Land, Australia): (a) Acceptable water goanna, (b) Unacceptable water goanna, (c) Acceptable crocodile. *After Morphy*

(177). In the end, the artist was prevented from continuing and someone else took over his work. Looking at the alternative motifs for water goanna and crocodile one has a strong impression that other details of the design are pertinent: the elongated digits of the goanna, the forked tongue, as well as the overall proportions of the figure, but without information from the artists this is merely speculation. Certainly, Morphy shows that the categories represented by the figurative motifs should be carefully investigated. He describes a test in which he abstracted a collection of motifs taken from bark paintings about which he already had information. Shown figurative motifs in isolation from their ground in the painting, artists could correctly identify them on only 48 per cent of the sample, even though they were in some cases taken from their own paintings! The possum was correctly identified in every instance but one. This, writes Morphy, is because the species has a unique schema, in which the animal's tail is shown curved over his back (see the possums in the Manggalili paintings of Djarrakpi). Likewise, the catfish is unique in having a motif which depicts whiskers at the fish's mouth and the garfish alone has a long narrow jaw barbed with teeth. Other fish species recognized in the Yolngu linguistic taxonomy do not possess unique figurative motifs, and the same is true of species of duck, turtle and goanna. Here the figurative style works with more general categories: generic turtles, fish, goanna and duck. Placed in a painting, a motif can be assigned to a single species because of the Durkheimian trait in Yolngu culture of assigning related species to opposite moieties. The clan design surrounding the motif makes it clear which species is denoted (173-6).

The figurative style of Yolngu bark painting thus has a distinctive way of categorizing experience, and of representing these categories with a set of alternative motifs or schemata. Each of these regular variations in design can be fully understood with reference to their place in the system of alternatives. Although they are motivated by the appearance of the depicted objects, this source of inspiration is in itself insufficient to explain the meaning of designs. Morphy makes the important observation that individual artists each have their own way of executing motifs and that, provided they contain the relevant elements, all can be identified correctly by onlookers. If the design lacks necessary identifying features, then it is criticized.

Geometric motifs, Morphy believes, contrast with figurative ones in having an *arbitrary* association with the depicted objects. This was the judgement Durkheim made of geometric art styles in Central Australia, although it differs (as Morphy comments) from Munn's opinion of Central Australian art. Morphy accepts that there can be a resemblance of form between a geometric motif and the class of

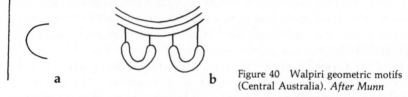

a   b   Figure 40   Walpiri geometric motifs
                      (Central Australia). *After Munn*

objects it depicts, but argues that this is too generalized to explain why geometric designs take the form they do. It is rather a kind of *post hoc* rationalization on the part of the Yolngu. 'The skin of a crocodile, the shell of a tortoise, the cells of a honeycomb and the fold marks in sheets of paperbark', items with totemic significance, '... are all said to show a formal resemblance to the Yiritja moiety diamond pattern' (212). Fire, another totemic entity, is seen represented in the colour of diamond clan designs: white pigment depicts ash blown in the wind, black depicts burnt-out bush and yellow, flames. Species of native bee are divided between the two moieties and so are honeycomb designs belonging to both moieties, but which possess the differences of form that allow them to be attributed to Dhuwa or Yiritja moieties. Perhaps the most telling evidence Morphy presents is that, while figurative motifs are

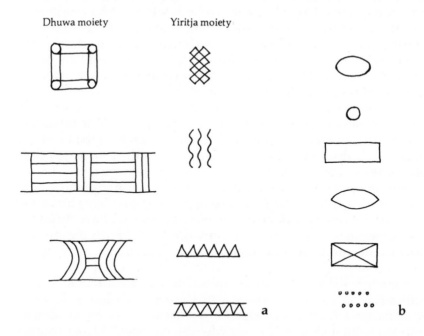

Figure 41   Yolngu geometric art (North-east Arnhem Land, Australia): (a) Clan designs, (b) Motifs replacing figurative designs. *After Morphy*

criticized according to their resemblance to depicted objects, the only criterion for judging geometric motifs is their conformity with 'established ancestral pattern' (170). It is, in other words, a matter of convention alone.

A geometric style is used for two purposes in Yolngu art. One of these is to reproduce designs signifying the clan to which a painting belongs. Clans belonging to a single moiety have similar designs: many Yiritja clans possess diamond shaped motifs while many Dhuwa clans possess motifs based on squares (fig. 41a). Further evidence for the purely conventional association of form and meaning in Yolngu geometric art comes from the fact that 'every informant agreed' on where the differences between related clan designs lay. 'These differences', writes Morphy, 'are essentially relational'. The significance of each is defined by its place in the set of alternatives. Citing the diamond designs of three Yiritja clans, he states: 'a Munyuku diamond should be larger than a Dhaḻwangu diamond, and a Gumaitj one should be elongated relative to both' (198). Diamonds with right-angled corners belong to groups emphasizing the sugar-bag dreaming while elongated ones are associated with the fire dreaming.

The second use made of geometric motifs is to depict ancestral events in such a way as to allow several meanings simultaneously to be assigned to each motif (see Chapter 3). Morphy insists on a distinction that Munn obscures: geometric motifs can have a multiplicity of meanings in different contexts, but only a sub-set of these potential meanings provide the 'multivalency' that such a motif possesses in the context of a single painting-type. Contrary to Turner's views on symbolism, there need be no reason to expect any meaningful cultural connection between all the potential meanings in the wider set, at which level geometric motifs may be compared to the phonemes of spoken languages. Phonemes form the set of sounds which give a characteristic flavour to the pronunciation of a language; but none of these sounds ever has a constant meaning, in that language. Likewise, the set of geometric motifs characteristic of Central Australian art (often made up of circles, arcs and straight lines) differs from the set typical of geometric art in North-east Arnhem Land, which includes diamonds, undulating lines and rows of dots.

The point is illustrated by the various potential meanings of the lens-like ellipse which provides the fourth motif in the accompanying diagrams (fig. 41b). The first three alternatives: ribs, bamboo grass and stakes of a fish trap, are taken from a single painting. According to the narrative depicted in this painting, the snake's ribs were transformed into a fish trap (190). The bamboo grass also referred to by Morphy in his caption to the painting presumably grows at the site of the ancestral trap and represents it in a different medium. The meanings *boat* and *sand sculpture*, however, come from a different set of paintings, and we have discussed the analogy between these two potential meanings in the previous chapter.

It is simplicity of forms in Yolngu geometric art that helps them to have many meanings at once (a point Munn drew attention to in Walpiri art), while the relative naturalism of Yolngu figurative art reduces this expression of multivalency. The two styles of Yolngu art thus satisfy different purposes and throw light on different aspects of Yolngu philosophy. Like the two styles of North-west Coast art, their co-existence helps to discount technical or intellectual constraints as the major determinants of style in the art of small-scale societies, revealing instead how cultures have devised sophisticated stylistic tools for the expression of their vision of the world. It is interesting to speculate that the Yolngu may perceive their geometric motifs in the same way that we perceive the 'duck/rabbit', 'flower/Maltese Cross' and other figures; that is, as optical illusions that switch their appearance from one to another of the alternative meanings within a given set; realizing in visual form the transformations of their philosophy. Whether or not this is the case Morphy makes it clear that the Yolngu deliberately exclude naturalistic clues from their geometric style, thus paralleling Gregory's explanation for the success of optical illusions. Conversely, in Yolngu figurative art, the artists appear to be doing what Gregory described as making us 'accept just one out of the infinite set of possible interpretations of a figure'. The characteristics of Yolngu geometric art suggest that we cannot, unaided, see another culture's art in the way that the members of that culture do — just as Hudson and Deregowski demonstrated the problems our own graphic styles pose for members of other cultures.

Rather than the purely conventional association of sounds and meanings characteristic of language, the forms of representational art are motivated by the appearance of their natural models. When an art tradition embodies a representational style, a field of study is thus opened up that is missing from language. Without committing the mistake of assuming that such objects merely imitate their models, or that of seeing in them an exact realization of the artist's mental image, it is still useful to investigate reasons why the tradition selects, transforms and organizes the appearances of the real world in the fashion it does. Style is one of the necessary components of visual communication but, like the other components we considered in Chapter 3, it acquires special qualities when it becomes part of art — qualities which express the artist's sensitivity to form and significance. Because of this it is possible to study how a culture fills the world around it with meaning and how different styles suit different purposes. Nonetheless, the danger of thinking we can understand other cultures' goals in our own terms is as great here as ever. It is easy to overlook the diversity of the many cultures that have been constructed from the universals of human behaviour.

5
Creativity of the artist

An Eskimo man was running from a summer camp on the tundra back to his village. As he ran, he saw a boat descending from the moon. In the boat he recognized the figure of a shaman who had died a short time before, who had also been a good runner. The dead shaman disappeared, and his place was taken by the grotesque figure of a man with one large eye, who danced to the runner, and was then replaced once more by the deceased shaman. The runner went home, upset to find he had been possessed by the spirit of the grotesque figure. When autumn came, he was himself accepted by his fellow villagers as a shaman.

The shaman's role was a central one in Eskimo religion. He was the doctor who diagnosed illness and advised the sick what they should do to restore their health. It was his task to act as an intermediary between the community and the supernatural world that controlled the lives of the animals on which the people depended for food and raw materials. It was also the shaman's duty to create festive dances performed at religious ceremonies, and masks worn by the dancers.

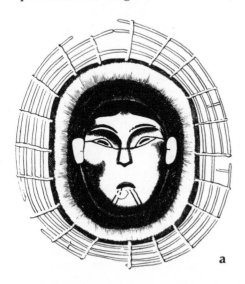

a

b

Figure 42 Eskimo masks: (a) Representing shaman's vision, (b) For secular entertainment. *After Blaker*

The purpose of these performances was to establish harmony between people and the world of spirits. The shaman's position was one he achieved, often after exhibiting symptoms of what we would diagnose as psychological disturbance. The incipient shaman was trained to adopt the cultural role to which his disturbing experiences qualified him. Some men became shamans while still young. Others achieved their position later in life, following some dramatic and testing event such as being cast adrift, accidentally, upon an ice-floe. (There is some debate in anthropology about whether shamans really have undergone mental upheaval, or simply learnt to manifest the symptoms of such a condition: see, for instance, Lévi-Strauss, 1963: 175-85 and Lewis, 1975.)

The particular skill of the shaman was his ability to make journeys between the mundane world, to which the rest of his community was confined, and the supernatural one. There, he could see the spirits that peopled Eskimo religion. Producing masks that depicted these spirits (fig. 42a) was one way in which the shaman made visible his experiences when he returned to Earth, translating a unique and individual vision into something the community could share. According to Ray, masks represented the spirits of animal species, or other beings with whom the shaman was in contact, but also — at the level of iconology perhaps — were a general reminder of the shaman's ability to keep people in touch with the unseen world directing their lives (Ray and Blaker, 1967).

A shaman wore his mask both in ceremonies and during individual curing sessions. Ray's opinion, based on the accounts of nineteenth-century European observers, is that the shaman would wear his mask particularly when he was dealing with illness or adversity that was seen to have been caused by human misdeeds. If the rules of Eskimo social life were broken, the spirits might retaliate by driving away food animals or causing storms, making the misbehaviour a matter of community concern. At such times, the shaman put on his mask and consulted, or pleaded with the spirits responsible (17-19). Masks of another kind were worn during festivals by people who were not shamans (fig. 42b). These masks represented individual animals: a raven or an eagle, for instance, or comic pictures of humans like the neighbouring Indians who were caricatured as lice-ridden and generally inferior to the Eskimo. All these were common experiences to the participants.

The shaman's mask, however, exemplifies the apparent dilemma of creativity: how can an individual experience be rendered in a form accessible to the community? The shaman who had acquired his position after experiencing the vision of the boat that descended from the moon instructed eight men each to carve a mask with the appearance of the dancer in the boat, and he taught people to sing and dance in the way that the spirit had shown him (12). Another man, who was accepted as a shaman after he had survived being marooned on an ice-floe, himself carved a set of masks which he distributed to other men, teaching them how to perform the accompanying dance. During the performance he was again possessed by the power of the Seal which he had encountered while adrift on the ice. He ordered a large sheet of ice through which a hole had been cut to be placed in the doorway of the hut where the dance was being displayed. Then he came up through the hole three times, like a seal blowing as it emerged from the sea. 'When he rose a fourth time the chief dancer harpooned [him] through the head. He bled profusely, and all present saw the weapon with attached line through his head. He then disappeared below the entrance hole, and the men pulled in the line with the harpoon on the end. Soon [the possessed man] reappeared as well as before' (13).

While the vision is personal to the shaman, in taking up his social role he must dramatize the experience in such a way as to give it public expression. One can, I think, guess that the dilemma is to some extent a false one simply because the vision itself may follow a pattern established by other shamans' accounts of their supernatural encounters, but it was nonetheless an individual experience of this cultural tradition. What is demonstrable is that the community recognized a certain code for depicting spirits on masks. While entertainment masks worn at festivals portrayed individual characters, the shaman's mask represented the collective spirit of a natural species such as the seal. The generic term for any non-human spirit among the southern Alaskan eskimo described by Ray was 'its human being' or 'its person', and the spirit could materialize in the form of a diminutive person. The supernatural quality of the apparition was, however, represented on masks by the regular ways in which it diverged from the human model: one side of the face was distorted, it had extra eyes (or only one), extra noses or ears (see plates 14a and b). Figure 42 (a) and (b) gives a comparison between a secular entertainment mask and one depicting a shaman's spirit.

Sometimes shamans carved their own masks, but more often they hired an expert carver to carry out the work for them (11). The shaman would base the form of the mask he commissioned partly on his personal vision but partly on the established traditional forms used to depict particular types of spirit. Sometimes the shaman would carve the face of the spirit on the mask, ,and leave the remaining work to another artist (50). Sometimes he would merely indicate the general form that the carving should take by placing a few guidelines on the surface of the wood. Ray argues that the often

Plate 14   North-west Eskimo masks:
(a) Fox and man. (b) Halibut and seal.
Inverarity Collection, British Museum

rudimentary nature of the shaman's directions demonstrate that every carver must have had a mental image of how a spirit mask should, in general, look. This does not prevent her from conceiving of a single vision becoming the basis for a new cultural tradition. 'Only the shaman's own mind and hands,' she writes, 'could approximate the transformation of his original dream into the first mask of its kind. The model, however, could easily become the prototype for subsequent masks, and might establish not only a norm for a carver's subsequent execution of a shaman's directions, but the basis of a cultural style' (51).

Aesthetic criteria were as important as those of iconography. If a shaman considered himself to be a good carver then he would certainly produce his own masks; the reason for seeking someone else to do the work was to ensure that the mask had a satisfying appearance (50). Like the Abelam and Yolngu, the Eskimo of Ray's study found a close connection between the aesthetic pleasure they perceived in a work of art and the control of spiritual powers. To influence the appropriate spirits and make them behave beneficently in the future, masks should be 'beautiful and exciting' (6) and they should be worn by the best dancers. Whoever made them, and whatever the bounds imposed by cultural convention, the limits of acceptable interpretation of the spiritual themes were wide and, in Ray's opinion, 'the result was a staggering number and variety of masks'.

The case of the Eskimo in southern Alaska appears to run counter to the popular image of art in small-scale societies, according to which such art is limited in its forms and unchanging in its patterns. The view was forcefully expressed in Lévi-Strauss' assertion that 'as much as an element of individualization intrudes into artistic production, the semantic function of the work tends to disappear'; individual creativity, in other words, is in small-scale societies alien to the expression of shared themes.

Just as people have in the past maintained that the beliefs of small-scale societies are nothing but a reflection of social structures, so the undoubtedly close relation between shared beliefs and social behaviour in such societies has led a number of writers to suggest that individual creativity has almost no role to play in ethnographic art; that it is rather concerned with upholding tradition. They would contrast such art with the constant change and discovery that they like to attribute to art in Renaissance and post-Renaissance Europe; ethnographic art is, they say, concerned merely with the portrayal of standard themes in standard fashions. It is difficult to know to what extent people dismiss the art of a certain culture as 'monotonous' and lacking variation simply through lack of acquaintance with the culture. It is certainly very difficult to assess what constitutes significant innovation to people of another society. In the second place, it is certainly true, as Guiart (in Biebuyck, 1969) pointed out, that some ethnographic art traditions embody far more variation than others. How far can such differences be explained in terms of social and cultural variation between different societies? The Eskimo case alone is sufficient to demonstrate that simplicity of economy and political system does not guarantee an immobile art tradition; like the Australian Aboriginals the Eskimo were traditionally hunters and gatherers. One of the more satisfactory ways of exploring limits on creativity is that adopted with respect to style in Chapter 4; that of comparing two different art traditions that co-exist as part of different institutional patterns in a single society but place different values on innovation (cf. Yoruba material discussed below, page 179ff.). Anthropologists have come to realize how false is the assumption that societies which lack a written history of change must necessarily be unchanging, and this must apply as much to art as to other aspects of culture. That it is a misunderstanding to consider individual creativity alien to the expression of shared themes has already been suggested in Chapters 3 and 4, and this final chapter will consider directly the place of the artist in relation to the cultural systems discussed in those chapters.

To confine oneself solely to the level of cultural generalities is to stay within the bounds of the tradition that visualizes individual members of society as nothing more than the vehicles through which standardized rights and duties are enacted, creating the pattern of social relations that is called (in Radcliffe-Brown's sense) the social structure. In recent years a number of anthropologists have shifted their viewpoint so radically as to present the individual actor as a calculating being who threads and manipulates his way through a tangle of obstacles quite outside himself that constitute 'the rules of the game'. Frederik Barth is perhaps the best-known exponent of this approach in anthropology (see e.g. Barth, 1967) but he himself has pointed out the theory's sources outside anthropology. Bailey has applied the theory to an understanding of political processes in Indian village communities and elsewhere (Bailey, 1969). The advantage of the approach is the recognition it gives to processes of social change, and the capacity of actors to assess the situation within which they act and decide how best to alter that situation. Yet, in setting up 'the rules of the game' as though they were disembodied realities, it surely ignores the fact that a culture has life only in as much as it forms the convictions and beliefs of a set of people, who act in certain ways because they accept those ways as *right*, or indeed in many cases cannot conceive of alternatives. Gellner opens his book *Thought and Change* with a quotation from Kant to the effect that a bird flying through the air, and feeling the resistance of the air against its wings, might fancy it could fly faster or more effortlessly in a vacuum. Neither can the artist think, nor express himself, except through a cultural tradition that both provides a vehicle for his creativity and determines the forms that it can take. The dichotomy between cultural tradition and individual innovation is a false one, which goes back at least to Durkheim's *Rules of Sociological Method* (1895), where the innovator is presented as a man out of step with his age, threatening the established order. This view is characterized in the following extract: 'To make progress, individual originality must be able to express itself ... According to Athenian law Socrates was a criminal ... However, his crime, namely the independence of his thought ... served to prepare a new morality and faith which the Athenians needed' (1964:71). This view is a popular one to apply to contemporary artistic innovators in our culture but it often seems to evaporate when, with time, one looks back on the innovators of past periods and sees that they were really close to the heart of their own times. In a sense, the problem of assessing the creativity of artists from an exotic culture stems from the *too distant* perspective we have of that way of life, making apparent uniformity obliterate the details of individual difference, just as members of other races themselves often look very much alike: it comes as a surprise to learn that they have the same difficulty in telling us apart. Even Durkheim, in a momentary lapse of taste and intellect, claimed that the lack of creativity in other cultures was exemplified by the physical likeness between the people who lived out those exotic lives (see parts of his *The Division of Labour in Society*).

Sources of creativity

What then, are some of the bases for creativity in the art of small-scale societies? A number have been mentioned in the course of previous chapters. One is simply the act required to give an idea tangible form. Another is the existence of elements of design which lie outside the semantic qualities of the art work, and which allow the artist to indulge in free variations, or permit selection from within a range of motifs, not all of which need be present to convey a particular message. At a more fundamental level lies the possibility of an artist's perceiving fresh parallels between realms of meaning, giving other members of his culture new insights into the nature of the order they detect in the world around them. It is scarcely a paradox that Shakespeare expressed his creative originality in the same language that millions of other English speakers used, and, likewise, wherever there is a visual grammar, artists working in that tradition have the possibility of producing innumerable fresh compositions that satisfy the requirements of comprehensibility to other members of the culture, and yet are original creations. At another level again, exists the kind of creativity denied to language by the conventional association of sound with meaning: that of the reduction of natural models to their representations in a restricted number of regular forms. At all these levels there exists a separate determinant: the attitude the artist and his audience hold towards the creation of new forms: how far do they accept the possibilities, which seem inherent in the perpetuation of an artistic tradition, for the creation of new works?

In many instances, it is true that the artist in a small-scale society is like a musician who gives repeated performances of a work of music whose melody has never been written down. This view, which stems from Wollheim's argument about *types* and *tokens*, is exemplified by cultures like the Kalabari and Lega, where a stock repertoire of cultural characters exists and artists are required to reproduce each as existing objects decay or are lost. Nonetheless, the artist's own manner of handling the medium will inevitably imprint a personal style on the object he or she creates; a personal style that may develop and change as the artist gains new insights or develops new technical skills, revealing the kind of creativity that Wollheim wrote about: the artist's interpretation of the work.

Thomson (1969) documents the evolution of a personal style in the work of a Yoruba potter, Abatan. When Thomson studied her work between 1962 and 1964 she was an elderly woman. She belonged to the Egbado, a subgroup of the Yoruba living in the south-west of the wider Yoruba territory. Her pottery was much sought-after and had spread throughout Egbado country and that of two neighbouring subgroups. The vessels she manufactured were of a distinctive type, made to be used in the cult of the spirit Eyinle. Eyinle's cult is said to have spread to the Egbado from the Oyo Yoruba. Eyinle is a legendary figure who, when his sons were thirsty, entered the earth and released a stream, from which they were able to drink. The two principal classes of object needed for the cult are an iron bracelet, which each cult member wears on the right wrist, and an earthenware pot which stands on a domestic altar. It is filled with water from a running source and contains stones used during initiation into the cult. The water represents the stream Eyinle created and it is the pots that Abatan made for her customers.

In some northern Oyo villages, writes Thomson, the Eyinle cult vessel is made according to an entirely non-figurative design, the lid decorated simply with a pair of intersecting arches (plate 15a). It is on such arches that the central figure on Abatan's pots is placed. In other areas, Thomson records, the lid is surmounted by a full-dress figure (plate 15b). Abatan's work is said to fall somewhere between the two extremes. He states that the central figure on the lids of her vessels represents the fertility promoted by Eyinle (142).

Abatan's career began when she was a young adolescent, during the last years of the nineteenth century. She received no formal lessons, learning simply from constant observation of her mother's work. Her mother, another famous potter, had in turn learnt from Abatan's maternal grandmother. Abatan first constructed one of the Eyinle cult vessels in the 1920s.

Thomson supplies two photographs of a vessel probably made by Abatan's mother (see figs. 43a). The lid is crowned by a group of figures: a dominant woman with a pronounced neck and a hairstyle in the form of two longitudinal ridges. The surface of the clay (cf. the side arch) is decorated with cross-hatched lines. In front of the main figures sit three children, among whom the central one holds a bowl. At the back is a model of a smaller child, holding onto its mother's back, whose cheerful expression contrasts with the seriousness of the other figures. In Abatan's early work ('phase one'), Thomson notes the following divergences from her mother's design (fig. 43b). The

Plate 15   Yoruba Eyinle cult vessels (Nigeria) showing variation in form: (a) Lid with crossed arches but no figure. (b) Lid with single figure holding bowl. *British Museum*

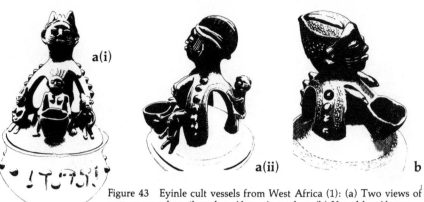

a(i)

a(ii)

b

Figure 43   Eyinle cult vessels from West Africa (1): (a) Two views of pottery vessel attributed to Abatan's mother, (b) Vessel by Abatan. Thomson's 'phase one'. *After Thomson*

elongated neck of the head crowning the arches has disappeared. The arches have been reduced in height. The hairstyle has been replaced by one which matches contemporary custom: the hair is dressed in a number of low ridges. The incised cross-hatching has been replaced by a design of impressed hollows. All the subsidiary figures have now been eliminated; the bowl is attached directly to the arch supporting the central head. At the same time, however, Thomson comments, a number of general features of her mother's style are retained by the younger woman: the expression of immobility on the figure's face; the raised decorations on the supporting arches.

In Abatan's later work ('phase two'), Thomson notes a number of changes: sometimes the central, minor figure holding the bowl is restored, although not the other children. The shape of the adult figure's face is changed; the mouth is broadened (fig. 44a). Most interesting, however, are the changes that followed a witch-finding cult in which much existing pottery was destroyed. A number of clients came to Abatan asking her to supply them with vessels like those her mother had made. Some brought the fragments of old vessels with them, which Abatan could copy: in such cases she revived the elongated neck and haughty expression of the central figure (fig. 44b). In other cases, where she was not supplied with a concrete model, Abatan combined elements of her own and her mother's style (cf. figs. 43 and 44a): two children are placed in front of the central figure, and an infant on her back is restored (fig. 44c); but sometimes the hairstyle remains in the modern form, and sometimes not.

Even from this very brief outline, it is possible to see how Abatan is in many ways enmeshed in a cultural framework, but how she still produces pottery readily identifiable as her personal work. She adopts a mode of representation much like her mother's, yet alters

a   b   c

Figure 44   Eyinle cult vessels from West Africa (2): (a) Vessel by Abatan. Thomson's 'phase two'. (b) and (c) Vessels by Abatan, Thomson's 'phase three': those made to replace pots destroyed during witch-finding cult. Note alternate hair styles and presence or absence of subsidiary figures. *After Thomson*

the form of the figure's head and the pattern of decoration. Changing hairstyles lead her to redress the pottery figure to keep in touch with fashion, without losing the generally maternal character of the composition. When asked by clients to modify her style in an attempt to imitate that of her mother, she is prepared to do so, but not entirely able to succeed. Within the demands of the cult for a pottery vessel with a removable lid to incorporate water and pebbles, she has realized objects with a unique, personal style.

In many artistic traditions there are some aspects of creative work which are not subject to the conventional demands of visual communication, but which allow the artist freedom in self-expression; perhaps not unlike the opportunities offered by the cadenza in a classical concerto. Self-decoration in Mount Hagen was taken as an excellent illustration of the complex order embodied in a system of visual communication, but even here there is scope for individual choice in the participants' preparation for display (see fig. 25). This is exemplified by the selection of painted designs available for decorating the face. There is a 'pool' of named designs referred to with figures of speech such as 'like an eddy in a stream', a 'furrow made by falling tears' or 'like the forked tail of an insect', but the choice of these designs, unlike the principle aspects of decoration, does not unequivocally mark out an actor's status in ceremony, nor do they possess magical significance (black paint, it will be remembered, drew the ancestors' support on the group, while red paint attracted wealth and alliances). Nor, the Stratherns suggest, is the terminology by which this pool of designs is known exactly codified: 'observers may pick on different features in their descriptions depending on how they "see" the designs' (1971:111).

The Stratherns are careful to point out that there are limits on how freely actors can select their face decoration. Women paint themselves more lavishly and profusely than do men; a composition judged overcrowded or slapdash on a man would be found appropriate on a woman. Men use single patterns executed in white, while on women red, yellow and blue predominate. At another level, the men who line up to dance as a single group at a ceremony show the value they give to a united front by conveying a certain uniformity in their choice of decoration, which is achieved at practice dances when people can see each other's styles of face-painting and revise their own accordingly (112). Clearly, too, one can infer from the existence of set names for designs that individual face decoration is built out of variations on cultural themes; but the fact that different people, seeing a design, may describe it differently, hints at the fluid character of this field: quite the opposite of the unequivocal oppositions in other aspects of Hagen self-decoration considered in Chapter 3. Each man tends to decorate himself in such a way that certain details of design distinguish him from other participants, or at least set him apart from his neighbours. A 'Big Man' makes particular efforts to arrange that he will stand out; a calculated gamble with the outrageous that may succeed, or may not; and if it fails, then his prestige is diminished, particularly since (as we have seen in other cultures) 'bad decorations are sometimes interpreted as a sign of disfavour on the part of clan ancestors, and no man wishes to appear to have incurred such disfavour' (*ibid.*). Choice is exemplified by the fact that there are no set terms for *combinations* of the named designs; as the Stratherns suggest, had specific compositions become recognized in this way, they 'might then have been considered appropriate to a particular dance and have restricted [the] person's choice of styles' (115).

It is difficult to select examples which illustrate only one of the various aspects of creativity outlined above, but I think it can be suggested that the Hagen case exemplifies something different from the instance of the Yoruba potter. Abatan was expressing her individuality in the manner in which she depicted essential elements of local iconography. While it appears that, in other corners of Yorubaland, potters had quite different concepts of how to execute a pot for the cult of Eyinle, Abatan was not alone in feeling a maternal figure (with or without children) was required. The essence of the Hagen case is, on the contrary, that face decorations are *not* part of the dominant message, but rather individual expressions of an aesthetic sense which cuts across the social motivations dominating self-decoration. The Stratherns compare alternative face-painting designs to alternative ways of pronouncing the sounds of language

(118); whether one be American, Australian or English, one speaks a common language, but with detectable differences which tell us something quite different than 'what is *being said*'. Linguists recognize that at a fine level even individual speakers have their own ways of forming sounds. Whether aesthetic motives are involved or whether we recognize such differences, with attractive metaphors like those of the Hageners' use of face decoration, might be questioned. Perhaps the parallel is therefore not an exact one.

There are several points in the course of preceding chapters where instances have been mentioned of the kinds of creativity illustrated by these two examples. Both Horton, writing of the Kalabari, and Biebuyck, of the Lega, referred to the wide variety of ways in which carvers represented common themes. Presenting evidence that the Kalabari judge carvings only in terms of 'semantic correctness' and not aesthetically, Horton compared the differences to differences of handwriting, an anology much like the parallel drawn by the Stratherns with individual differences of pronunciation. Horton's example is actually closer to that of Abatan's personal style, since it concerns the way carvers represent elements of meaning essential to the sculpture — but they do have some choice in which motifs to include, to convey these essential elements of meaning. Biebuyck, although he too draws an anology with language, suggests the Lega value the creative realization of a new embodiment of a type like 'Mr Many-Heads' (fig. 8), just as her customers appreciate the personal renderings of the Eyinle pot which Abatan and her mother manufactured. The Yolngu material also discussed in Chapter 3 parallels that on the Kalabari in illustrating how artists may choose from a body of motifs to express elements of meaning, while the further discussion of Yolngu style in Chapter 4 reveals individual differences of stylistic expression in Yolngu art, like those of the African potter and sculptors.

Because these types of creativity are not concerned with the aspects of the art work that must be present to achieve visual communication, it could be argued that they do not contradict Lévi-Strauss' assertion that creativity is incompatible with communication in the art of small-scale societies. Perhaps creativity can only occur in these peripheral areas; personal quirks in the articulation of a common language or decorative frills on the fabric of communication?

The next type of creativity comes close to refuting this view. The vast possibilities offered for individual expressions by the existence of a visual grammar demonstrate that creativity is rather an essential component of many art traditions. From the Lévi-Straussian perspective Yolngu bark painting would surely appear a dramatic paradox: a small-scale society composed of family bands with little development of a political hierarchy, subsisting by hunting and gathering and expressing a desire to uphold the unchanging, ancestral order of the Dream Time, which nonetheless produces an endless variety of bark paintings (fig. 30). True, these paintings express certain themes, and embody certain rules, but since these rules contain a visual grammar the creation of new compositions seems almost a necessary part of the tradition; variety is predicated by the need individually to formulate each visual statement freshly. It is worth recalling here Wollheim's view that aesthetic pleasure is created by the judicious mixture of satisfied expectation and surprise at new variations as the structure of the art work unfolds. Morphy suggests that there is a parallel between the creation of new paintings by the Yolngu and the philosophical reflections of senior men upon their own religion. This also reminds one of Aristotle's definition of art. 'Insights that are the result of individual introspection by senior men about the meaning of symbols can become part of the formal body of knowledge that subsequent generations are taught' (Morphy, *op. cit.*: 252). As Aristotle put it, 'to be a master of metaphor ... is a sign of genius'. Even the simple traditional compositions of Central Australian geometric art provide some scope for the creation of new compositions. Munn illustrates the fact during her discussion of women's ritual designs (in Munn, 1973). When performing ritual, Walpiri women paint designs on their bodies that represent ancestral heroes. The arrangement of motifs is guided by the shape of the body, but this framework still leaves room for a variety of modes of combining or multiplying a fixed and limited set of forms. Munn cites the case of a design-theme that depicts an opossum ancestor sitting beside a rock hole. The ancestor appears, in characteristic form, as an arc like that someone might impress on the sand as they sat cross-legged, while the rock hole is depicted as an oval. Munn found various ways of composing the subject (fig. 45): sometimes one rock hole was shown, sometimes several; in one instance, symmetry is created by having two opposed 'sitting-figure' motifs while, in a more subtle case, the rock holes

Figure 45 Walpiri women's body-painting (Central Australia). *After Munn*

i   **ii**   **iii**   **iv**

become an extension of one side of the 'sitting figure', completing the line of the arc. Wherever a visual grammar of form or content exists, such creativity is possible.

It may be that some traditions preserve certain fixed compositions, in the way that Saussure recognized the establishment of certain phrases in language, whose component words remain stuck together however the phrase is used. Humphrey's material on Buryat *ongon* (page 96) suggests these visual compositions generally have a set form, even though their parts are related according to a visual grammar. Nonetheless, Humphrey does record that new *ongon* can be created within the established tradition. She writes: 'there are known cases of the invention of ongon by individuals. Here, a new combination of units, couched in the ongon *language*, becomes institutionalized and becomes a stereotype' (1971:274, Humphrey's emphasis). She mentions two: 'kitten, son of the cat ongon', which was created as a kind of joke at the time of collectivization, but which survived for several years, and the 'two Khori girls ongon' which, writes Humphrey, appeared in the mid-nineteenth century and has since become widely established.

While the Yolngu case suggests vigorous individual creativity, the Buryat instance shows that even individually-created compositions of this kind can acquire a standardized form as successive artists take them over. It is therefore possible to put forward a different argument for the incompatibility of individual creativity with traditional or folk art. The proposition is expressed by A. L. Lloyd, in his study of *Folk Song in England* (Lloyd, 1975). It is not Lévi-Strauss' position, and seems rather to derive from an aspect of Marxist theory that views genuine folk art as the collective creation of the people. True, although a master and his pupils sometimes work together, art is rarely created by a people's committee. Lloyd is able to quote instances where loggers, drovers and frontier guards collectively composed songs (*op. cit.*: 129), but this is not his real argument. Lloyd's view is based on the essential difference between literate and non-literate cultures. Since non-literacy is often cited as one of the defining characters of the small-scale societies studied by anthropology, his view is a relevant one to the present discussion.

In support of his position he refers to the International Folk Music Council, which considered folk music essentially to be 'the product of a musical tradition that has been evolved through the process of oral transmission'. The reason is that it is only in the absence of a documented orthodox version handed down by the composer that the variations and improvements of subsequent performers can have equal validity as realizations of the work, until its eventual form becomes the work of many contributors. Of course, folk music reflects 'variation which springs from the creative impulse of the individual or the group' (note the Durkheimian opposition of individual to collectivity!), and Lloyd admits that, 'Nowadays it is generally conceded that most of the ballads are made by individuals and subsequently reshaped to some extent by the mass of people in the course of being handed on'. His interpretation of this fact, however, is that the group participates not in their creation but in their diffusion (129). The Folk Music Council insisted, in a similar vein, that 'the term [folk music] does not cover composed popular music that has been taken over ready-made by a community and remains unchanged, for it is the re-fashioning and recreation of the music by the community that gives it its folk character'. Once popular compositions are written down by their authors or distributed on record, the audience may still accept or reject the work but successive performers, it is alleged, no longer have the opportunity to modify the composition until in the end it becomes the product of the community, not a single individual.

It is clear that this does constitute an important difference between oral and literate traditions (one that seems to invite a comparison with the contrast between apparently unique works of Renaissance masters and the repeated themes of African sculpture) but it is not, I think, accurately expressed as a contrast between individual creation and collective stereotypy. Literate and oral cultures are alike in living only through embodiment in the words and actions of people. Conversely, like Kant's bird winging through the air, individuals participate in social life only through the medium of culture. Lloyd provides good evidence that in folk song, as in the art of small-scale societies, every fresh creation expresses elements of already-shared culture. No innovation could, or should, materialize outside a shared, cultural tradition but equally cultural traditions demand an act of creation to give them tangible form. It could therefore be argued (and to some extent, I would do so) that the difference between creating a new work and giving a new realization to an old one is simply a difference of degree.

Lloyd writes: 'We know folk singers are capable of making new poems; and the use of traditional commonplaces, so that hands are almost bound to be lilywhite, cheeks are like the roses red, the outlaw's men are merry ... does not affect the poem's claim to originality'. More subtly, he quotes with approval a view reminiscent of Wollheim's, that what the performer of folk songs carries in his mind 'is not a note-for-note accuracy of a written tune; but rather an ideal melody ... which is responsive to the momentary dictates of feeling or verbal necessity'. He adds, 'Traditional performers no less than the performers of fine-art music show varying degrees of skill, talent, taste and imagination' (64). Finally, Lloyd provides his own evidence that successive creations within a cultural tradition may possess a common structure which is realized in images that change with the contemporary context: the struggle is there, whether of warrior against dragon, outlaw against forester, or ploughboy against the rich girl's parents (132). 'Clearly enough they [ballad makers] drew on oral tales, folk legends local or international, the tragedies and comedies of real life, and also on their own artistic imagination and fantasy' (141).

The final source of creativity among these suggested above is the tension, inherent in representational art, between imitation of appearances and the use of limited, regular forms. Swinton (1978) discusses the aesthetics of Inuit (Canadian) Eskimo sculpture in terms of this principle. Aesthetics is for Swinton not just a concern with the pleasing or beautiful, but 'sensuous cognition' (76). In support of the relevance of his definition to Inuit sculpture he cites the modern Eskimo term for printing and carving, which translates: *making a diminutive likeness or model* (cf. 80); it refers to objects that are well-made rather than objects that are beautiful. Swinton's account of Eskimo artistic philosophy matches well with Carpenter's (see page 27). 'Ultimately, quality resides in the successful achievement of giving tangible reality (i.e. form) to subject matter' (83; Swinton's parenthesis). 'Things and events change and cannot be known beforehand. They become real only after they have actually been experienced' (85). The major principle of Inuit aesthetics is, writes Swinton, 'the desire to be as "real" as possible and to achieve this ... through sensuous or tactile means' (71). It is clear that to be 'real' does not entail the slavish reproduction of actual dimensions; sensuous cognition is expressed through the simplification of forms, and some sculptures even portray fantasy objects: grotesque animals and animal spirits (see Swinton's figures 5 and 6, *op. cit*). The essential qualities of the subjects are emphasized: 'textures become more smooth or rough depending on one's needs ... the body action or experience becomes translated into form through increased tensions, bulging volumes, intensified proliferations of shapes' (86).

Incentives to continuity and change

The creative production of new forms appears, it has been argued, to be intrinsic to the perpetuation of many, if not all artistic traditions. What may vary widely is the rate at which such change occurs. Whether it consists of variations on a fixed theme, elaboration towards the baroque or progressive refinement of simple geometric forms, the rate at which new forms are established depends on many factors in the artists' cultural environment. The context may favour conformity with tradition or promote innovation. Sometimes artists compete for a market by seeking to create new and striking designs. To illustrate this Guiart (*op. cit.:* 85-6) cites a case of New Guinea pottery traded for essential subsistence goods from other villages. Nubian house decoration, to be considered in detail below, is a further excellent example. Casting of *edan* figures for the Yoruba Ogboni cult illustrates the contrary situation: here there is considerable effort to adhere closely to established forms (fig. 14). The brass smith must be an older man who works according to methods surrounded by ritual, to produce figures with an established iconography. His work is judged by an official of the cult lodge, the *Apena*, who can reject a casting if he finds it technically ill-made, lacking in the required motifs or stylistic qualities. It is the *Apena* who decides whether a son can follow his father as a brass smith, so controlling the craftsman as well as his products (see page 69). The Ogboni smith is far removed from the Eskimo shaman in his scope for creative expression, but even he manages to incorporate some individuality into his work. Extreme pressure towards continuity does not destroy, merely dampens creativity. The *edan* figures illustrated by Williams and Morton-Williams show significant variations of form, and Williams recognizes this. Although the artist 'is not in a position to take liberties with symbol and meaning' he writes, 'his personal instinct for form, proportion and finish would be certain to distinguish his work' (*op. cit.:* 144).

What social factors help to make the Ogboni tradition so different from that of Eskimo shamanism? The Ogboni cult, it will be remembered, was a stabilizing influence on Oyo government; it was an exclusive body that had rejected the speculation and appeasement of the Orisha cults for a secret knowledge which gave deeper understanding of order, and what threatened it, in the world. This knowledge was carefully guarded from society at large and, in many ways, inverted the principles of popular Yoruba cosmology. The unique position of the Ogboni cult depended on the complexity of the Oyo political system; the cult was constituted as a corporate group with its own internal hierarchy, and initiation ceremonies. There exist a number of other corporate cult groups in Oyo with complementary functions, whose members worship different spirits — such, for instance, as Eshu the Trickster or the various Orisha. Eskimo society, on the other hand, is uncentralized and possesses fewer differentiated social roles. Shamans work as intermediaries between men and the spirit world according to a generalized set of duties: curing illnesses of many kinds, ensuring the prosperity of animal species on whom the community depended for food; duties that in a complex system like that of the Yoruba would almost certainly be divided among a number of experts with distinct status. Eskimo shamans, moreover, do not band together as a discrete group with a specially-constructed headquarters housing ceremonial objects.

It is not, however, just a question of political complexity. The Yoruba culture which produced the Ogboni cult also produced the complementary Orisha cults whose carvings are full of innovation and anecdotal reference to everyday life. Other hunting and gathering cultures, like those of the Australian Aborigines, have exclusive, secret cults. On admission to a cult lodge from which women and children are excluded, Aboriginal youths are shown rock paintings and the carved sacred objects of which Durkheim wrote. Prehistoric rock engravings found in Australia suggest that, in general terms, the style of decoration used on these objects is one which has persisted in Aboriginal culture, unchanged for thousands of years (see Mulvaney, 1969:176).

Both Ogboni cult members and Eskimo shamans have access to spiritual knowledge or experiences from which members of the populace at large are excluded. But they contrast strikingly in that whereas Ogboni cult knowledge is deliberately withheld from the majority, and this exclusivity enhances the cult's autonomy as a force of social control, the Eskimo shaman attempts to communicate his experience to validate his position and to perform his role in ensuring that the whole community benefits from the satisfactory relation he seeks to engineer with the spirit world. I assume that each new shaman will try to establish his claim to play the part by showing that he has something new and different to offer, in terms of spiritual contact; quite the opposite of the Ogboni cult member.

It is a corollary of the fact that both Ogboni cult members and Eskimo shamans have a role which distinguishes them from others in their social system that the associated art objects have in both cases a special inconography to express the ideas linked with that role. In the Ogboni case this iconography is understood only by cult members; in the Eskimo case everyone knows how to 'read' the difference between a distorted spirit mask and a realistic entertainment mask. It is evident that processes exist in the two cultures, processes of education and initiation, which assist the spread or restriction of this understanding. In both cases there is some degree of shared knowledge about the spirit world to which the art objects contribute by giving it tangible expression but, in the shaman's case as well as that of the Ogboni, there is some degree to which this sharing is restricted. It would be rash to assume that every Ogboni cult member believes exactly the same thing about Onile, but there is an orthodox notion that all cult members are privy to a definite body of knowledge which is deliberately taught on initiation. The lack of variation in Ogboni sculpture correlates with this principle of uniform belief, and the stress on order and stability in social life. In the Eskimo case, on the other hand, the shaman is expected, without detailed instruction, to experience a personal vision. Since he must give the vision tangible form in a way which his community will understand there must be a balance between uniqueness and convention: the shaman fails completely to convey his personal, visionary experience only to the extent that conventions and techniques of carving are inadequate to represent it.

These two examples seem to exhibit, in one instance, unequivocal appreciation of innovation, leading to a 'staggering variety' of art objects, in the other, an exclusive aim towards continuity of tradition in which no liberties with form may be taken. It is interesting to compare them with one particular culture's attitude in which people show an ambivalence towards innovation. The ambivalence derives partly from the culture's unwillingness to admit that its art forms change regularly while nonetheless remaining conscious that its present forms might be improved. This is the case of the Abelam, the New Guinea culture studied by Forge. The Abelam live in the southern foothills of the Prince Alexander mountains, to the north of the Sepik. They have an elaborate art tradition associated with the cult of the clan spirits. 'The Abelam artist works within fairly narrow stylistic limits sanctioned by the total society in which he lives' (Forge, 1967:81). It was generally insisted that the design of carvings, representing the clan spirits, executed at the time of Forge's fieldwork was in 'the ancestral style'. Yet Forge found carvings being used which (from genealogical information concerning the carvers) he estimated to be 80 or 100 years old. These were invariably carved in a style different from that of the more recent figures. 'The current style of painting does not fit happily on forms intended for different designs ... Normally, however, the stylistic difference does not worry anyone; it is simply ignored; only when the impertinent ethnographer holding an artist firmly by the wrist has pointed out all the differences will he admit their existence' (83).

Even if innovations are rapidly assimilated to the 'ancestral style', this does not mean that no one notices them when they first occur. On the contrary, they may cause heated debate before being accepted or rejected. Forge argues that artists discuss and evaluate their work in aesthetic terms, while men at large in the community are more concerned with the effectiveness of designs (as a component in ritual) in ensuring the community's future prosperity. As noted before, Abelam art is executed both on the front of large, ceremonial cult houses built by the community (fig. 4), and on carved panels placed within them. When competitive displays of yams are made at ceremonies involving the cult houses, both artists and their community seek to impress the guests who come from other villages with the magnificence of the decorations expressing the desire to make an impression on the visitors (71).

One of Forge's examples of innovation is particularly interesting because it seems to show a departure from convention so radical that it could not be assimilated by the community. A boy who found a curious growth on a tree in the forest decorated it to resemble a human head. This was not well-received by his fellow-villagers (81). Two other examples concern variations on the local form of composition according to which ceremonial house-fronts were decorated. In one instance, the artists commissioned to do the work decided to abandon the design traditional to the community in favour of that used by another village ten miles away, because of the greater length of the long yams grown in the latter village. The change was 'not a great success — the bottom row of [ornamental] heads, which was the principal innovation, was badly painted ... The explanation offered for the bad painting [referred to the fact that] one of the artists died a week later after the painting had been completed; the sorcery that killed him had obviously been working in him and prevented him and his fellows from correctly realizing the super-natural energy inherent in the design' (81-2). Other innovations, however, may be accepted. In one case two artists painting the front of a ceremonial house introduced a narrow band of decoration representing a stylized pattern of leaves which, although similar to the traditional form, had some obvious differences. 'Some of the older men were against it; [but] the two artists and their helpers were adamant — they were both of high reputation and no alternative artists were available; in the event this innovation was much admired in the surrounding villages. The artists were courted by people from other villages who wished to be able to call on them for houses in the future' (81). Two failures and one success story.

The remainder of the chapter will discuss two detailed studies of artistic creativity, one (from New Guinea) examining the role of the artists in a context relatively unfavourable to innovation, the other (from north-east Africa) documenting the rapid evolution of an untraditional art form.

Individual creativity in a conservative context: the Asmat

To appreciate the role of individual creativity in Asmat art, the artist and the work he produces must be placed in their cultural context. The Asmat are a New Guinea people, living in villages close to the south coast on the former Dutch, western half of the island (now Irian Jaya). Gerbrands (1967) deals only slightly with their social structure, but it appears that each village community is an autonomous social group with a certain amount of internal unity and significant internal divisions. The smallest social unit seems to be the extended, patrilineal family. A number of such families, related to each other by kinship ties of one sort or another, are linked by the participation of their menfolk in a group called the *yeu*, whose activities centre around a large meeting house from which women and children are excluded. Young unmarried men spend most of their time there. Families belonging to a single *yeu* live in a single quarter of the village. In the village in which Gerbrands lived there were three *yeu*. The ceremonial house has a number of hearths, one for each constituent family and a central one to represent the united group. Poles carved in the representation of ancestors sometimes stand next to each hearth (28).

Wood is the dominant material of Asmat technology. Stone tools have to be imported from mountainous areas far inland, and there is no clay locally available from which to make pots; in fact the Asmat have no pottery at all. Wood provides not only fuel but the material from which weapons, houses, canoes and paddles are constructed; canoes are essential in the Asmat's swampy, coastal environment. The sago palm tree, moreover, is the chief source of food, yielding an edible pith and harbouring edible beetle grubs.

Traditionally Asmat culture was one in which men achieved status through headhunting. Headhunting had considerable ritual status; some of its imagery was referred to in Chapter 1, page 21. The importance of wood and of headhunting in the lives of the Asmat is conveyed in the symbolism of Asmat culture, and carving provides one of the vehicles through which this symbolism gains tangible expression. Gerbrands writes that *man* and *tree* are almost 'interchangeable concepts' to the Asmat. According to one of their creation myths, people came into being through the agency of a culture hero called Fumeripits, who built a great meeting house and carved a large number of wooden figures of men and women with which to fill it. Fumeripits then began to beat his drum, and as he did so the wooden figures gradually came to life (33-5). Thus, although the modern Asmat woodcarver cannot repeat Fumeripit's miracle, he still occupies a special place of respect in Asmat culture. Nowadays, says Gerbrands, women create bodily life and the woodcarver spiritual ('supernatural') life in the imagery of his carving. Primarily, the carver produces images of headhunting, and to the Asmat, headhunting is the source of life for the community (35); an irony of cultural thought. A second aspect of the tree-equals-person imagery is the idea of the sago palm as a woman: just as the child is created in the womb, so the sago palm, when split open, reveals pith and grubs.

The fruit of the palm tree is identified with the human skull. Thinking of themselves as dark-skinned headhunters, the Asmat consider that dark-plumed birds who eat the fruit are fellow headhunters. Thus the white-tailed hornbill and the black wing cockatoo are special symbols of headhunting, and are frequently represented in Asmat art. The sea pelican is apparently also taken as a symbol of the headhunter: he is black and white, although not fruit-eating (30). Another identification crucial to the imagery of headhunting is that between man and the praying mantis (*wènèt*). This identification is based on the human-like behaviour of the mantis — the way it moves its limbs — and the resemblance of its body and limbs to bits of wood: it is like a piece of wood come to life. Moreover, the female bites off the head of the male during or directly after mating.

The art objects produced by the Asmat are divided by Gerbrands into two categories: the ancestor carvings which are specially produced for ritual and (traditionally) left afterwards to rot in the forest; and decorated but durable utility goods: spears, paddles, signal horns used to give warning of a headhunting attack. Drum handles are frequently carved with an assemblage of the different headhunter motifs: mantis, hornbill, cockatoo or pelican (33); and the heads of these birds also sometimes appear on the decorated prows of canoes, or on bamboo signal horns. It is the mantis which is the most pervasive image. Frequently it is portrayed in a human-like style, so that it appears as a simplified, squatting figure viewed from the side (fig. 46a). When two such simplified mantis representations are joined back-to-back, the resulting image is called a *kavé* — the word for ancestor. The decorative 'wave' pattern seen on Asmat spears is identified by them as a series of highly geometricized mantises (*wènèt*) (fig. 46b i). On the other hand, some artists portray the mantis in a way that, by the inclusion of detail, more clearly identifies it as an insect rather than a man (fig. 46b ii). It is, if you like, a more naturalistic, less geometric style, symptomatic of the work of certain artists.

The status of the woodcarver in Asmat society is to some extent an achieved one, an important fact, because his position therefore depends on the recognition of the skills he possesses by fellow

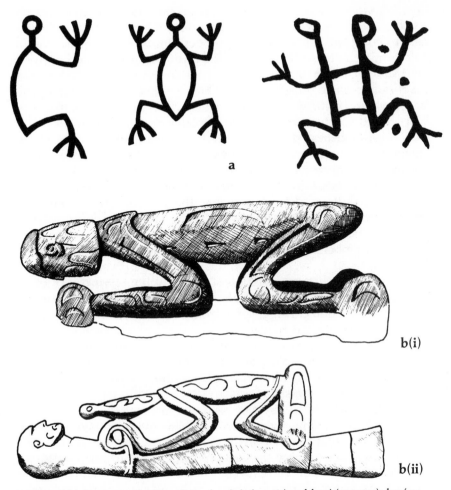

Figure 46   (a) Asmat carving (New Guinea): *wènèt* (mantis) and *kavé* (ancestor); *kavé* as two *wènèt* joined back-to-back, (b) Schematic man/mantis figure of Asmat canoe prow; naturalistic mantis. *After Gerbrandts*

members of his community. The artist always remains a man who, under normal conditions, carries out the ordinary daily activities of preparing sago, hunting and fishing and (in the past) headhunting (36). Equally, every man in the community can manufacture utensils in wood; carving canoes, paddles, digging-sticks and sago-pounders. The recognized artist is essentially someone who is approached by others to produce a carving which is required for use on ritual occasions. Such a man is distinguished by the term *wow-ipits* (*wow* = wood carving; *ipits* = human being). While he is carving the drum, shield or ancestor pole he has been commissioned to produce, the man who has commissioned him takes over the daily tasks the artist would otherwise perform, and during the many days it may take to complete the work also supplies him with delicacies like the hind foot of a pig or the larvae of the capricorn beetle which grow in the trunk of fallen sago palms. The artist may have a better than usual house, since those for whom he has worked will provide their labour when he turns to this major task. Gerbrands states that it is, however, the deference accorded him during daily interaction that most distinguishes the established *wow-ipits* from his fellow villagers. Although the artist appears to gain recognition of his skills through commissions in the first of the two realms of artistic expression isolated by Gerbrands, it would appear that he first reveals his skills in the other realm, that of decorating utilitarian objects. Certainly much of the work photographed and discussed by Gerbrands belongs to this field, and he is able to quote evaluations by other members of the community, on the artists' contributions here.

The man who has achieved his status as a *wow-ipits* has received no organized training. Although every man possesses a practical knowledge of wood carving, some from boyhood show an interest in carving non-utilitarian figures in soft wood, and such boys can be seen spending hours at a time watching established artists at work. Sometimes the young observer is allowed to execute some of the preparatory cutting of a log to be carved, but Gerbrands never saw them receive direct instructions. Social recognition of an artist's worth begins within the circle of his own kin, since the ritual carving with which he is primarily concerned when commissioned by others is that of representing their shared ancestors. Once he has received commissions, presumably, he has a confirmed status; and Gerbrands *did* see younger but recognized artists receiving suggestions or instructions from older *wow-ipits*, even in tasks they had done before. Finally, important artists are those who are commissioned by people outside their own kin group. How is such an artist chosen? Gerbrands asserts that the choice is based solely on aesthetic criteria. 'The average Asmat finds it difficult to express in words why at a given time one artist is preferred to another. In the eight months of my stay [in one village], however, I observed a specific preference for particular woodcarvers several times, a preference which was clearly based on the better aesthetic qualities of their work' (37). However, as will be seen below, there is at least one other criterion which may affect Asmat judgements.

Gerbrands compares the work of a number of young and old Asmat artists, discussing both the aesthetic quality of their work (according to his own, and sometimes also native judgements); and the distinctive use of images and decorative motifs that characterize each artist's work. Following the scheme set out earlier in the chapter, the following sources of creativity may be recognized in Asmat art. Artists possess locally recognized differences in the degree of technical skill with which they execute their work; some achieve flowing lines and uniform compositions while others do not. Choice may be made from within the range of images that convey the themes of Asmat culture — Gerbrands shows that there are social pressures acting differently upon young and old artists in this respect. A third inspiration, at which he hints, is the possibility that different artists may perceive different symbolic equations in the religious imagery. His exigesis of the actions of an artist named Bapmes, at a ritual, and Matjemos' approach to a carving should be referred to (cf. 42, 43 and 53). To clarify the account, we will cite just a few of the men whose work Gerbrands documents, and consider a limited selection of their work with reference to the topic of this chapter.

Gerbrands collected examples of traditional art forms, including signal horns and decorated boat prows. Many of the latter were what he terms 'pseudo-prows' constructed as ornamental items for indigenous exchange and not destined to be attached to a canoe. He also commissioned exotic pieces which placed demands on the artists unlike those imposed by local tradition. This rather curious action has useful results, because it reveals just how difficult it is for an artist to step outside his own culture. One project initiated by the anthropologist was the construction of legs for a table he wanted. When this failed to materialize he requested the artists to decorate the would-be legs with traditional designs. He also attempted to commission small, free-standing ancestor figures, and requested artists to illustrate the motifs they used, in felt-pen drawings.

One man who impressed Gerbrands was the young carver, Matjemos. Matjemos was rated, in the eyes of both the anthropologist and his community, a good artist. Gerbrands describes him at work on one of the 'table legs': 'With a proficient hand and a sharp eye for a balanced distribution over the surface he filled in each of the panels with a rather crowded linear pattern'. Native recognition of his skill was evident in the fact that when a new men's house was being built in his ward, Matjemos was the one who was commissioned to carve the ancestor pole for the central hearth shared by the whole group, as well as the pole for his own extended family hearth. Matjemos had only one revenge killing to his credit and, since other wood carvers of similar age and status were asked only to carve the poles for their own family hearths, Gerbrands argues that the extra commission must be a direct expression of the young man's prestige as an artist. He praises the variety of decoration

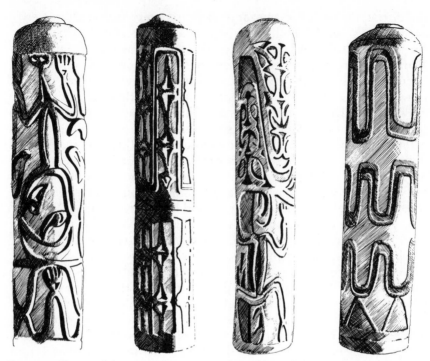

Figure 47   Variety of decorative compositions of signal horns by Matjemos (New Guinea). *After Gerbrandts*

in Matjemos' work, illustrating a number of his signal horns and pointing out how some are decorated with a restrained wavy line while others have their surface completely covered by a small, uniform rectangular motif and on yet others, man/mantis figures extend themselves (fig. 47). For all this diversity, he notes, fellow villagers could always identify Matjemos' work by its characteristic style, which gave continuity among the variety of his decorations (81).

The second artist, Bishur, is older but considered not to be so good. Bishur himself says to Gerbrands while carving his 'table leg', 'I'm afraid you will think it very bad'. Gerbrands considers that Bishur's work lacks the 'flowing certainty' of that by Matjemos and others and describes how he works hesitantly and over-cautiously, as if afraid of making a mistake. From amongst the available decorative motifs, Bishur shows a preference for the (evidently) most sacred *wènèt-kavé* (mantis-ancestor); indeed it was he who first pointed out the link between the two to the anthropologist. The *wènèt-kavé* motif appears on a shield and on signal horns illustrated by Gerbrands. Realistic *wènèt* (mantises) are carved for canoe prows by Bishur.

Tarras is another older wood carver but he, in contrast to Bishur, is considered by the villagers to be their best artist. His work is characterized by a particular leaf-like motif (96). Gerbrands considers Tarras is definitely more skilled than Bishur, but he does not consider him the best artist of the village; arguing that the villagers' judgement was swayed by Tarras' age and prestige in headhunting — a suggestion which evidently contradicts the earlier claim that artists are evaluated on aesthetic grounds alone! At any rate, he suggests, Tarras was thought to be particularly close to the spiritual world portrayed by the artists in their symbolic motifs (102).

Itjembi is an artist of about the same age as Matjemos. When one of the leaders of the village was asked to single out the best-carved of the 'table legs' he selected those of Matjemos and Itjembi: 'He considered the wide grooves Matjemos had made between the panels unusually successful'. In Itjembi's work he praised the balanced distribution of the decoration known as 'Ghostly Fingers' (108). Itjembi's favourite motif is an S-shaped design representing the human body (109), although the anthropologist implies not everyone knew its significance when he writes that the motif was 'generally denominated by the vague term *was*, particularly by those who lack a thorough knowledge of the symbolic significance of the motifs'.

Finally the work of a third young carver is mentioned, to contrast it with the originality of Matjemos and Itjembi. Bifarji's work was readily identifiable by his constant use of a single scroll-like motif (see Gerbrands' plates 110-13) in which the surface of a cylinder to be decorated is divided into two oval panels separated by two half ovals, filling them with a looped motif and occasional stylized birds' heads (118). His ancestor figures were evidently equally uniform; and Gerbrands notes Bifarji's tendency to copy the work of the older, highly-rated Tarras.

How, then, does individual creativity become manifest in Asmat culture? Gerbrands writes that in all the work produced for him a great variation in individual interpretation was evident, ranging from the 'highly personal' to the 'unimaginative imitation of others'. However, the work produced falls clearly into two categories, for some was purely traditional (the bamboo signal horns and boat prows), while other tasks were new (the felt pen drawings and the small free-standing ancestor figures). Obviously the constraints will be different in the two cases.

Gerbrands points to two constraints operative in the traditional work. The younger artists feel a conflict between, on one hand, the sacredness of the ancestor and headhunting motifs which makes them appropriate to wood carving, and on the other, a fear of using them on secular objects like paddles and signal horns (163). Thus, while younger artists show a tendency to abstract decoration, Bishur unabashedly 'filled in the space [of his carvings] with figures of the mantis, representations of ancestors, with other motifs such as the black king cockatoo and the hornbill ... [and] did so with a naturalness which can only be explained by a deep sense of intimacy with the world of ancestors and ghosts' (95). The second constraint is evident in a comparison of Matjemos and Itjembi with Bifarji: some within a single generation, are more inventive in their combination and selection of available motifs than are others.

By contrast, the attempt of Gerbrands to get artists to produce small, free-standing ancestor figures placed severe constraints on all who tried it. The problem is that the usual ancestor figures are neither small nor free-standing, as they are carved for the men's ceremonial houses (fig. 48a). The only small representations of

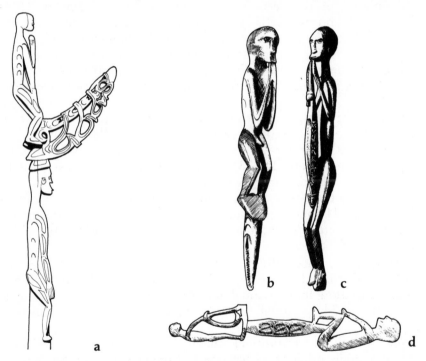

Figure 48   Attempts by Asmat carvers to satisfy Gerbrandts' request for a free-standing ancestor figure: (a) Traditional ancestor figure made for men's ceremonial house, for comparison, (b) Small ancestor figure standing on beak of bird (Ndojokor), (c) Small ancestor figure holding boat/penis derived from paint-mixing bowl (Ndojokor), (d) Two ancestor figures with vestigial paint-mixing bowl between them. *After Gerbrandts*

ancestors are those sometimes incorporated into the handle of a paddle, the ends of a paint-mixing bowl or the prow of a canoe. The principal difficulty in the way of visualizing a free-standing figure is that there is no flat surface in the Asmat house on which such a figure could be stood; hence the reason that in the ceremonial house the large ancestor figures are carved out of the upper length of poles. Gerbrands comments: 'However simple it may appear to be, this assignment went far beyond the limits of the cultural pattern' (164). The strength of the force which a lack of experience of alternatives places upon an artist seeking or requested to innovate is one of the hardest things to visualize cross-culturally.

It is notable that only Bifarji, the unoriginal young artist, managed to produce a free-standing figure for Gerbrands (see plate 96, but note also plate 101 and text, p.125 of Gerbrands, *op. cit.*) . All the others, presumably because they were better integrated into the limits and opportunities of the local tradition, found it difficult to separate such a figure from the context in which it would normally appear. Ndojokor, a talented older artist whose work, like that of Tarras, was imitated by younger carvers, produced figures ending in a stick or on the beak of a bird (fig. 48b), or grasping a small boat/penis derived from the paint-mixing vessels (fig. 48c). Matjemos produced figures set on a minuscule boat or grasping a non-existent pole.

Gerbrands describes how he attempted to present the Asmat artists with a visible example of what he wanted after an 18-year-old, beginner artist brought him a carving based on the typical paint-mixing vessel but with outsize ancestor figures on either end and a minuscule bowl in the middle (fig. 48d). Gerbrands called a number of established artists together and publicly sawed off the figures from the vessel, then stood them upright: he says 'the result evoked hearty laughter', but he asked his interpreter to explain he wanted them to produce the same thing. Whereupon everyone duly came back with carvings combining outsize ancestor figures joined by a vestigial paint vessel (plates *op. cit*. p.167). In this instance, it was only two of the youngest and not-yet-established carvers who constructed anything that approximated to what Gerbrands had sought, but these two were evidently restrained by their elders and betters from bringing him anything else. He guesses that some of the older villagers had made it clear to the very young carvers that the privilege of offering Gerbrands their work and particularly the associated profit in valuable goods, were to be reserved for the older men (165).

The Asmat case reveals a pool of talent and creativity among the artists of a single, small community with a relatively restricted artistic tradition. It shows how artists possess recognized differences of skill, but how, often, their reputation partly depends on other qualities such (in this instance) as age and prowess at headhunting. There are rewards for artistic excellence in the commissions that it brings, the prestige and the possession of a superior house. The local tradition includes sources of inspiration in religious imagery from which artists may select, and a body of decorative motifs from which each carver takes his characteristic designs. Despite these opportunities for the expression of creativity, Asmat artists found difficulty in carrying out requests which took them beyond traditional work. Their attempts to satisfy Gerbrands' exotic demands almost inevitably consisted of modified forms of work with which they were familiar. If it is accepted that such a pool of talent, which can only gain expression through established media, is typical of art even in small-scale societies, the question may be put: what happens when, far from valuing continuity with tradition, the local culture offers an opportunity for innovation? What sources of new work are available to the artist, and how does he present these to the public? The last example documents such a case.

Individual creativity in an innovative context: Nubian house decoration

Marion Wenzel's study of house decoration in Nubia (Wenzel, 1972) was carried out in an area straddling the border between Egypt and the Sudan, which was due to be flooded by the Aswan Dam. Her work was carried out in the early 1960s, taking in villages in the extreme south of Egypt and extending 100 miles into the Sudan (see map fig. 49). In the north of this region, both the entrances to houses and the inside walls of rooms were elaborately decorated with paintings and mud sculptures. Farther south the designs used in these contexts were simpler. Wenzel's purpose was to record the art and discover its significance before it was destroyed by flooding the dam.

When she arrived in the area, it was her belief that the art was the contemporary expression of a long cultural tradition yet, as she studied it, she discovered that to a great extent the forms seen in the north had existed only since the 1920s, and that they had been initiated by one man, Ahmad Batoul. Other men had copied Batoul, competed with him for recognition from the public and in the end superseded him ... his final work was simply to prepare the mud ground on which one of his rivals then painted his successful designs.

From the point of view of house decoration the area that was to be flooded by the Aswan Dam could be divided into two zones,

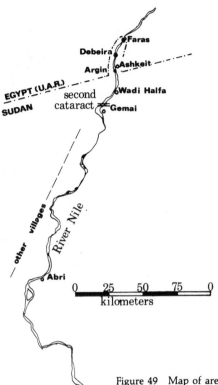

Figure 49   Map of area of Nubian house decoration. *After Wenzel*

separated by the second cataract of the Nile. The impassable stretch
of river formed a barrier to the spread of culture traits and those who
would have carried them. To the north of the second cataract, on the
Egyptian border, house decoration became a specialized trade during
the 1920s; but 40 years later the communities for the next 75 miles
south, up the Nile, gave some clue as to what the situation farther
north must have been like in the early 1920s. If, in the south, a
builder decorated a house which he had just completed he expected
nothing more than a tip when the work was finished. If asked to
plaster and decorate an already-constructed house he would be paid;
but to erect a building itself earned him more money and often took
less time. Rather than lose money by wasting his time on decoration,
the builder would prefer to leave that task to a professional
decorator. The decorator's job was less secure; plastering was a job
which the women of the house could do themselves. The plasterer's
best prospect was to attach himself to a well-established builder. If he
lacked such a patron he sometimes added decoration to his plastering
without being asked to do so and he was paid nothing. The
decoration was only a kind of advertisement for his plastering work.

If the people liked his decoration he might be asked to do more plaster work and, ultimately, he might receive extra payment for the decoration (77).

By 1925 things were already different in the area of Wadi Halfa, to the north of the cataract. The occupation of plasterer and decorator had become prestigious. By 1940, most of those who had been noted decorators during the '30s were hiring others to apply the plaster, and working as professional artists at decoration alone. Far from aspiring to achieve a traditional position, like the *wow-ipits* of the Asmat, the Nubian house decorators had created a new status for themselves. Carpentry also became a specialized occupation. As each man worked at fewer tasks, the composition of designs became more elaborate and each individual artist developed his distinctive style of decoration. To describe, and partially to explain, this process, Marion Wenzel discusses three aspects: (1) the traditional themes in house decoration; (2) the innovative contributions of various artists, and (3) the response to these by those who commissioned them.

As Wenzel points out: 'The environment which allowed menial craftsmen to develop into professional artists required a predisposition of the local inhabitants towards art, which would lead them to hire professionals' (47). Sometimes, indeed, a householder who did his own work could afford particularly brilliant pigments that, had he spent money hiring a professional, he would have been obliged to forego. Local Sudanese Nubians still frequently decorated their own houses; there were distinctive styles characteristic of men, women and boys. The men favoured designs celebrating pilgrimage to Mecca (54). Women's work consisted of painting horizontal wall friezes and decorating house entrances. Wenzel divides their work into two types of composition, 'type A' and 'type B'.

It was a traditional practice to hang a number of objects upon the walls of rooms. Objects used in the wedding ceremony of the householders (mats and basket lids) were hung on the wall 40 days after the wedding, and could not be removed afterwards for more than 7 days without ritual precautions (26). If the originals wore out they were replaced. Other objects were hung on walls in order to avert the evil eye. Such objects had to be bright and startling: mirrors, car headlamps, shells or saucers. The form of decoration Wenzel terms women's 'type A' consisted of a painted band which was said to imitate a mat. The painted design thus appears to derive from the still-extant custom of hanging actual mats upon the wall (67). Baskets were sometimes hung from such a mat and within the painted band representing a mat were placed circles and crosses, said to represent basket lids. Actual basket lids were decorated with a cross, acknowledged locally to be a vestige of the times when Nubia subscribed to Christianity (29). At two localities informants themselves interpreted the painted motif as a skeuomorph: 'Women used to hang up baskets round the room for decoration; they dropped this and replaced it with painting' (74).

Wenzel's category 'type B' decoration is similar. The painted frieze still consists of a double bar, enclosing circles and crosses, but here there are domes, topped by circles or crescents, above the horizontal band (fig. 50). These domes were sometimes said just to be a traditional design, sometimes to represent the tombs of holy men and thus to confer protection on the occupants of the house.

Traditionally, there was little decoration on the outside of the house (fig. 51). It was customary to place small mud relief designs of wild animals on the wall, most frequently representations of the crocodile (92). On the top of the wall above the entrance might be put a crocodile or antelope head, to divert the evil eye from the entrance itself. For the same reason, there would be saucers or plates set into the plaster of the wall, above the doorway. The plates would be decorated with a little painting executed by the women who set them there. In the days before plates, shells were used. Wenzel cites a number of accounts by informants; for instance: 'He remembers the old houses were very small and not decorated ... He had no decoration in his house; he did not like it. But in 1913-14 his lady ordered the plates to be put up, and he found on his return [from Egypt] that all the saucers to the teacups were absent'. China plates appeared in about 1896: 'before plates, women used shells ... Plates appeared with Europeans, after they conquered the area' (93).

Relief decoration north of Wadi Halfa became a locally-acknowledged art form with the work of Ahmad Batoul, who established the style of the 1920s and '30s. His work was copied by others, notably by a man called Jabir Bab al-Kheir and the latter's student Hasan Arabi. Hasan Arabi was extremely successful, and introduced new designs, departing from Ahmad Batoul's motifs.

Figure 50 Nubian interior decoration: traditional women's style, Wenzel's 'type B'. *After Wenzel*

Figure 51 Nubian house front decoration: traditional women's style. *After Wenzel*

Others (like Jabir Bab al-Kheir) were less so, and Ahmad Batoul himself was eventually reduced to working as assistant for Hasan Arabi.

Batoul, the original innovator, was born in Egyptian Nubia in about 1912. He seems to have begun work as a plasterer, assisting an older builder when about 15 years old. At this time, it had become the practice for the plasterer himself to set dinner plates and saucers in the house wall if the women of the house asked him to do so. Batoul's original contribution was to offer to make some special mud relief work around the plates he set, thus relieving the women of the task of painting the surrounding area themselves. Someone recalled: 'When [he] started this work, some people laughed at him and criticized him, because this is the work of women' (96). In his early decoration Batoul both borrowed from the style and motifs used by the women, and in turn influenced them: they adopted his innovations. On doorways his early work used the domes, sometimes with crescents poised on their tops, which characterize the work of the women's interior designs of 'type B'. Other decorations he put on house doorways were simply an elaboration of the designs women put on the entrances to their houses; he added vertical columns to either side of the doorway. An interior room decorated by Batoul at this time simply has horizontal bands, between which are placed a line of domes. It differs from the friezes painted by the women only in that the women placed the domes above the painted bands. This kind of variation suggests a parallel with the simple sort of 'ringing the changes' on established compositions that Munn documented in Walpiri women's body decoration. By 1931, Batoul was being paid to make his mud relief around house entrances, and work from this period shows that his style developed rapidly (fig. 52). No longer did he devise variations on established designs, but instead, following the internal logic of traditional compositions, created increasingly baroque elaborations upon them. On doorways, the number of columns either side of the entrance proliferated, and so did the arches and domes represented in relief above the door. He then transferred these newly-devised designs to the interior decoration of rooms, and adopted a triangular punch to cut incised patterns in the relief, giving his compositions a more delicate appearance.

Between 1928 and 1935 Batoul also introduced a new design to the outside house wall: the portrayal in relief of a lion with a sword on either side of the decorated entrance. Wenzel suggests that this design may have been taken from the Egyptian marriage chests on which it frequently appears, and which were locally highly-valued objects during the early years of the century. This development seems

Figure 52 Ahmad Batoul: development of house entrance design. *After Wenzel*

therefore not to come from the grammar of local design, but rather to be an external contribution. It is possible, however, that its acceptability stemmed from a local precedent, the small reliefs of wild animals which people remembered seeing on house fronts at the beginning of the century (112). Although Batoul had adopted the lion-with-sword design to make his own work stand out from the imitators, the innovation was not at first universally accepted: 'We laugh[ed] at Batoul sometimes saying these lions carry a sword and lions cannot carry a sword' (109). Because Batoul adopted the motif to set his work apart from those who had begun to copy him, this — in turn — stimulated them to rival him with alternative designs. Jabir Bab al-Kheir recalled: 'then I made this painted lion, not with a sword but with a gun, to overcome this competition ... Then he [Batoul] said, "No lions without teeth and eyes", and started putting them in specially ... I introduced men shooting lions as competition to Batoul. As I liked firearms and shooting, I introduced crocodile shooting in competition to the lion with the sword' (111). As Wenzel notes, it was the rivalry between the artists (presumably to seek more, and better commissions) which provoked this fresh burst of development upon a theme.

Ahmad Batoul's work went into a decline after 1940. He dropped the lion motif, and began to leave commissions unfinished. One informant reported that when asked to complete his works, Batoul quarrelled with his clients and abandoned it. Hasan Arabi (the successful pupil of Jabir Bab al-Kheir) was called in to complete the reliefs.

Jabir Bab al-Kheir was the son of a slave, who had been brought to the region from the south. Al-Kheir himself was born in Debeira, and began his career as an artist when he decorated the house in which he lived (the house of his 'patron') with 'a woman's head with horns, just for fun' (116). Al-Kheir was less successful than Batoul. He worked just between 1929 and 1948, only sufficiently long to save enough to purchase one cow. He never gained enough to become married, and in 1964 Wenzel found him living alone in an undecorated hovel — although 'he had always kept a small talismanic packet of green powder paint in the pocket of his robe' (120). Al-Kheir 'took great pride in his work and held to his own strict standards of how he wanted it to look. For these standards, he was willing to suffer unpopularity'. Batoul had included moulded horn shapes on top of some of the pillars in his early decoration to house entrances. Batoul later dropped this motif, but al-Kheir retained it. He explained to Wenzel: 'people don't ask for horns, I put them if I feel like it. Horns came with the beginning of this art' (122). After 1944 al-Kheir refused to set saucers into the plaster amongst his designs. He announced that saucers were old-fashioned and that they spoiled his compositions because they had a surface texture different from the rest of the design. He preferred to make white circles instead. 'This, according to his clients, was too much to accept. They felt it was more important to have saucers on doorways than to have relief designs, *since saucers were necessary to divert the evil eye*' (123, my emphasis). They also felt he spent too much time on his work. In 1947 al-Kheir fell the victim of sorcery, and was ill for three months. Shortly afterwards his tools disappeared, and he retired from house decoration until invited to decorate the wall of a house occupied by an American expedition in the area in 1964.

Hasan Arabi, the student of al-Kheir who eventually came to

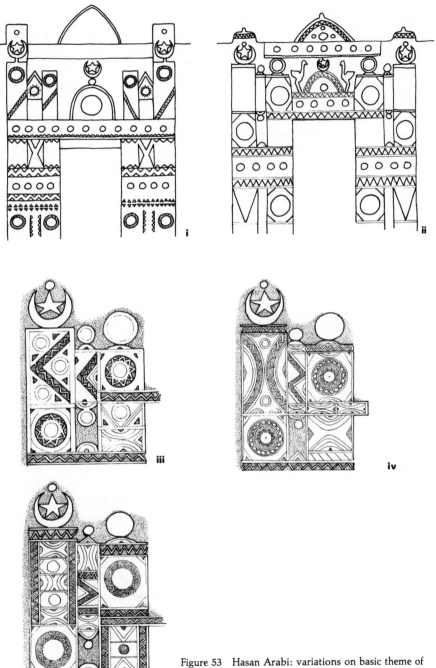

Figure 53   Hasan Arabi: variations on basic theme of
house entrance design. *After Wenzel*

employ Batoul as his assistant, began with a formula for the decoration of house entrances which allowed numerous developments on a basic organizational theme (fig. 53). The theme is clearly a derivation of the style evolved from the traditional women's pattern by Batoul but one that allows continuous generation of variants, rather than the progressive elaboration required by Batoul's technique. Two broad columns flank either side of the entrance, crossed by horizontal bands of circles and saucers. The outer columns were surmounted by circles and stars, and a pair of long-legged birds facing each other above the lintel. Like the man with whom he had worked, al-Kheir, Hasan Arabi felt he knew better what formed a pleasing design than did his clients. Hasan Arabi, however, was successful in effecting a change in public taste. He began modelling his reliefs in the natural colours of sand and mud but, after requests from his clients, used first white, then colour, on house fronts. Yet he came to the conclusion that colours 'did not look well on house exteriors', and reverted to the use of white. Since few of the saucers offered him by householders were white, he followed al-Kheir in substituting white circles in lime. Unlike al-Kheir, however, he convinced people that this was a good thing.

In decorating house interiors, Hasan Arabi began by applying bands of coloured geometric design (which can be said to resemble the traditional women's decoration to some extent); but later turned to motifs which he took from imported European biscuit tins. As with the marriage chests, the tins appear to provide inspiration to a local artist looking for a new and distinctive design to incorporate into his work. The designs he adopted in the 1940s were typical of tins manufactured ten to twenty years earlier. Wenzel points out that, being a luxury item in the shops of Cairo and Khartoum, such tins might well have taken some time to be sold, and then would probably be bought by European residents who would in turn pass them on to a Nubian servant only some time later, when the tin was empty. The servant himself might not bring the tin back to his home village until he retired from employment in the capital (150-1).

House decoration came to an end when the villagers were removed from the area to be flooded, and settled many miles away in small concrete houses built for them by the government. Yet already, by the late 1950s, the fashion for elaborate decoration was beginning to die. Wenzel was told: 'The custom of making painted or relief decoration outside the house is becoming old, and people are now satisfied with decoration inside the house only' (175). Whether or not interior decoration would continue in the new habitat was uncertain. Al-Kheir at least had been inspired to begin again, partly by Wenzel's interest in his old work.

What Wenzel has so well documented from the period when the art flourished is how the search for more work, and competition among themselves, encouraged artists to follow through the possibilities that traditional design offered for creative composition, and look for further inspiration in exotic forms brought to the region. The artists express the aesthetic pleasure they found from their work, but the rest of the community (like that of the Abelam) was often more concerned with the more useful aspects of house decoration, averting the evil eye with shining plates or fierce animals. Thus, although much of their new work grew out of local tradition, Nubian house decorators were confronted with the need to 'educate the public' or lose their position through lack of popular support. But the artists did not have sole access to aesthetic values. Some villagers decorated their own houses. Others criticized the work of one artist because it was not symmetrical, telling Wenzel that 'only those people hired him who could not afford someone better' (153), and so the community must have helped shape the progress of individual inspiration through its participation in shared values.

This chapter opened by outlining the artistic role played by Eskimo shamans in southern Alaska. It was suggested that the shaman apparently faced an impossible task in first experiencing a unique, individual vision, but then frequently needing to commission others to translate his personal experience into an expression of it which his community could understand. The task was made possible by the fact that there existed established conventions for depicting the spirits shamans encounter — not in fixed forms, but rules of composition and iconography which made possible what the anthropologist termed 'a staggering number and variety of masks'. It was argued that the opposition of individual experience to collective tradition was therefore a false one, albeit one long-established in anthropology. A recapitulation of various aspects of the anthropology of art that had been described in preceding chapters showed that creativity is, at many levels, a necessary part of the perpetuation of perhaps all shared art traditions. Despite the richness and diversity of the art created by human cultures around the world, artists everywhere are constrained and stimulated by certain common aims, common problems and common procedures. Instead of setting our own culture apart from those of the small-scale, non-literate communities sometimes called 'primitive', perhaps we could thus learn from their accumulated experiences.

References

Attneave, F. (1974) Multistability in perception. In Held, R. (ed.), *op. cit.* 91-9.

Bailey, F.G. (1969) *Stratagems and Spoils.* Oxford, Blackwell.

Banton, M. (ed.) (1966) *Anthropological Approaches to the Study of Religion.* London, Tavistock (ASA Monograph series).

Barth, F. (1967) On the study of social change. *American Anthropologist,* **69**, 661-9.

Barthes, R. (1967) *Elements of Semiology.* Trans. A. Lavers and C. Smith. London, Cape.

Bartlett, F.C. (1932) *Remembering: a study in experimental and social psychology.* Cambridge, University Press.

Bateson, G. (1973) Style, grace and information in primitive art. In Bateson, G., *Steps to an Ecology of Mind.* St Albans (England), Paladin. 101-25.

Beattie, J. (1966) Ritual and social change. *Man* (n.s.), **1**, 60-74.

Biebuyck, D. (ed.) (1969) *Tradition and Creativity in Tribal Art.* Berkeley, California University Press.

Biebuyck, D. (1973) *The Lega: art, initiation and moral philosophy.* Berkeley, California University Press.

Blackwood, B. (1961) Comment on Haselberger's method of studying ethnological art. *Current Anthropology,* **2**, 360.

Blundell, V., and Layton, R. (1978) Marriage, myth and models of exchange in the west Kimberleys. In Specht, J., and White, J.P. (eds.), *Trade and Exchange in Oceania and Australia. Mankind,* 11(3). Sydney, Australian Museum. 231-45.

Boas, F. (1955) *Primitive Art.* New York, Dover.

Bohannan, L. (1958) Political aspects of Tiv social organisation. In Middleton, J., and Tait, D. (eds.), *Tribes without Rulers: studies in African segmentary systems.* London, Routledge. 33-66.

Bradbury, R.E. (1957) *The Benin Kingdom and the Edo-Speaking People of Southwestern Nigeria.* Ethnographic Survey of West Africa, pt. 13. London, International African Institute.

Carpenter, E. (1961) Comment on Haselberger's method of studying ethnological art. *Current Anthropology,* **2**, 361-3.

Cory, F. (1956) *African figurines: their ceremonial use in puberty rites in Tanganyika.* London, Faber.

Cutting, J.E., and Eimas, P. (1975) Phonetic feature analysis and the processing of speech in infants. In Kavanagh, J.F., and Cutting, J.

(eds.), *The Role of Speech in Language*. Cambridge, Mass., M.I.T. Press. 127-48.

Deregowski, J.B. (1972) Pictorial representation and culture. *Scientific American* (November 1972), 82-8.

Deregowski, J.B. (1973) Illusion and culture. In Gregory, R.L., and Gombrich, E.H. (eds.), *op. cit.* 160-91.

Durkheim, E. (1915) *The Elementary Forms of the Religious Life*. Trans. J.W. Swain, London, Allen and Unwin.

Durkheim, E. (1947) *The Division of Labour in Society*. Trans. G. Simpson. Glencoe, I11., Free Press.

Durkheim, E. (1964) *The Rules of Sociological Method*. Trans. S.A. Solovay and J.H. Mueller. Glencoe, I11., Free Press.

Emery, W.B. (1965) *Archaic Egypt*. Harmondsworth, Penguin.

Escher, M.C. (1972) *The Graphic Work of M.C. Escher*. London, Pan/Ballantine.

Evans-Pritchard, E.E. (1937) *Witchcraft, Oracles and Magic among the Azande*. Oxford, University Press.

Fagg, W. (1970) *Divine Kingship in Africa*. London, Trustees of British Museum.

Finley, M.I. (1966) *The Ancient Greeks*. Harmondsworth, Penguin.

Firth, R. (1939) *Primitive Polynesian Economy*. London, Routledge.

Firth, R. (1952) The social framework of primitive art. In Firth, R., *Elements of Social Organization*. London, Watts. 155-82.

Forde, C.D. (1948) *Habitat, Economy and Society*. London, Methuen.

Foreman, W., and Dark, P. (1960) *Benin Art*. London, Hamlyn.

Forge J.A.W. (1965) Art and society in the Sepik. *Proc. Royal Anthropological Institute*, 1965, 23-31.

Forge, J.A.W. (1967) The Abelam artist. In Freedman, M. (ed.), *Social Organization: essays presented to Raymond Firth*. London, Cass.

Forge, J.A.W. (1970) Learning to see in New Guinea. In Mayer, P. (ed.), *Socialization: the approach from social anthropology*. London, Tavistock. 269-91.

Fortes, M. (1940) The political system of the Tallensi. In Fortes, M., and Evans-Pritchard, E.E. (eds.), *African Political Systems*. Oxford University Press for International African Institute. 239-71.

Fraser, D. (1972) The fish-legged figure in Benin and Yoruba art. In Fraser, D., and Cole, H. (eds.), *op. cit.* 261-94.

Fraser, D., and Cole, H. (eds.) (1972) *African Art and Leadership*. Wisconsin, University Press.

Friedman, J. (1975) Tribes, states and transformations. In Bloch, M. (ed.), *Marxist Analyses and Social Anthropology*. London,

Malaby (ASA Studies series, 2). 161-202.

Gardiner, A. (1966) *Egypt of the Pharaohs*. Oxford, University Press.

Geertz, C. (1966) Religion as a cultural system. In Banton, M. (ed.), *op. cit.* 1-16.

Gell, A. (1975) *Metamorphosis of the Cassowaries*. London, Athlone Press (LSE Monograph series).

Gellner, E. (1964) *Thought and Change*. London, Weidenfeld.

Gennep, A. van (1960) *The Rites of Passage*. Trans. M.B. Vizedom and G.L. Caffee. London, Routledge.

Gerbrands, A.A. (1967) *Wow-Ipits: eight Asmat carvers of New Guinea*. The Hague, Mouton.

Gombrich, E.H. (1960) *Art and Illusion: a study in the psychology of pictorial representation*. London, Phaidon.

Gombrich, E.H. (1972) The visual image. *Scientific American* (September 1972), 82-96.

Goodnow, J. (1977) Schemas and variations: concepts and techniques from analyses of children's drawings. In Ucko, P.J. (ed.), *op. cit.* 66-72.

Goody, J. (1961) Religion and ritual, the definitional problem. *British Journal of Sociology*, **12**, 142-64.

Greenhalgh, M., and Megaw, V. (eds.) (1978) *Art in Society: studies in style, culture and aesthetics*. London, Duckworth.

Gregory, R.L. (1966) *Eye and Brain: the psychology of seeing*. London, Weidenfeld (World University Library series).

Gregory, R.L. (1973) The confounded eye. In Gregory, R.L., and Gombrich, E.H. (eds.), *op. cit.* 49-95.

Gregory, R.L. (1974) Visual illusions. In Held, R. (ed.), *op. cit.* 48-58.

Gregory, R.L., and Gombrich, E.H. (eds.) (1973) *Illusion in Nature and Art*. London, Duckworth.

Grube, G.M.A. (1974) *Plato's Republic*. Indianapolis, Hackett.

Guiart, J. (1969) The concept of the norm in the art of some Oceanian societies. In Biebuyck, D. (ed.), *op. cit.* 84-97.

Harmon, L.D. (1974) The recognition of faces. In Held, R. (ed.), *op. cit.* 110-12.

Haselberger, H. (1961) Method of studying ethnological art. *Current Anthropology*, **2**, 341-84.

Held, R. (ed.) (1974) *Image, Object and Illusion: readings from The Scientific American*. San Francisco, Freeman.

Hertz, R. (1960) *Death* and *The Right Hand*. Trans. R. and C. Needham. London, Cohen and West.

Horton, R. (1960) A definition of religion and its uses. *Journal of the Royal Anthropological Institute*, **90**, 201-26.

Horton, R. (1964) Ritual man in Africa. *Africa,* **34,** 85-104.

Horton, R. (1965) *Kalabari Sculpture.* Lagos, Department of Antiquities.

House, A.H., and Hardie, C. (1956) *Aristotle's Poetics, a course of eight lectures.* London, Hart-Davis.

Hudson, W. (1960) Pictorial depth perception in subcultural groups in Africa. *Journal of Social Psychology,* **52,** 183-208.

Humphrey, C. (1971) Some ideas of Saussure applied to Buryat magical drawings. In Ardener, E. (ed.), *Social Anthropology and Language.* London, Tavistock (ASA Monograph series). 271-90.

Humphrey C. (1973) Some ritual techniques in the bull-cult of the Buryat Mongols. *Proc. Royal Anthropological Institute,* 1973, 15-27.

Kelly, G.A. (1963) *A Theory of Personality: the psychology of personal constructs.* New York, Norton.

Kuhn, T.S. (1962) *The Structure of Scientific Revolutions.* Chicago, University Press.

Lane, M. (1970) *Structuralism, a reader.* London, Cape.

Layton, R. (1970) Myth as language in Aboriginal Arnhem Land. *Man* (n.s.), **5,** 483-97.

Layton, R. (1971) Patterns of informal interaction in Pellaport. In Bailey, F.G. (ed.), *Gifts and Poison.* Oxford Blackwell. 97-118.

Layton, R. (1977) Naturalism and cultural relativity in art. In Ucko, P.J. (ed.), *op. cit.* 33-43.

Leach, E.R. (1961) *Rethinking Anthropology.* London, Athlone Press (LSE Monograph series).

Lévi-Strauss, C. (1960) *Entretiens avec Claude Lévi-Strauss.* Paris, Plon. (French text by Georges Charbonnier; my translation of extracts cited).

Lévi-Strauss, C. (1963) *Structural Anthropology.* Trans. C. Jacobson and B.G. Schoepf. New York, Basic Books.

Lévi-Strauss, C. (1966) *The Savage Mind.* London, Weidenfeld.

Lewis, I.M. (1975) *Ecstatic Religion: an anthropological study of spirit possession and shamanism.* Harmondsworth, Penguin.

Lienhardt, G. (1961) *Divinity and Experience.* Oxford, University Press.

Linton, R. (1936) *The Study of Man.* New York, Appleton-Century-Crofts.

Little, K. (1966) The political system of the Poro. *Africa,* **35,** 349-65, and **36,** 62-71.

Lloyd, A.L. (1975) *Folk Song in England.* St Albans (England), Paladin.

McElroy, W.A. (1952) Aesthetic appreciation in Aborigines of Arnhem Land. *Oceania,* **23,** 81-94.

Macintosh, N.W.G. (1977) Beswick Creek cave two decades later: a reappraisal. In Ucko, P.J. (ed.), *op. cit.* 191-7.

Malinowski, B. (1948) *Magic, Science and Religion and other essays.* Glencoe, I11., Free Press.

Morphy, F. (1973) *Anthropological and other interpretations of changes in art from the North-west Coast.* M. Phil. thesis, University of London.

Morphy, F. (1977) The social significance of schematization in North-west Coast American Indian art. In Ucko, P.J. (ed.), *op. cit.* 73-6.

Morphy, H. (1977) *Too Many Meanings.* Ph.D. thesis, Australian National University.

Morphy, H. (1977b) Schematization to conventionalization: a possible trend in Yirrkala bark paintings. In Ucko (ed.), *op. cit.* 198-204.

Morphy, H. (1977c) Yingapungapu — ground sculpture as bark painting. In Ucko (ed.), *op. cit.* 205-209.

Morphy, H. (1978) *Manggalili Art. Paintings by the Aboriginal artists Narritjin and Banapana Maymuru.* Canberra, Faculty of Arts, Australian National University.

Morphy, H. (1979) Past and future in land rights poster. *Aboriginal News* 3, no. 6. Canberra, Department of Aboriginal Affairs.

Morton-Williams, P. (1960) The Yoruba Ogboni cult in Oyo. *Africa,* 30, 362-74.

Morton-Williams, P. (1964) The cosmology and cult organization of the Oyo Yoruba. *Africa,* 34, 243-61.

Mountford, C.P. (1961) The artist and his art in an Australian Aboriginal society. In Smith, M.W. (ed.), *The Artist in Tribal Society,* London, Royal Anthropological Institute (Occasional Papers, 15). 1-14.

Mulvaney, D.J. (1969) *The Prehistory of Australia.* London, Thames and Hudson.

Munn, N. (1966) Visual categories: an approach to the study of representational systems. *American Anthropologist,* 68, 936-50.

Munn, N. (1973) *Walpiri Iconography.* Ithaca, Cornell University Press.

Neisser, U. (1974) The processes of vision. In Held, R. (ed.), *op. cit.* 4-11.

Newcomer, P.J. (1972) The Nuer are Dinka: an essay on origins and environmental determinism. *Man* (n.s.), 7, 5-11.

Noton, D. and Stark, L. (1974) Eye movement and visual perception. In Held, R. (ed.), *op. cit.* 113-22.

Panofsky, E. (1955) *Meaning in the Visual Arts.* Harmondsworth, Penguin.

Petrie, H., and Petrie, W.M.F. (1953) *Ceremonial Slate Palettes.* British School of Egyptian Archaeology, paper LXVI.

Radcliffe-Brown, A.R. (1952) *Structure and Function in Primitive Society.* London, Cohen and West.

Ray, D.J., and Blaker, A.A. (1967) *Eskimo Masks: art and ceremony.* Washington, University Press.

Rock, I. (1974) The perception of disoriented figures. In Held, R. (ed.), *op. cit.* 71-8.

Sahlins, M.D. (1961) The segmentary lineage: an organization of predatory expansion. *American Anthropologist, 63,* 322-45.

Sahlins, M.D. (1974) *Stone Age Economics.* London, Tavistock.

Saussure, F. de (1959) *Course in General Linguistics.* Trans. C. Bally and A. Sechehaye. London, Owen.

Segall, M.H., Campbell, D.T., and Herskovits, M.J. (1966) *The Influence of Culture on Visual Perception.* New York, Bobs-Merrill.

Shapiro, M. (1953) Style. In Kroeber, A.L. (ed.), *Anthropology Today.* Chicago, University Press. 283-311.

Southall, A. (1976) Nuer and Dinka are people: ecology, ethnicity and logical possibility. *Man* (n.s.), **11,** 463-91.

Stanner, W.E.H. (1963) *On Aboriginal Religion.* Oceania Monographs 11.

Stevenson, R.F. (1968) *Population and Political Systems in Tropical Africa.* New York, Columbia University Press.

Stevenson-Smith, W. (1958) *The Art and Architecture of Ancient Egypt.* Harmondsworth, Penguin.

Strathern, A., and Strathern, M. (1972) *Self-Decoration in Mount Hagen.* London, Duckworth.

Swinton, G. (1978) Touch and the real: contemporary Inuit aesthetics. In Greenhalgh, M., and Megaw, V. (eds.), *op. cit.* 71-88.

Tambiah, S.J. (1968) The magical power of words. *Man* (n.s.), **3,** 175-208.

Terray, E. (1972) *Marxism and 'Primitive' Societies.* Trans. M. Klopper. New York, Monthly Review Press.

Thomson, R. (1969) Abatan: a master potter of the Egbado Yoruba. In Biebuyck, D. (ed.), *op. cit.* 120-82.

Trigger, B.G. (1968) *Beyond History: the methods of prehistory.* New York, Holt, Rinehart.

Turner, V.W. (1962) *Chihamba, the White Spirit.* Manchester, University Press (Rhodes-Livingstone Institute paper 33).

Turner, V.W. (1965) Colour classification in Ndembu ritual. In Banton, M. (ed.), *op. cit.* 47-84.

Turner, V.W. (1967) *The Forest of Symbols: aspects of Ndembu ritual.* Ithaca, Cornell University Press.

Ucko, P.J., and Rosenfeld, A. (1967) *Palaeolithic Cave Art.* London, Weidenfeld (World University Library series).

Ucko, P.J., and Dimbleby, G.W. (eds.) (1969) *The Domestication of Plants and Animals.* London, Duckworth.

Ucko, P.J. (ed.) (1977) *Form in Indigenous Art.* Canberra, Australian Institute of Aboriginal Studies.

Weber, M. (1947) *The Theory of Social and Economic Organization.* Glencoe, I11., Free Press.

Wenzel, M. (1972) *House Decoration in Nubia.* London, Duckworth.

Willett, F. (1972) Ife, the art of an ancient Nigerian aristocracy. In Fraser, D., and Cole, H. (eds.), *op. cit.* 209-26.

Williams, D. (1964) Iconology of the Yoruba edan Ogboni. *Africa,* **34**, 139-66.

Wilson, B. (ed.) (1970) *Rationality.* Oxford, Blackwell.

Wollheim, R. (1970) *Art and its Objects.* Harmondsworth, Penguin.

Index

Index

poetry: 130−1
symbolism: 112
visual grammar: 113−14, 186
visual imagery: 100
fig. 22
BUSHMAN, KALAHARI, subsistence 82−3
Bwami cult (among Lega)
and lineage segments: 53, 60
comparison with Ogboni cult: 63 64
comparison with Poro cult: 81
control of wealth through: 52, 55
goals of: 8
grades in: 51
initiation into: 48, 49−50, 52, 56−8, 59, 60
proverbs: 48

calligraphy: 7, 27
capitalism: 45, 83
car-ownership: 38
Carpenter, E.: 27, 68, 188
cartography: 6, 103−4, (123−4), 130
children's drawings: 162
Chomsky, N.: 138
clan, definition of: 47
classification, cultural systems of: 87, 100, 107, 112, 165
colour
perception of: 136−8
significance of: 101, 107, 108, 111−12
Cook, Captain J.: 153
cubism: 143
culture: 15, 111, 117; see also classification, cultural systems of
Cutting, J.E. and Eimas, P.: 138−9
cyclical developments
in art styles: 77, 143
in government: 84, 85
in society: 45

Dark, P.: 3
density gradients: 147−8
depth, perception of: 145
Deregowski, J.B.
on naturalism: 144−5, 148, 170
on split representation and twisted persepective: 152, 157, 158
DIDA: 84
diffusion: 74, 76, (210)
DINKA
ritual: 39
songs: 19
Duchamp, M.: 6
Durkheim, E.
on distinctive features of social life: 31, 93−4

on innovation: 178, (187)
on population and social change: 79
on religion: 31, 32, 36−7, 86, 132
on totemic art: 89, 90, 91−2, 121, 190
on totemism: 32, 86−8, 90−1, 101, 129, 134, 167

Edan (brass figures from Ogboni cult): 64, 67, 189; Plate 3; fig. 14
EGBADO YORUBA, Eyinle
cult: 179−82, 183; figs. 43, 44
EGYPT, CLASSICAL: 144, 151
EGYPT, PROTODYNASTIC
iconography and visual grammar: 116−23, 151
political development of: 114−15
registers: 125
visual metaphors in art: 21
figs. 6, 27, 28
Emery, W.B.: 117
equilibrium, social: 45
Ernst, Max: 21
Escher, M.C.: 161
ESKIMO, ALASKAN
cosmology: 173−4
masks: 173−6, 190, 212; Plate 14; fig. 42
shamanism: 172−6, 189, 190
ESKIMO carving, aim of: 27; Plates 1, 2
ESKIMO, INUIT, aesthetics: 188
ethology: 38
Evans-Pritchard, E.E.: 35, 36
Eyinle cult: Plate 15; see also EGBADO YORUBA
evolution
in art: 1, 79, 123, 144, 158
in political structures: 143
in religion: 32, 34, 38, 39
of society: 45, 82

Fagg, W.: 69−74, 77−9, 143−4
family, the: 43
feedback: 45
fetishes: 6
feudalism:43
figurines: 6, 42, 43
Finley, M.I.: 4
Firth, R.
on aesthetics: 11, 15
on 'reading' visual images cross-culturally: 23, 25
on social context of art: 41
on style: 151
folk music: 186
Forde, C.D.: 79
Forge, J.A.W.

Index

Kant, I.: 178
Kelly, G.: 99–100
Kuhn, T.S.: 33

Leach, E.R.
  on communication in ritual: 93
  on comparative anthropology:43
leadership
  in centralized chiefdoms: 49, 84
  in relation to production and
    exchange: 83, 100
  in uncentralized societies: 45, 47,
    49, 82, 84, 100
LEGA
  cultural 'types' expressed in
    sculpture: 28, 179
  economy: 7
  evaluation of sculpture: 9–10, 12,
    25, 179
  iconography of sculpture: 23
  leadership among: 50, 60, 83, 84,
    85
  mnemonic function of carvings:
    59, 86
  ownership of art objects: 48,
    53–5, 60
  ownership of ivory: 72
  parallel content of art forms: 20
  patrilineal descent among: 47
  proverbs: 20–1, 49, 59, 60, 109,
    132
  use of natural objects in ritual: 8,
    9, 108
  use of sculpture in ritual: 59, 108
  figs. 3, 12, 13
  see also Bwami cult;
    Mr Many-Heads
Lévi-Strauss, C.
  analysis of Baudelaire sonnet with
    R. Jakobson: 19, 132
  critique by Marxists: 43–4, 45
  on art and communication: 93–4,
    97, 176, 184
  on cultural symbols: 107
  on exchange systems: 43
  on myth: 43, 88, 128
  on shamanism: 172
  on structuralism: 42, 99, (138)
  on totemism: 87, 88
Lewis, I.M.: 172
Lienhardt, G.: 19, 39
lineage
  and centralized authority: 61
  dynamic aspect: 58
  segments: 47, 52
Linton, R.: 15–16
Little, K.
  on cyclic development in chiefdoms
    84–5

  on Poro cult: 81
Lloyd, A.L.: 186, 187
'lost wax' technique of brass casting:
  69, 72
Löwy: 141, 142, 148

McElroy, W.A.: 13
MacIntosh, N.G.W.: 147
MAGDELENIAN: 1
magic
  among Azende: 35, 36
  among Hageners: 182
  among Tiv: 51
  among Trobrianders: 38
  among Yoruba: 65
Magritte, R.: 21
Malinowski, B.
  critique of Durkheim on religion:
    37
  on social analysis: 74
MAMPRUSI: 45
Many-Heads, Mr (Lega carving type):
  29, 48, 184; fig. 8
marriage, economic significance of:
  56
Marx, Karl
  on contradictions in belief systems:
    35
  on social change: 45
  on surplus production: 82, 83
Marxist interpretation of folk music:
  186
masks: 42, 43
  Eskimo: 173–6, 190
  Plates 11, 12, 14; figs. 11, 36, 42
medium (influence of): 4
Meillassoux, C.: 81, 83–4
metaphor
  among Lega: 8, 109, 128
  as characteristic of art and poetry:
    5, 35, 185
  relation with aesthetics: 130, 132
  visual in Kalabari and protodynastic
    Egyptian art: 21–2
  visual in Western and Asmat art:21
mnemonic devices, in art and ritual:
  39, 59, 86
Moby Dick: 111
mode of production: 80–1
models
  religious: 32, 36
  scientific: 33, 40, 132
  sources of: 32
Morphy, F.: 155
Morphy, H.
  on Durkheim's analysis of religion:
    86
  on totemism: 87
  on Yolngu bark paintings: 88, 90,

224

Index

religion
  definition of: 33
  Durkheim on source of: 32
  evolution of: 34, 38, (39)
Renaissance: 3
  motifs, parallel with West Africa:
    74
  style: 143, 151
  uniqueness of art objects: 25, 176,
    187
ritual: 25
  and art: 36, 40
  as mnemonic device: 39
  effects of: 38, 39, 40
  expressive function of: 38, 93
  purpose of: 37
  symbolism in: 39
ritualized behaviour, in animals: 38
road signs: 6, 113, 142, 149, 157
rock art: 3
Rock, I.
  perception of handwriting: 153
  perception of shapes: 139−40, 146
Rosenfeld, A.: 3
Rutherford, E.: 33

Sahlins, M.
  on 'domestic mode of production':
    82−3
  on lineage structure: 80
  on Polynesian chiefship: 84
  on social evolution: 82
Saussure, F. de
  on conventional phrases: 186
  on linguistic signs: 27, 91
  on onomatopoeic languages: 91
  on 'speech': 93, 106
  on syntagmatic and associative
    relations: 127
'Scorpion' mace head: 116−17, 151;
  fig. 27
Shakespeare: 178−9
shamanism: 172−6, 189, 190
shape, perception of: 139−40, 146;
  fig. 33
Shapiro, M: 134, 141−4, 148, 151
sign (linguistic): 27, 91
signifier and signified
  continuous variation in: 103
  in art generally: 93, 165, 178
  in Buryat art: 98
  in Hagen art: 105, 106−7
  in Kalabari art: 95
  in language: 91, 103
  in Yolngu art: 165−6
skeuomorph: 205
sociology: 1
Socrates: 178
songs, social functions of: 41

Southall, A.: 80
'speech', defined: 93
  equivalent in art: 94
Spencer, B. and Gillen, F.J.: 32, 125
split representation: 152−7; figs. 37,
  38
Stanner, W.E.H.: 33
Stevenson, R.F.: 79
Stevenson-Smith, W.: 117
Strathern, A. and M.
  critique of V.W. Turner: 111
  on art as a mode of expression: 100
  on Hagen face decoration: 182−3
style: 4, 133
  and mental image: 141, 144
  as evaluative term: 142
  characterization of: 134
  cultural functions of: 163
  emotional suggestiveness of: 141
  in Australian Aboriginal art: 134,
    163; Plates 9, 10; fig. 32
  personal: 181
  relation to aesthetics: 141
  special qualities in art: 170
Swinton, G.: 188
symbolism
  as characteristic of art: 5, 86, 112
  as characteristic of culture: 86, 107,
    133
  distinguished from representation:
    70
  'dominant' symbols: 110
  universal: 107
syntax: 106
  see also grammar; visual grammar

TALLENSI
  cult organization: 64
  leadership among: 45, 49, 52, 83
Tambiah, S.J.: 38
technical process
  and form: 134
  and imitation of model: 93, 141
  and style: 77
  as source of rhythm and balance:
    16
  fig. 31
technological knowledge: 35
  among Azande: 36
  among Trobrianders: 38
Terray, E.: 80−1, 83−4
Thompson, D.: 164−5
Thomson, R.: 179−81
THOMSON INDIANS, decorated leggings:
  17
TIKOPEA, songs: 41
TIV
  age-grading among: 51, 80
  expansionism: 80